T5-AVN-310

INSIDE POLITICAL CAMPAIGNS

INSIDE POLITICAL CAMPAIGNS

Theory and Practice

Karen S. Johnson-Cartee
and Gary A. Copeland

Introduction by Dan Nimmo

Praeger Series in Political Communication

Westport, Connecticut
London

Library of Congress Cataloging-in-Publication Data

Johnson-Cartee, Karen S.
    Inside political campaigns : theory and practice / Karen S.
Johnson-Cartee and Gary A. Copeland ; introduction by Dan Nimmo.
      p.   cm.—(Praeger series in political communication, ISSN
1062–5623)
    Includes bibliographical references and index.
    ISBN 0–275–95587–7 (alk. paper)
    1. Political consultants—United States. 2. Communication in
politics—United States. 3. Campaign management—United States.
I. Copeland, Gary. II. Title. III. Series.
JK2281.J639   1997
324′.0973—dc20   96–21249

British Library Cataloguing in Publication Data is available.

Library of Congress Catalog Card Number: 96–21249
ISBN: 0–275–95587–7
ISSN: 1062–5623

First published in 1997

Praeger Publishers, 88 Post Road West, Westport, CT 06881
An imprint of Greenwood Publishing Group, Inc.

Printed in the United States of America

The paper used in this book complies with the
Permanent Paper Standard issued by the National
Information Standards Organization (Z39.48–1984).

10 9 8 7 6 5 4 3 2 1

Copyright Acknowledgments

The authors and the publisher gratefully acknowledge permission for use of the following material:

"The 1994 deGraffenried 'Long Name' Ad." Used by permission of Ryan deGraffenried.

"The 1990 Helms 'Martin' Ad." Used by permission of Jesse Helms.

"The 1994 Kerrey 'No AK47 Needed' Ad." Used by permission of Bob Kerrey.

Every reasonable effort has been made to trace the owners of copyright materials in this book, but in
some instances this has proven impossible. The author and publisher will be glad to receive information leading to more complete acknowledgments in subsequent printings of the book and in the
meantime extend their apologies for any omissions.

To my husband Michael who shares my love of politics and who shares my love of winning and to Gary and Susan Copeland, fellow travelers on the treacherous road of Alabama politics.

Karen Johnson-Cartee

To the two most influential teachers I had at California State University, Fresno—George Diestel and R. C. Adams. From them I learned to be both a teacher and a scholar. Whenever I lecture while standing on a table, I think of George. Whenever I measure the margins on a student's paper, I think of R. C. What they gave me I hope to pass to my students.

Gary A. Copeland

Contents

Political Advertising Transcripts

Note: Titles may not be those given by the political consultants.

Series Foreword

Those of us from the discipline of communication studies have long believed that communication is prior to all other fields of inquiry. In several other forums I have argued that the essence of politics is "talk" or human interaction.[1] Such interaction may be formal or informal, verbal or nonverbal, public or private, but it is always persuasive, forcing us consciously or subconsciously to interpret, to evaluate, and to act. Communication is the vehicle for human action.

From this perspective, it is not surprising that Aristotle recognized the natural kinship of politics and communication in his writings *Politics* and *Rhetoric*. In the former, he establishes that humans are "political beings [who] alone of the animals [are] furnished with the faculty of language."[2] And in the latter, he begins his systematic analysis of discourse by proclaiming that "rhetorical study, in its strict sense, is concerned with the modes of persuasion."[3] Thus, it was recognized over 2,300 years ago that politics and communication go hand in hand because they are essential parts of human nature.

Back in 1981, Dan Nimmo and Keith Sanders proclaimed that political communication was an emerging field.[4] Although its origin, as noted, dates back centuries, a "self-consciously cross-disciplinary" focus began in the late 1950s. Thousands of books and articles later, colleges and universities offer a variety of graduate and undergraduate coursework in the area in such diverse departments as communication, mass communication, journalism, political science, and sociology.[5] In Nimmo and Sanders' early assessment, the "key areas of inquiry" included rhetorical analysis, propaganda analysis, attitude change studies, voting studies, government and the news media, functional and systems analyses, technological changes, media technologies, campaign techniques, and research techniques.[6] In a survey of the state of the field in 1983, the same authors and Lynda Kaid found additional, more specific areas of concerns such as the presidency, political polls, public opinion, debates, and advertising to name a few.[7] Since the first study, they also noted a shift away from the rather strict behavioral approach.

A decade later, Dan Nimmo and David Swanson argued that "political communication has developed some identity as a more or less distinct domain of scholarly work."[8] The scope and concerns of the area have further expanded to include critical theories and cultural studies. While there is no precise definition, method, or disciplinary home of the area of inquiry, its primary domain is the role, processes, and effects of communication within the context of politics broadly defined.

In 1985, the editors of *Political Communication Yearbook: 1984* noted that "more things are happening in the study, teaching, and practice of political communication than can be captured within the space limitations of the relatively few publications available."[9] In addition, they argued that the backgrounds of "those involved in the field [are] so varied and pluralist in outlook and approach, . . . it [is] a mistake to adhere slavishly to any set format in shaping the content."[10] And more recently, Nimmo and Swanson called for "ways of overcoming the unhappy consequences of fragmentation within a framework that respects, encourages, and benefits from diverse scholarly commitments, agendas, and approaches."[11]

In agreement with these assessments of the area and with gentle encouragement, Praeger established the Praeger Series in Political Communication. The series is open to all qualitative and quantitative methodologies as well as contemporary and historical studies. The key to characterizing the studies in the series is the focus on communication variables or activities within a political context or dimension. As of this writing, nearly forty volumes have been published, and there are numerous impressive works forthcoming. Scholars from the disciplines of communication, history, journalism, political science, and sociology have participated in the series.

I am, without shame or modesty, a fan of the series. The joy of serving as its editor is in participating in the dialogue of the field of political communication and in reading the contributors' works. I invite you to join me.

Robert E. Denton, Jr.

NOTES

1. See Robert E. Denton, Jr., *The Symbolic Dimensions of the American Presidency* (Prospect Heights, Ill.: Waveland Press, 1982); Robert E. Denton, Jr., and Gary Woodward, *Political Communication in America* (New York: Praeger, 1985; 2nd ed., 1990); Robert E. Denton, Jr., and Dan Han, *Presidential Communication* (New York: Praeger, 1986); and Robert E. Denton, Jr., *The Primetime Presidency of Ronald Reagan* (New York: Praeger, 1988).

2. Aristotle, *The Politics of Aristotle*, trans. Ernest Barker (New York: Oxford University Press, 1970), p. 5.

3. Aristotle, *Rhetoric*, trans. Rhys Roberts (New York: The Modern Library, 1954), p. 22.

4. Dan Nimmo and Keith Sanders, "Introduction: The Emergence of Political Communication as a Field," in *Handbook of Political Communication*, eds. Dan Nimmo and Keith Sanders (Beverly Hills, Calif.: Sage, 1981), p. 11-36.

5. Ibid., p. 15.

6. Ibid., pp. 17-27.

7. Keith Sanders, Lynda Kaid, and Dan Nimmo, eds., *Political Communication Yearbook: 1984* (Carbondale: Southern Illinois University, 1985), pp. 283-308.

8. Dan Nimmo and David Swanson, "The Field of Political Communication: Beyond the Voter Persuasion Paradigm," in *New Directions in Political Communication*, eds. David Swanson and Dan Nimmo (Beverly Hills, Calif.: Sage, 1990), p. 8.

9. Sanders, Kaid, and Nimmo, *Political Communication Yearbook: 1984*, p. xiv.

10. Ibid.

11. Nimmo and Swanson, "The Field of Political Communication," p. 11.

Acknowledgments

We would like to thank Julian Kantor, the archivist at the University of Oklahoma Political Commercial Archives, who provided invaluable assistance to us in locating particular examples of campaign ads. Rosie McMahill served us well as a dedicated research assistant. We hope that some of the searches for arcane references that we requested of her will help her in her new law career.

Special thanks go out to Robert Denton and the people at Greenwood Publishing Group for having sufficient confidence in our work that they would publish two different books of ours in the same year.

We also want to publicly thank Dan Nimmo for taking time during his London vacation to write the introduction for this book. There are any number of things more interesting to be doing in London than writing introductions for other people's books.

As usual, thanks to our spouses and families. Preparing two manuscripts within the same year was tough on us and our families. We usually write our books in the office at Karen's house. This means that Michael can see Karen more frequently than Susan sees Gary. On the other hand, Michael has to listen to us cursing crotchety computers, damning the University of Alabama's library and interlibrary loan's inability to work on our timetable, the derisive remarks about other people's work that strikes us as bad or, as Karen usually refers to it, bizarre, and the exasperation of looking for some convention paper that is lost among the thousands of pages of resource materials that are scattered in meaningless clumps about the office. Susan is spared these experiences.

Introduction

Inside Political Campaigns: Theory and Practice is the third volume published by the authors in this decade. Their output comprises a trilogy surveying the background, character, effects, and future of contemporary electoral campaigns now driven principally by the imperatives of political advertising. The first two volumes, *Negative Political Advertising: Coming of Age* (1991) and *Manipulation of the American Voter: Political Campaign Commercials* (1997), are painstaking, copious taxonomies of various forms of political commercials. This third volume endeavors to trace the sources of professional campaign wizardry by encapsulating the theories and concepts that practitioners and scholars alike claim to guide and rationalize consultants' magical weaving of strategies, tactics, and techniques into a "winning tapestry of political communications."

Given the current proliferation of "political consulting campaigns" at all political levels—incorporating diverse candidates, appeals, and electorates—the authors' effort to codify the explosion of consultant activity constitutes a daunting challenge. The purpose of this introduction is to raise a set of questions implied by the current state of political consulting. Each series of questions points to the formidable nature of the authors' enterprise; moreover, it provides a few selective criteria to assess whether political consulting campaigns are indeed informed by general political theory.

IS POLITICAL CAMPAIGN CONSULTING PROFESSIONAL?

If the size of the fees charged by leading political consultants, the number of trees felled to publish scholarly and trade books about

political consultants, and the amount of airtime devoted to documen-
taries and talk about political consultants are indicators, then
Johnson-Cartee and Copeland are correct in their opening assessment
that the "mystery surrounding political consultants and what they do
. . . fascinates." A partial source of that fascinating mystery lies in
the consultants' capacities for bridging seemingly polar worlds—one
constituted by the scientific findings of political science, advertising,
and public relations; the other by the aesthetic renderings sparked by
intuitive, instinctive impulses of talented artists.

In describing the tasks of the political campaign consultant,
Johnson-Cartee and Copeland employ the felicitous metaphor of the
"concert violinist." As informed and skilled artists, contemporary consultants are both bookwise and streetwise, balance reason with emotion, and combine quantitative and qualitative insights. By implication, the consultant has the fortunate capacity to synchronize the left
and right hemispheres of the brain—analysis with synthesis, melody
with harmony, sequence with simultaneity. Little did C. P. Snow re-
alize when, in 1959, he posed to the world his puzzle of "two cultures,"
one of scientists and another of literary writers "who had almost
ceased to communicate at all" (p. 2), that with the maturing of the
campaign consulting industry, technical wizards would emerge who
join the two cultures through the specialized avocation of political
communication.

Assuming for the moment that political consultants are analogous
to concert violinists, one implication is that a set of standards, criteria, and touchstones common to the endeavor of political consulting
has evolved that permits, first, consultants themselves, and second,
their candidate-clients, to distinguish a quality performance from one
by a rank amateur, that is, employing the authors' root metaphor, the
sensitivities, skills, and talents that differentiate the accomplished
concert violinist from the mere violin player that travelers toss coins
to in subway porticos. Given the status of political campaign consultation at century's end, is such an implication justified?

Generally, as the documentation of the first two chapters of the
Inside Political Campaigns: Theory and Practice attests, the shift in
emphasis from the era of organizational politics to media-age politics
in major office campaign management has been sizable. However,
whether it has been accompanied by a parallel evolution in
separating the virtuoso consultant from the tyro politico is
problematic. Hence the first question: is political campaign
consulting professional? A quarter of a century ago it was possible to
state, apparently without refutation, since no published review took
the assertion seriously enough to mention it, that "although aspiring
to professional status, campaign management is still a craft without

theoretical underpinnings and lacking common guidelines" (Nimmo, 1970, p. 66). To ascertain whether the evolution of political campaigning has been accompanied by consultant professionalism requires a precise view of the nature of professionalism itself. This is particularly true when persons routinely pass themselves off as "professional" in every occupation: auto parts sales, pay-for-play sports, termite eradication, civil and criminal law, medicine, classroom teaching, ethnic cleansing, and so forth.

In 1933 philosopher Alfred North Whitehead published a volume in a trilogy of his own, three works unified by his common theme of "understanding the nature of things," a theme dating back to the works of Empedocles, Epicures, and Lucretius. Beginning with *Science and the Modern World* (1925) and *Process and Reality* (1930), but especially in *Adventures of Ideas* (1933), Whitehead offered the argument that one mark of a civilized society is the effort to fashion a balance between unbridled authority and unrestricted liberty. A key element in that "golden mean" is the proliferation and "wide distribution of institutions founded upon professional qualifications and exacting such qualifications" (p. 71).

In his 1933 volume Whitehead was specific in his understanding of the nature of a profession: "Here the term Profession means an avocation whose activities are subjected to theoretical analysis, and are modified by theoretical conclusions derived from that analysis" (p. 72). Theoretical analysis seeks to define both the purposes of the avocation and how activities can and should be adapted to the attainment of those purposes: "Thus foresight based upon theory, and theory based upon understanding the nature of things, are essential to a professional" (p. 72). The "antithesis" to a profession, argued Whitehead, is the "Craft." A craft is any avocation based upon "customary activities" that are modified by the "trial and error of individual practice." Granted, the distinction between profession and craft "is not clear-cut"; yet, professions involve theoretically derived collective standards of performance, and crafts stem from individual claims and demonstrations of skill (p. 73):

Perhaps the most important function of these institutions is the supervision of standards of individual professional competence and of professional practice. . . . Whatever is done can be subjected to the test of general professional opinion, acting through this network of institutions. (p. 77)

IS THERE A POLITICAL CONSULTING CAMPAIGN THEORY?

The verdict of whether political consulting is professional thus rests on a prior question, namely, are consultant activities "subjected to theoretical analysis" and are they "modified by theoretical conclusions derived from that analysis?" Moreover, is there a "canalization of a variety of occupations" (Whitehead's phrase, p. 72) into a consulting profession? Aside from the concepts that inform consultants' "understanding of the nature of things," such as public opinion, news mediation, polling, political leadership, and so forth, is there a profession wide distribution of common "understanding of the nature of things?" Without theory and without common understanding, at least in Whitehead's view, consulting consists of mere "customary activities" and the "trial and error of individual practice," not a professional avocation.

Chapters 3 through 6 of *Inside Political Campaigns: Theory and Practice* provide a detailed inventory of the principal concepts and research findings available to political consultants in specialized areas. Presumably many political consultants apply these concepts and findings in their practice on behalf of candidates. The picture that emerges from the authors' accounting reveals that there is less a systematic theory of political campaigns that provides a basis for common theoretical analysis than a patchwork of disparate concepts, some compatible and others contradictory. Certainly the evolution of campaign technology has witnessed an increasingly sophisticated craftsmanship, but is that alone sufficient for professional development?

For example, in the absence of an ideological patterning in American political culture, consultants face the task of adjusting, from election to election, their customary activities of campaign advertising and manipulation of news coverage to shifting circumstances of public agendas, moods, sentiments, and impressions (Chapters 3 and 4). Granted, the adjustments may be justified as "responsive" to popular demands. Yet, without a general theory of responsive, let alone responsible, consulting, political consultants run the risk familiar to military generals that is, fighting the current war based on outdated lessons learned from past conflicts. Or, in constructing leader-follower relations, again from one campaign to the next, consultants acting as "dramatists" (Chapter 4) rewrite scripts and plotlines not with a common view of what constitutes quality dramatic performance but in adjustment to the overnight critical reviews provided by the op-ed columnists, television commentators, and talk show hosts. And, as the authors of *Inside Political Campaigns: Theory and Practice* demonstrate in Chapters 5 through 7, attitude change, communication effect theories, and other features of the voter persuasion paradigm (Nimmo & Swanson, 1990), although throwing "limited effects" proponents on the scrap heap of history, possess their own limits in generating professional theory. Grounded as they are in derivative, summative variable analysis, they largely ignore the multiplier effects inherent in what the authors properly emphasize as the "synergism" characteristic of campaigns qua campaigns.

Professional standards, criteria, and touchstones not only provide institutions with means of judging quality performance—thus separating, say, the modern internist from the patent medicine hawker—but also ways of detecting ethical versus unethical behavior. "The organization of professions by means of self-governing institutions," wrote Whitehead, "places the problem of liberty at a new angle. For it is now the institution which claims liberty and also exercises control" (1933, p. 73), not the individual craft worker or entrepreneur. As Johnson-Cartee and Copeland demonstrate in their concluding chapter, political consulting is an avocation very much in its infancy as a self-governing institution. The bulk of campaign regulation comes not from craft-based ethical standards (the American Association of Political Consultants "Code of Professional Ethics" not withstanding) but from externally imposed federal, state, and local authorities. If the threat of additional external regulation is to be thwarted, it behooves political consultants to subject their actions to, and modify them in light of, systematic ethical analysis. If, of course, there is a serious desire to replace the trial and error of the craft with the theoretical underpinnings of a profession.

HOW IS POLITICAL CONSULTING THEORY BUILT?

In his succinct little work *The Art of Political Manipulation* (1986), political scientist William Riker argued that the conventional liberal arts of logic, grammar, and rhetoric have long formed the basis of our conventional understanding of the nature of politics, especially campaign politics. Logic concerns the truth-value of assertions, grammar their communications-value, and rhetoric the persuasion-value. Logic, grammar, and rhetoric evolved initially through the cataloging and inventory of practical knowledge and its applications in each field. "But in recent times philosophers and scientists have recognized cataloguing and inventorying are not enough." After the initial phase of development in logic, grammar, and rhetoric came efforts to systematize. This required construction of a more general theory "to investigate the subjects without waiting for the more or less accidental and random developments in the practice of the arts" (p. x). When that stage of development arrived, applied theory offered new insights into practice. For example, primitive medicine's "customary activities" (in Whitehead's words) cured, or failed to cure, by hit or miss, by "trial and error." Cataloging, inventorying, systematizing, and theorizing led to preclinical theoretical sciences whose contexts are now requisites to learning medical practice.

Johnson-Cartee and Copeland capture well the cataloging and inventorying phases of theory building that are the state of the science and art of political consulting campaigning. Each chapter of their work constitutes an exhaustive accounting of research concepts, variables, findings, and sources pertaining to the various specializations that comprise major office campaign management in the era of media-age politics. If that accounting contributes to Riker's next stage—systematizing and general theory building—then the authors' compilations will be a step forward. Before rendering that judgment, however, one additional question needs to be asked: does campaign activity sufficiently rest upon logic, grammar, and rhetoric so as to *require* theory building in the tradition of those disciplines? Or is there another way?

William Riker argues that there is another way. He calls it the "heresthetic":

Heresthetic is a word I have coined to refer to a political strategy. Its root is a Greek word for choosing and electing. While it is related to rhetoric, the art of verbal persuasion, still heresthetic differs from rhetoric because there is a lot more than eloquence and elegance involved in heresthetic. (p. ix)

Like logic, grammar, and rhetoric, the heresthetic involves the use of language to accomplish some purpose—to arrive at truth in the case of logic, to communicate in the case of grammar, and to persuade in the case of rhetoric. The purpose of heresthetic is to manipulate. Where heresthetic differs as a discipline, in addition to purpose, is in the generation of appropriate theory. Heresthetic, the art of manipulating rather than truth seeking, communicating, or persuading, argues Riker, reversed the developmental pattern common to logic, grammar, and rhetoric. Instead of building theory via accumulation, that is, practices, singular theoretical implications, then general theory, with heresthetic first there was a general theory (social choice theory), then practical applications derived from and informed by that theory.

Consider for illustrative purposes Riker's example of Abraham Lincoln's manipulation of his opponent, Stephen A. Douglas, 1858 and 1860. In his 1858 debates with Douglas that marked the race for a U.S. Senate seat from Illinois, Lincoln posed Douglas a question: "Can the people of a United States Territory, in any lawful way, against the wish of any citizen of the United States, exclude slavery from its limits prior to the formation of a state constitution?" The purpose of the question was, as with most campaign stratagems, not to discover truth (logic), not to clarify concepts (grammar), and not—as so much of current consultant campaign "theory" implies—to persuade voters, be they rank and file or state legislative members, to choose Lincoln. Rather, the purpose was to ensnare Douglas in a trap, to manipulate Douglas into placing himself in a catch-22 situation. Douglas had a choice: answer the question in the affirmative—that territorial legislatures could exclude slavery—pleasing northern Democrats and, in all likelihood, winning the Senate seat. But Douglas would thereby alienate southern Democrats and throw away any chance for the presidency in 1860. Or, Douglas could respond in the negative to Lincoln's question. If he did, he would appear to be a tool of the southern Democrats, lose the Senate seat in 1858, but enhance his chances in 1860. Either way, Douglas's choice would eventually defeat him. Douglas chose "Yes," was reelected to the Senate, helped split the Democratic party in 1860 (for the remainder of the century and beyond), and lost the presidency to Lincoln by a plurality.

What Lincoln did—as his own political campaign consultant—was pose not a rhetorical dilemma designed to change minds of an audience, but a heresthetic dilemma "to structure the decision-making situation to the speaker's advantage and the respondent's disadvantage" (Riker, 1986, p. 8). Political manipulation, not persuasion, is the principal focus of a campaign. One need not accept Riker's view that social choice theory is a sufficient catchall to embrace the diverse and proliferating avocation of political consulting. Social choice theory is but one possibility. One could argue, for example, that viewed through the lenses of a heresthetic approach to campaigning rather than the conventional persuasive one, the total body of Kenneth Burke's dramatistic theory, Jacques Ellul's *la technique*, or Johan Huizinga's ludenic theory might provide more suitable bases for approaching strategic decision making.

The key question of whether heresthetic analysis applies to contemporary political consultant campaign theory depends in part on whether *any* body of general theory, in fact, underlies and serves as a guide for consultants. The burden of the careful analysis contained in *Inside Political Campaigns: Theory and Practice* is that, as yet, no heresthetic applies. Rather, consultants rely on a hodgepodge of received wisdom, conventions, shared techniques, and values combined with largely atheoretical findings from diverse bodies of political science, advertising and public relations, and communication research.

In the last quarter of a century, political scientists belatedly rejected the earlier conventional wisdom that campaigns contribute minimally to electoral outcomes. However, having accepted the possibility that campaigns make a difference, it is curious that, in Marshall McLuhan's phrase, "progress and advanced thinking is nearly always

of a rear-view mirror variety" (McLuhan & Fiore, 1968, p. 126). As
the research reported in *Inside Political Campaigns: Theory and
Practice* indicates, the bulk of studies in public opinion, political
leadership, communication effects, and political advertising still
examine, with varying rigor, individual differences primarily within
the framework of the voter persuasion paradigm. Studies, both by
academic scholars and political consultants, predominantly examine
whether campaign messages—advertising, news accounts, publicity,
orchestration, and other mediation forms—affect, and are affected by,
individual voters' attitudes, images, schema, information processing,
and so forth.

Unfortunately, piling studies on one another, useful as the exercise may be for scholarly and consultant resume building, is not necessarily theory building. In spite an "all deliberate speed" pace of theory building in the last quarter of a century of campaign studies, the
result is akin to the theoretical sophistication attributed by Riker to
the evolutionary stage of logic, grammar, and rhetoric before craft
personnel grasped that "to develop practical subjects, it is necessary,
as it turns out, to systematize them. . . . [T]his requires general theory
about each of the subject matters" (p. x).

Training programs in political communication, those housed both
in academic institutions and in the campaign consultant environment,
apply the art and science inherited from campaign research. They too
eschew serious efforts to construct a heresthetic of strategic collective
decision making. As in research employing the concept, "strategy"
aims at teaching means that achieve persuasive, not manipulatory,
results. Instead of privileging theory-based applications of strategic
manipulation, programs, workshops, and conferences stress the nuts-
and-bolts methods and gimmicks that influence individual voting
choices. Similarly, perusal of leading academic journals and consultant trade magazines provides numerous insights in the Dale Carnegie
tradition of how to win friends (financial backers) and influence people (voters), but a theory of political consultant campaigning is yet to
emerge.

Many lessons can be drawn from the Johnson-Cartee/Copeland
classifications of consultant practices, media presentations, sources of
public opinion, leadership types, communication effects, applications,
and ethical issues. Certainly one is that the concert violinist may be
but a fiddle player, untutored in musical theory, masquerading as a
virtuoso after all. Setting aside the absence of political correctness in
Socrates' dialectic in Plato's Book X of *The Republic,* his statement
offers a succinct judgment of the contemporary consultant-candidate relationship:

And whenever any one informs us that he has found a man who knows all the arts, and all things else anybody knows, and every single thing with a higher degree of accuracy than any other man—whoever tells us this, I think we can only imagine him to be a simple creature who is likely to have been deceived by some wizard or actor who he met, and whom he thought all-knowing, because he himself was unable to analyze the nature of knowledge and ignorance and imitation.

Dan Nimmo, Visiting Scholar
Department of Political Science
Baylor University

Chapter 1

The Evolution
of Political Campaigning

The task of a political consultant is to weave magic—a winning tapestry of political communications that ultimately leads to victory. The contemporary political consultant must be a master of scientific research methods and applications (political science, marketing, advertising, and public relations) and yet remain an artist who creates products based not only on research findings but also on a gut instinct for politics (see Theis, 1968, p. 8). It is an odd combination. It's as if the mind of a consultant has to be separated into two parts: one side is guided by educated reason, governed by years of technical, even scientific, training; the other side is the domain of emotional instinct. Political consulting is similar to the artistry of the concert violinist. A concert violinist once explained that during a performance, one side of the mind must concentrate on the technique of playing while the other side must be receptive to the emotional feelings evoked by the music. Being able to do just one is not sufficient; it is the difference between a violin player and a concert violinist. Just as artistic talent cannot be quantified, one cannot begin to quantify political savvy on the part of a consultant. It is an unusual talent; a talent often misunderstood and frequently debated. Perhaps that is why there is so much mystery surrounding political consultants and what they do. It cannot be quantified, therefore it fascinates. And what people don't understand, they either fear or admire. The nationally recognized political consultant who is both a political animal and a master of modern research methods and applications is a very hot commodity.

Before the heyday of modern political consultants, advertising agencies did the bulk of what is now referred to as major office campaign management, which includes the campaigns for president and U.S. Senator. This was true through the 1968 presidential election. The shift from traditional advertising agencies to modern-day political consultants occurred for a number of reasons. The advertising agencies themselves preferred to distance themselves from national political campaigns. Frequently, business clients had been offended by the agency's work for political candidates. The political campaign season interrupted the day-to-day operations of the company, and more often than not, the political work was not very profitable (see Hill, 1984). But most important, after the 1968 election, the political rules changed dramatically, and these changes required new skills that the typical advertising agency could not provide (see Blumenthal, 1980). Enter the modern political consultant.

Professional political consulting was born in California in 1933. Clem Whitaker and Leone Baxter joined forces to form Campaigns, Inc. Whitaker, a former reporter and public relations man, and Baxter, a chamber of commerce executive, made a successful team. The duo won 93 percent of the first seventy-five campaigns they managed (Nimmo, 1970; Sabato, 1981). Since that time political consultants have been called many things: "hidden persuaders" (Packard, 1958), "political persuaders" (Nimmo, 1970), "mind managers" (Schiller, 1973), "image merchants" (Hiebert, Jones, Lotito, & Lorenz, 1971), "media masters" (Wolfson, 1972a, 1972b, 1972c), "candidate makers" (Blumenthal, 1980), and even "political advertising hitmen" ("Political Advertising Hitmen," 1980).

Sabato (1981) has defined a political consultant as "a campaign professional who is engaged primarily in the provision of advice [campaign strategies and tactics] and services (such as polling, media creation, and production, and direct-mail fund raising) to candidates, their campaigns, and other political committees" (p. 8). Two types of political consultants have been identified: *generalists* and *specialists*.

A generalist consultant advises a candidate on most or all phases of his campaign and coordinates most or all aspects of the technology employed by the campaign. A specialist concentrates on one or two aspects of the campaign and peddles expertise in one or two technological specialties. (Sabato, 1981, p. 9)

Most political consultants today are specialists either emphasizing political polling or media production and placement (see Consultants Scorecard, 1986; Sabato, 1981). Political pollsters and media consultants constitute the majority of this profession; some political consultants work only in the areas of campaign management, campaign finance, or direct mail (see Sabato, 1981).

Just as consultants may be typed based on the advice or services that they perform, they may also be typed according to their ideological orientation or their party affiliation. Consultants are "spread all across the [political] spectrum, but most work within circumscribed parameters—as moderate Republicans or liberal Democrats, for instance" (Blumenthal, 1980, p. 27).

Hagstrom (1992) reported in a 1984 *National Journal*-sponsored survey of national consultants "that every serious candidate running in a contested race [for president, U.S. Senate, or state governorships] had hired a pollster and a media consultant" (p. 5). More recently, Hagstrom (1992) reports that this practice has spread to "city hall, state legislatures, and statewide offices of all types" (p. 5).

Although political consulting has certainly grown in the past twenty years, the circle of top-flight political consultants is really quite small. In 1986, *Campaigns and Elections* identified all Democratic and Republican media and political polling consultants that participated in the 1986 campaign season. In order to be included in their list, the firm must have managed at least one statewide race. *Campaigns and Elections* identified 23 Democratic media consultants, 13 Democratic polling consultants, 16 Republican media consultants, and 5 Republican polling consultants. The journal also identified two bipartisan media consultants and three bipartisan polling consultants (see Consultants Scorecard, 1986). Hagstrom (1992) estimated that "there has emerged an elite of approximately 40 polling and media firms employing about 100 professionals who have worked for winning governors and senators in at least two states" (p. 6). Morris and Gamache (1994) reported the top ten media consultants in the 1992 congressional races by the amounts of fees earned (see Figure 1.1).

Although prominent national political consultants are the norm for gubernatorial and U.S. Senate races, such political consultants rarely sign on with presidential campaigns. Hagstrom (1992) writes:

Working for a presidential candidate brings great prestige to a firm, but it is risky from a business standpoint. Presidential campaigns and candidates are highly demanding, and by the nature of the system, a majority of presidential candidates lose their primary elections. If a consultant goes to work for a candidate for president, he or she must either take fewer statewide candidates or neglect those candidates during the presidential primary season. And if the presidential candidate loses the primary, then the firm may be without enough work to sustain its staff or be forced to take clients it normally would have rejected as being undesirable or poorly financed. (pp. 6-7)

Candidates frequently hire nationally known consultants in order to bring credibility to their campaign. This is especially true for viable challengers who must convince their financial backers that they can offset the advantages of incumbency by running a high-tech media campaign. In addition, an incumbent who is in trouble may hire

one of the national consulting elite to signal supporters that the candidate knows the campaign is in trouble and is willing to make every
available effort to turn things around (see Hagstrom, 1992).

Figure 1.1
Top Ten Media Consultants in the 1992 Congressional Races

Rank	Company (Location)	Fees Earned
1.	Squier/Eskew/Knapp/Ochs Comm. (Washington, D.C.)	$12.5 million
2.	Greer, Margolis, Mitchell & Assoc. (Washington, D.C.)	$11.1 million
3.	National Media (Alexandria, VA)	$10.0 million
4.	Multi-Media Services Corp. (Alexandria, VA)	$9.3 million
5.	Target Enterprises (Hollywood, FL)	$9.1 million
6.	Campaign Group (Philadelphia, PA)	$8.2 million
7.	The Media Group (Washington, D.C.)	$7.1 million
8.	Fenn & King Communications (Washington, D.C.)	$5.8 million
9.	The Garth Group (New York, NY)	$5.6 million
10.	Morris & Carrick (New York, NY)	$5.1 million

Note: Dollar amounts have been rounded.
Source: Morris & Gamache, 1994, p. 85.

The elite political consultants do not manage the majority of
political campaigns in the United States for a variety of reasons.
Local candidates and some members of Congress still rely on a favorite
advertising agency in their home district to "handle the election"
rather than turn to a political consultant. Frequently these advertising agencies have a history of interest in political races, and they are
readily identified by their prominent positions in electoral contests
over the years. This is not to say that candidates who hire advertising agencies receive the same type of services as candidates who hire
political consultants. The advertising agency will run a political
campaign much in the same way as it would a product campaign.
Other reasons that top political consultants do not manage the major-

ity of campaigns are that the consultants do not have the time and, typically, the candidates do not have the money to attract them. Many local and state races do not retain a full-time political consulting firm because they simply can't afford it. Some campaigns hire college professors in the fields of political science, marketing, and communication to serve as part-time consultants to the candidate when the campaign can not afford the services of a full-time or national political consultant. Other candidates may rely exclusively on volunteers to manage their campaigns.

The political consultant is a modern-day phenomenon—a business/politics/communication hybrid. The consultant runs a specific campaign tailored for the individual candidate based on relevant political science, marketing, public relations, and advertising theory and research. This does not mean to suggest that a political consultant is necessarily better than an advertising agency. Many electoral situations do not require all the sophisticated tools of a trained political consultant. Different levels of electoral races in different campaign settings require different campaign management strategies (Nimmo, 1970).

THE EVOLUTION OF POLITICAL CAMPAIGNING

In order to understand the evolution of political campaign communication management, we must first examine the evolution of the American political process. As the role of political parties changed through the years, the characteristics and style of political campaign management also evolved. We believe that American campaign history may be divided into two eras: the organizational politics era and the media-age politics era.

Almond and Coleman (1960) maintained that there are a number of functional political requisites for any political system. These political "input" functions include: political socialization and recruitment, interest articulation, interest aggregation, and political communication (see Almond & Coleman, 1960). These functional categories are fulfilled in different ways at different times in different political systems (see Almond & Coleman, 1960) by different organizations, individuals, institutions, and so on.

An Era of Organizational Politics

We term what Nimmo and Savage (1976) have called "Old Politics" the era of organizational politics, as this label more readily identifies the most significant characteristic of this period. During this time, the political party fulfilled the functional "input" political requisites for society. According to Nimmo and Savage (1976), the political party served as the means of contacting voters. The party machine recruited candidates, mobilized voters, and shaped policies. Through the use of patronage, party bosses influenced voters. The party organization or machine can best be described by militaristic metaphors in that it was characterized by hierarchical command and discipline (Jensen, 1968). It operated as a military fighting machine, and the war was politics.

Potential political leaders were chosen among the rank and file of the party, and once selected, the future leader began a long political apprenticeship. Candidates were, in essence, groomed by the party. Usually candidates for high-level offices such as governor, senator, or congressional representative had other successful careers at lower-level elected offices. In this way, the party maintained a tight control over political leaders, ensuring that elected officeholders had a history of political experience to draw upon and would hold the party's interests as their top priority. Candidates were given access to an internal party campaign organization that was financed by party dues or donations.

The political party served as the primary link between the people and their government. Voters contacted local party officials if they had complaints about government services, policies, and so on. In this way, the majority of voters believed that they had a direct line to the center of power, for they had a party representative who intervened on their behalf. Thus the party organization served as a means for citizens to participate in the political process, and political interests were articulated through the party organization.

Particularly in the big cities, the party organization worked as a well-oiled military machine, hence the name "machine politics." When there were fires, party officials appeared on the scene, helping the victims with food, clothes, and money. At weddings, local political leaders frequently made an appearance and gave the newlyweds a cash wedding gift. On holidays, party leaders often helped the local voters celebrate by giving out hard liquor. And when a loved one died, the party man was always there to pay his respects. In short, the party "took care of" their people. The party also maintained close contact with the voters by sustaining a strong patronage system that provided jobs and thus financial security to many of the party faithful (see Crotty & Jacobson, 1980). Elected officials had strong community ties because of this process. Political interests were articulated through the political party organizations and aggregated by the political parties on the floors of American legislative bodies at the local, state, and federal levels.

During the organizational politics era, the political parties reached the voter through personal contact (door-to-door canvassing, local rallies, parades, whistle-stop tours), party pamphlets, and a party-owned or party-controlled newspaper (see Johnson, 1981; Nimmo & Savage, 1976). American newspapers during this time were either in the party organism stage or parallelism stage of newspaper development. During the party organism stage of newspaper development, the party either owned or controlled the newspaper through political cronies. By 1800, American newspapers were in the party organism stage of newspaper development. With the reactions to the excesses of the muckraking era of Pulitzer and Hearst and with the growth of expensive newspaper technology, the party organism stage of media development in the United States began to end in the late nineteenth and early twentieth centuries.

The second stage of newspaper development that occurred during the organizational politics era was the parallelism stage. A newspaper is said to be parallel to a party by being "closely linked to that party by organization, loyalty to party goals and the partisanship of its readers" (Seymour-Ure, 1974, p. 173). Such newspapers voluntarily follow party lines, for they are no longer owned or controlled by political parties. However, there is a consistent correspondence between party views and newspaper copy. Thus, the political parties of the organizational politics era greatly benefited from the newspapers of the day.

During the organizational politics era, party identification determined how an individual would vote. According to DeVries and Tarrance (1972), during the 1940s, the most significant factors in determining how a person would vote in a presidential election were (in descending order) party allegiance, group allegiance, assessment of the candidate's personality and consideration of issues. Elections were primarily viewed as contests between the competing parties. However, by the 1960s, this had changed dramatically, for an assessment of the candidate's personality and the issues associated with a candidate had surpassed party and group allegiance in importance. By 1976, split-ticket voting, "another measure of the instability of partisan attitudes and contemporary politics" (Crotty & Jacobson, 1980), had reached about 25 percent of all votes cast in the United States (see Crotty & Jacobson, 1980).

According to Jensen (1968), techniques associated with the new politics era began to appear in presidential elections as early as 1916, but it was not until the 1960s that the organizational politics era faded away from the national scene. However, remnants of the organizational politics era remain in low-level races in some states.

The Era of Media-Age Politics

During the media-age politics era, the mass media system dominates the fulfillment of the functional input political requisites: political socialization, recruitment, interest articulation, interest aggregation, and political communication. This era may be called the media age, for it is truly a political age dominated by mass-communicated messages. No longer do people experience politics firsthand through their association with low-ranking party officials. People obtain political information through the eyes and ears of the mass media. Furthermore, people experience what Horton and Wohl (1956) have called a para-social interaction in that politics is experienced through mass media presentations (especially television), and people then feel as if they have participated in the political process without any direct contact with the system itself. Thus, the desire for involvement in the political process is satisfied by the para-social experience. In their own minds, many viewers carry on imagined dialogues with political actors that appear on television. They often feel as if they have told the mayor, governor, or even the president their "two cents." Thus they have experienced the illusion of political participation, of vicariously making their views known to political leaders.

Jamieson (1988) argues that television has transformed both the substance and style of American political discourse. She suggests that television has changed the "intensity, style, tone, and even length of political discourse" (Jamieson, 1988, p. 56). Gone are the days of fiery orators and larger than life personalities who presented high drama on the campaign trail. Instead, there is a new style of political rhetoric, which Jamieson terms the "new eloquence," that is more conciliatory and conversational—calm, soft, and warm. This "new eloquence" became necessary and appropriate for television audiences, because television is far more "intimate" (Brummett, 1988) than a campaign stump speech to 500 people. The style appropriate for television is one that would be found appropriate in a person's living or dining rooms. We call this a connected style in that the motive or the intent of the communicator is to "connect" with the individuals in this audience. It is an attempt to build bridges between political leaders and the voters through the utilization of relational communication messages. This does not mean, however, that the political leader is a spineless, passive individual. On the contrary, Americans demand energetic and aggressive public figures. It does inform as to how that energy and aggression must be delivered—in a way that is not offensive as if it were to be delivered in one's home. This is far different from the style of orators of old, who had an interest in appearing above and beyond the people.

Graber (1980) has concluded that with "the advent of television and its ready availability in every home, the spread and improvement of public opinion polling, the use of computers in election data analysis" (p. 157), and the use of sophisticated political advertising and impression management strategies, the political party has declined in influence. This decline has "vastly enhanced the role of the mass media in elections" (see Graber, 1980, p. 157; Nimmo & Savage, 1976; Perry, 1968; Swanson, 1972). Elections have become increasingly media affairs rather than party affairs.

As early as 1969 Alexander observed that

manipulation of the media has become as important, and sometimes more important, than control of a party organization, especially for those seeking statewide or national offices, and campaign technicians and professional persuaders have replaced the organization men of former days in the campaign hierarchy. An organization can be purchased or men can be employed who can decrease the need for foot soldiers in the battle for ballots. Contemporary politics is focused on the candidate, not the party. (pp. 259-260)

Thus political consultants are "the new directors of the American political drama" (Blumenthal, 1980, p. 27) who reach voters directly, in effect by mass-merchandising their candidates. Gone are the militaristic metaphors associated with "machine or organizational politics," and in their place are mercantilist metaphors that speak of "selling candidates" to selected "target markets" with specific "demographic and psychographic profiles" (see Nimmo & Savage, 1976). Yet even though the consultants have adopted the mercantilist language of the commercial advertiser, the way in which they "sell" their candidates is far different from the way they sell soap.

In the United States, candidates no longer have to serve an apprenticeship period before rising to the top. Political candidates can bypass party organization by hiring political consultants to create an instant campaign organization (see Crotty & Jacobson, 1980). Therefore, many successful candidates have little or no political experience. The quintessential example of this is Ross Perot, who mounted an independent run for the presidency in 1992 based upon his ability to spend his own vast personal wealth.

Campaign organizations are candidate centered, technocratic, and short-lived (Crotty & Jacobson, 1980). No longer is the party the center of operations. The campaign organization belongs to and focuses on the individual candidate. The operation of the campaign organization is based on technology. Computer analysis of voting trends and sophisticated survey research techniques dominate the work of the organization. The campaign structure or organization is temporary, for it disappears the day after the election.

Political Campaign Finances

No longer are party dues the primary source of campaign funding. Rather, campaigns are financed through individual contributions, personal wealth, and political action committees. Qualified presidential candidates also rely on governmental public funding to wage their political races.

Acquiring political consultants, instant campaign organizations, and television advertising is a very expensive enterprise. Indeed, the high costs associated with television advertising and modern polling techniques necessitates that a candidate be well financed. "The ability of a candidate to raise money remains a strong consideration. Wealthy candidates have an advantage because they can draw on personal resources. Activities and statements likely to alienate donors are shunned" (Graber, 1980, pp. 161-162; see also Alexander, 1969). Thus, those that remain are candidates who have either inherited or personally amassed considerable wealth and those candidates who are financially well connected and willing to run on a "least objectionable" platform of Milquetoast positions in order to finance the new techniques required in media-age politics.

Campaigns are increasingly expensive to wage. From 1968 to 1976, presidential campaign expenses increased over 250 percent. In 1976, federal funding of presidential campaigns amounted to 72 million dollars (Crotty & Jacobson, 1980). In 1980, "Carter and Reagan got $29.4 million each and independent candidate John B. Anderson $4.2 million" ("Campaign Finance Debate," 1988, p. 122). For the 1984 general election, Ronald Reagan and Walter F. Mondale each received $40.4 million. The Federal Election Commission (FEC) distributed $35.1 million in matching funds in the 1984 presidential primaries ("Campaign Finance Debate," 1988). In 1988, $92.2 million was spent by the two major party candidates for the presidency (Sorauf, 1992).

Besides the public funding for presidential elections, political action committees (PACs) have also become an important source of both direct contributions and independent spending in modern elections. In 1992, PACs spent nearly $189 million on federal elections (Markerson & Goldstein, 1994). "Independent spending for presidential candidates went from $1.6 million in the 1976 elections to $13.7 million four years later" ("Campaign Finance Debate," 1988, pp. 120-121). "The FEC reported that independent spending in the 1984 presidential election amounted to $16.7 million" ("Campaign Finance Debate," 1988, p. 121). The FEC reported that independent spending in the 1988 presidential election amounted to $20.4 million (Sorauf, 1992).

The increase in independent spending has meant an increase in the amount of negative political advertising aired. Research has shown that independently sponsored negative ads are effective in negatively impacting on targeted candidates (see Garramone & Smith, 1984; Kaid & Boydston, 1987). The majority of independent expenditures goes toward negative political advertising (Johnson-Cartee & Copeland, 1991a; see also Garramone, 1985a; Garramone & Smith, 1984; Jamieson, 1984; Merritt, 1984; Sabato, 1981). "In the 1982 elections, most independent spending went for negative ads. About $4.6 million of the nearly $5.8 million spent by independent individuals and groups went for such ads" ("Campaign Finance Debate," 1988, p. 121).

If political action committees are important in the financing of presidential campaigns, they are indispensable in U.S. Senate, congressional, gubernatorial, and other statewide races. For example, during the 1983-1984 campaign season, the average House incumbent received 43 percent of his or her campaign funds from PACs, and the average Senate incumbent received 24 percent of his or her funds from PACs ("Political Action Committees," 1986). During this same election time period (1983-1984), Democrats received a greater percentage of their total campaign treasury from PACs than did Republicans; Democrats received 46 percent and Republicans received 37 percent of their respective campaign funding from PACs ("Political Action Committees," 1986).

Political action committees directly contribute to campaigns and also independently spend money for the benefit of candidates. Indeed, "PACs may not contribute more than $10,000 to one candidate, up to $5,000 in the primary elections and another $5,000 in the general elections" ("Campaign Finance Debate," 1988, p. 120). In 1984, PACs gave $104.9 million to House and Senate races ("Political Action Committees," 1986); 72 percent of that went to incumbents ("Political Action Committees," 1986). In 1986, PACs gave $132.2 million to House and Senate races; 67 percent of that went to incumbents ("Campaign Finance Debate," 1988). Today the great majority of PAC dollars go to finance incumbent campaigns (Markerson & Goldstein, 1994, p. 10).

In *Buckley v. Valeo* (1976), the Supreme Court held that PACs are not limited in the amount that they can independently spend on the behalf of a given candidate (see Johnson-Cartee & Copeland, 1991a). In 1984, the Federal Election Commission reported that $16.7 million dollars was independently spent by political action committees on behalf of presidential candidates. Less than one million dollars was spent on behalf of Walter Mondale; the remainder was spent in support of the incumbent, Ronald Reagan ("Campaign Finance Debate," 1988).

The national political parties themselves have indirectly aided the destruction of their status as the candidate's support mechanism for electoral success. Since 1972, the presidential nominating conventions have allowed for greater participation on the part of the rank and file; however, the reforms that allowed for this opening of the process have at the same time "contributed to the continued erosion of the party system by weakening the parties' control over their most vital function, the nominating process" (Crotty & Jacobson, 1980, p. 25). The increased use of party primaries (the selection of delegates and/or presidential nominees through popular vote) has also weakened the party's control over the nominating process.

Since 1968, the number of presidential primaries has fluctuated; however, the general trend has been upward ("1988 Delegate Selection," 1988). And "although Iowa and about 18 other states select national-convention delegates through caucuses or conventions—mass meetings of party members—primaries are by far the more important method" of delegate selection ("1988 Delegate Selection," 1988, p. 34). Primaries—either delegate-selection primaries or presidential nominee preference primaries—now account for the majority of convention delegates ("Presidential Primaries," 1988). The number of delegates selected through the primaries has increased from around 38 percent in 1968 to 75 percent in 1988 (see "1988 Delegate Selection," 1988). The opening of the nominating conventions to the parties' rank and file and the selection of the majority of delegates by party primaries, while democratically admirable, have led to the neutralization of the "role and influence of the party" (Crotty & Jacobson, 1980, p. 250; see also "1988 Delegate Selection," 1988).

The Role of the Media in the Media-Age Politics Era

In the media-age political era, media technology and media professionals overpower the political parties in communica.ing political information to the public. Nimmo (1978) has identified two professional political communicators involved in this process: promoters and journalists. Promoters are "hired to advance the interests of particular clients" (Nimmo, 1978, p. 29). Journalists are "employees of news organizations that link news sources and audiences" (Nimmo, 1978, p. 29; see Lippmann, 1965). Pollsters are also professional political communicators, but, depending on their employer, they can also be categorized as either promoters or journalists.

In order to understand the significant role of the journalist in media-age politics, the role of modern communication media must be examined. For the most part, American newspapers have entered the independent participancy stage of newspaper development (Johnson,

1981). With a few exceptions, no longer do newspapers recite a party doctrine in their copy. Although the newspaper organization may endorse a candidate or party in editorials, the news reporters attempt to present an independent journalistic perspective in their copy. Journalists bring up issues, they spark political debate, and in short they serve as political actors in the ever enlarging ring of American politics.

It is also important to remember that television is a relatively recent, although revolutionary, event on the political landscape. The three national commercial television networks (ABC, CBS, and NBC) are federal systems that were built as a result of linking local or regional stations together. Individual television stations, by federal regulation, retain responsibility for their programming.

The presidential election of 1952 saw the first television political advertising (Carroll, 1980; Crotty & Jacobson, 1980). And it was not until 1963 that the 30-minute nightly network newscast common today was offered to the American public (Patterson, 1980). The nation still continues to see the development of news programming at both national and local levels. Morning, noon, evening, and Late night news programming has become common in most television markets.

Since the late 1960s, television network news has become a multimillion dollar enterprise. The profitability of news operations at local television stations has caused major changes in news operations in the last two decades. The news menu has greatly expanded to meet the demands of interested advertisers and the news-hungry American public. After his success with turning a small television station, WTBS, into a nationally viewed superstation, Atlanta media mogul Ted Turner created the first satellite-delivered, 24-hour all news network (CNN). Since its inception in 1980, CNN has grown to become a worldwide influence in the gathering, processing, and delivery of news information. Perhaps its impact on world affairs and world politics was not truly appreciated until the fall of 1990, when the buildup of tensions in the Middle East over Iraq's invasion of Kuwait led to the U.N. resolution that condemned Saddam Hussein's actions and ultimately led to the Persian Gulf War. Both Saddam Hussein and the Bush administration watched CNN to determine how the war was proceeding.

Findings by Roper Research Associates indicate that television has been the dominant source of news for the American public since 1963 (Roper, 1969) and in November 1992, television was reported as the primary source of news for 82 percent of post election respondents (Gersh, 1992). In addition, the public evaluates television as being more credible than other available news sources (Roper, 1969). Research has shown that the public indicates that it gains "its clearest understanding of national candidates and issues from television by more than two-to-one over newspapers" (Alexander, 1969, p. 258). Accordingly, an estimated 50 to 75 percent of campaign budgets for major political offices is spent on the production and the dissemination of television advertising (see Kaid & Davidson, 1986; Patterson, 1983). Thus, the majority of political information pertaining to major campaigns that voters receive comes from television.

Broadcast and print journalists have an image of themselves "as independent, fearless, and professionally neutral conveyors of information: Vital links in the chain of democratic governance" (Crotty & Jacobson, 1980, p. 73). Reporters are involved in what Entman (1981) termed surrogate representation: "the enforcement of government responsiveness to the public by pressing politicians to explain candidly their actions, motivations, and plans" (pp. 81-82). In short, the news media see themselves as watching out for the public's interest—or more cmmonly, the "watch-dog" theory of the press. Yet surrogate representation takes the notion of the watchdog theory of the news media one step further, for the news media have now sought to become the arbiters of the political system (see Grossman & Kumar, 1981). Grossman and Kumar (1981) explain:

News organizations have become actors of considerable significance in the American political system. They play a number of important public roles including influencing the selection and removal of those who hold office, determining the public perception of the importance of many issues and interpreting the significance of a leader's activities. Nonetheless, news organizations are neither traditional political actors nor are they a fourth branch of government. What might be said of them is that they strive to become the arbiters of the political system. . . . Collectively and individually, news enterprises act as if they set the ethical norms for candidates and the criteria by which policies shall be evaluated. In sum, these organizations attempt to establish the criteria of rectitude for political operations in the United States. (p. 302)

The news media have "supplanted the political party as the main conduit between" political leaders and voters (Crotty & Jacobson, 1980, p. 67). This is especially true of television. Smith holds that "television has acquired the additional function of being the register of which historic events are significant, and the process of event—news coverage—critical assessment—point scored—voter influence begins to feed upon itself" (1976, pp. 196-197). Clearly, then, the mass media serve as the main linkage between people and government, and the mass media articulate interests to the people, creating for them an interest agenda. Similarly, the media supervise the presentation of competing issues and personalities. In the media's self-appointed role as political arbiter, political interests are aggregated not in the halls of a legislative body but rather in the newspaper copy and on the broadcast airwaves. Political demands are negotiated not in back offices but on front pages.

Consequences of the Media-Age Politics

Doris Graber (1980) has identified four major consequences of the new media-age politics. According to Graber, the media age has created a decline in party influence over elections. Campaigns are now centered on candidates rather than parties. Party affiliation remains important only in low-involvement, low-visibility campaigns on the state and local levels (see Graber, 1980). Second, as we have discussed, the mass media personnel have become powerful political arbiters in that they actively "influence the selection of candidates and issues" during the course of a campaign season (see Barber, 1974; 1978; Graber, 1980; Nimmo & Johnson, 1980). Mass-mediated news reports set the tone and structure of an electoral contest. By distinguishing between the front-runners and the also-rans, by playing the expectation game, by signaling the stops, starts, and falters in a candidate's campaign, by treating the campaign as a horse race, the news media define and give character to the mediated political campaign (see Barber, 1974, 1978; Combs, 1980; Nimmo & Combs, 1983; Nimmo & Johnson, 1980; Sigal, 1978; Weaver, 1976). The acknowledgment of the news media's power in defining the presidential campaign of 1988 became so great that the news media themselves developed a name for what they were doing: spin doctoring. In other words, news reporters and political figures (candidates, political consultants, former leaders, etc.) were the spin doctors of the '88 campaign by placing a slant, or "spin," on the discussion of campaign events, happenings, and so on. As early as 1976, Roger Mudd used a billiard's metaphor when he called this practice putting "English" on the ball. Mudd said, with respect to Iowa's precinct caucuses: "The English that is applied to these results is going to be applied by the media and the politicians themselves. It's not exactly the precise figures that will be important; it's whether the media and the politicians agree that this man won and this man lost" (quoted in Sigal, 1978, p. 469).

Graber's third major consequence of the media-age politics is a change in the "types of candidates likely to be successful" (1980, p. 161). Candidates must be attractive, dramatic, and have access to money. Media-age politics has a very harsh requirement in that one must be telegenic—the right hair, the right face, the right clothes, and the right personality (see Glass, 1985; Rosenberg, Bohan, McCafferty, & Harris, 1986; Rosenberg & McCafferty, 1987; Stokes, 1966).

Candidates recognize that "the news media seek out the dramatic—the dramatic events and the dramatic men" (Alexander, 1969, p. 261). For this reason, politicians work with consultants on re-training themselves for television. In Chapter 4, we discuss the numerous areas with which consultants work in order to improve candidate presentation and communication style.

The "fourth major aspect of the media-age politics is the fact that mass media coverage—has become the pivot around which campaigns turn" (Graber, 1980, p. 162; see also Carey, 1976). Pseudo-events (which may include such things as public appearances, trips, talk show appearances, rallies, parades) are prepared with one thing in mind—media coverage, and, in particular, television coverage. The creation of pseudo-events (Boorstin, 1961; Nimmo, 1970) or medialities (Robinson, 1981a; Ranney, 1983), which are "events that take place mainly to be shown on television—events that, in the absence of television, would not take place at all or would take place in a different manner" (Ranney, 1983, p. 23) are important campaign devices.

Candidates may engage in meaningless activities merely to provide attractive, action-oriented pictures. Most of these pictures are deliberately packed with symbols to convey stock messages quickly and easily. For instance, showing candidates with old people, or black workers, or college students proclaims affinity for these groups. . . . Many campaign events are now staged as prime-time, live coverage television spectacles. (Graber, 1989, pp. 204-205)

"Campaigners design methods for getting exposure on newscasts; some of the best practitioners of the political art claim that a few minutes on the evening news are worth all the rest of the publicity they can get—or can buy" (Alexander, 1969, p. 260). Alexander (1969) concluded that "television has changed the political campaign, changed the political candidate, and, in fact, changed the entire nature of the political discourse. Television has reordered the political campaign" (p. 260; see also Carey, 1976).

Beside the effects on the political candidate and the candidate's campaign staff, there are also effects on American society. Political candidates have bypassed political parties by hiring political consultants, who create instant campaign organizations and finance them primarily through public funding, PAC contributions, or the candidate's personal wealth. Thus, American political leaders have prevented the less affluent citizen from participating in any political organization that might affect the political leader and therefore provide a vehicle for political expression (see Crotty & Jacobson, 1980).

Little interpersonal contact exists between political leaders and their constituents. With the growth of the welfare state and the civil service, patronage is virtually dead as a political linkage between parties, party members, and sympathetic constituents. This lack of contact between ordinary citizens, political parties, and political leaders breeds dissatisfaction. The average citizen has no input in the party decision-making processes. "The disturbing decline in voter turnout in recent decades suggested to some analysts that increasing numbers of Americans had become disconnected from the world of politics and government." ("Why America Doesn't Vote," 1988, p. 139). In addition, party allegiance has weakened, particularly among whites (Abramson, 1987). "Surveys by the University of Michigan's Survey Research Center/Center for Political Studies indicated that the percentage of whites who strongly identified with either the Republican or Democratic parties dropped from 36 percent in 1960 to 23 percent in 1980; in 1984, the figure rose to 29 percent, but that was still 7 percentage points less than it was in 1960" (as reported in "Why America Doesn't Vote," 1988, p. 139). Thus, only one out of four American voters considers himself/herself to be a "strong partisan" (Nie, Verba, & Petrocik, 1979). This lack of political allegiance has concerned researchers for more than a decade. "Without political parties, the average man has no effective means of political expression; therefore, he becomes politically alienated. An alienated society is a prime breeding ground for demagoguery" (Crotty & Jacobson, 1980, p. 253).

In Summary

Clearly the organizational politics era and the media-age politics era are ideal types that have been constructed by political scientists and other researchers who have observed American political behavior over the past 100 years (Nimmo & Savage, 1976). These ideal types explain national politics much more effectively than they explain, say, the political behavior surrounding local elections for such offices as constable or district attorney. It is safe to say that the modernization of political campaigning started on the presidential level and has filtered down through other major political campaigns. Gubernatorial and senatorial campaigns have been quick to use the techniques of media-age politics. Congressional campaigns have been slower to turn to the use of professional political consultants; however, the primary reason behind that hesitancy is the lack of a strong financial base. In 1984, the average congressional campaign total expenditure was $391,954 (see "Controls on Political Spending," 1985). In 1992, that figure was roughly the same at $390,387 (Morris & Gamache, 1994). However, campaigns involving prominent congressional leaders, independently wealthy candidates, or those occurring in large metropolitan areas with expensive media costs frequently spend well above the average. In 1992, an independently wealthy Republican candidate in California, Michael Huffington, spent $5.43 million dollars to win California's District 22 congressional seat. Dick Chrysler spent $1.76 million in a Michigan congressional race, and Linda Bean spent $1.44 million in a Maine congressional race; but despite their large war chests, both Chrysler and Bean lost in 1992 (Markerson & Goldstein, 1994). As congressional campaigns become better financed and as more incumbents retire, an increase in the use of media-age techniques can be expected (see Goldenberg & Traugott, 1984).

Modern American political campaigns are no longer party creations but rather are the products of mass-media-age politics. And as such, they are high drama. And it is the modern-day political consultant who directs the drama. As Clem Whitaker used to tell his clients, "put on a fight, and, if you can't do that, put on a show" (Alexander, 1969, p. 277).

Chapter 2

Modern Political
Communication Consulting

Although there are a wide variety of specialized consultants, this work focuses on the political communication consultant. Modern political communication consultants are said to be the "direct descendants" of public relations professionals (Nimmo, 1970); much of what they do is borrowed from commercial advertising and marketing. In addition, the influence of the more traditional academic enterprise of political science and its subfield of political communication should not be forgotten. After all, political consultants are in the business of politics. In order to understand the political utilization of various concepts borrowed from public relations, advertising, and marketing, we must place them in their appropriate context—the political campaign. We will now briefly consider political campaigns as organized political behavior.

A POLITICAL CAMPAIGN

Combs (1980) suggests that a campaign is "a planned and deliberate series of actions or operations designed to bring about a particular purpose" (p. 138). "A campaign suggests execution of a dramatic script, theatrical action, the dramaturgy of united effort, the persuasion and mobilization of an audience" (Combs, 1980, p. 138). The building blocks of the political campaign are quite simply political talk, or "the creation, re-creation and transmission of significant symbols through communication" (Nimmo, 1978, p. 371). Significant symbols in this context are the shared political symbols common to a political culture. According to Nimmo (1970),

Symbols are selected and employed to impress a large audience, evoke a sympathetic response from spectators, identify the candidate with the most cherished traditions, rules, and folk heroes of his party and of America, and convey a sense of relevance, meaning, timeliness, and appropriateness to what the candidate is saying. (pp. 27-28; see also Edelman, 1964, pp. 95-113)

Campaign Functions

Gronbeck (1978) and Trent and Friedenberg (1983) have identified a number of campaign functions. Although the political party no longer serves as a military organization, researchers frequently liken the candidate's campaign organization to a military organization. In the eyes of the news media, the campaign period serves as a "test" or a "trial of battle" for the candidate. During the campaign, the voters are able to determine if the candidate has "the right stuff" to hold public office. The credibility and viability of the candidacy is determined through the trials of the campaign such as fund-raising, public appearances, and campaign debates (Trent & Friedenberg, 1983).

In addition, the campaign satisfies the ritualistic activities necessary to reaffirm the legitimacy of the government in general and the elected officials in particular (see Gronbeck, 1978; see also Combs, 1980; Trent & Friedenberg, 1983). Campaigns encourage people to get involved in the electoral process; they invite participation (Gronbeck, 1978). The degree to which people choose to participate may vary from contributing to money to a campaign, to discussing political issues with friends, to reading or watching news concerning the campaign, to examination of individual political ideas and values, or even to the single task of voting. The result is the same; when people get involved, when they attend to a political campaign or when they vote, they perceive their government as representing them. Therefore, it becomes more legitimate in terms of its exercise of authority over them. It is important to remember that often what voters view as "participatory" is really illusory, as they have achieved that participation through a para-social experience. Except for the physical act of voting, the voters' participation is often more fiction than real.

Some voters do participate and are part of the social construction phase of opinion development. Those individuals who join civic, political, and religious groups often come into contact with candidates for public office as a result of this group membership. Candidates frequently address such groups as part of their public relations campaign. In addition, voters and the media have a chance to interact with candidates during public debates. Given these circumstances, a mutual exchange among the candidates, media personnel, and voters may well occur. This process of mutual exchange dramatizes public issues and establishes the political agenda of the campaign. Often the social-political-economic priorities of the election are decided upon through this process of negotiation. Through this process, a candidate's leadership style and issue priorities are dramatized not only for the public but also the media. However, it is important to remember that the universe of active, participating individuals is really quite small; less than 30 percent of the American population may be characterized as belonging to the social construction phase of opinion construction, that is, less than 30 percent is actively involved in civic, religious, or political groups (see Nimmo, 1978).

Campaign Message Goals

According to Nimmo (1978), there is a threefold goal to political campaign messages. First, campaign messages are directed at the party faithful to encourage them to vote. Second, campaign messages are directed at those who may be independent but who are likely to be predisposed toward the candidacy, and the campaign messages are then used to crystallize their latent support. And third, the campaign messages are directed at the opposition in an effort to convince normally hostile voters that for this one election they would be better off voting for a candidate of another party.

Campaign Plan

A political campaign is organized behavior, and as such, it must be carefully planned and executed. The campaign plan is developed to detail the campaign organization, the financial plan, the research strategy (voters, issues, opposition), and the details concerning message development and dissemination plans. However, the plan is adaptive; it evolves as new ingredients, new inputs, and new evidence surface. It is affected by a number of variables: the campaign setting, the candidate status, the party status, and the candidate style.

Campaign Setting

Political campaigns have different characters depending on the level of the electoral contest. The campaign setting "determines many things about the contest itself—the amount of money spent, the campaign resources available, the comprehensiveness of organization, and so forth" (Nimmo, 1970, p. 30). The level of the campaign determines to some extent the degree of campaign visibility and the amount of voter involvement. Thus it can be expected that presidential campaigns are dissimilar to congressional campaigns, just as congressional campaigns are dissimilar to district attorney races.

High/Low-Involvement Elections

Political contests may be classified as to the degree of voter involvement or interest in the race. High-involvement elections are those elections where voters have commitments to a given position or "concern with a specific stand on an issue" (Rothschild, 1978, p. 60). Low-involvement elections are those elections where voters have merely a "concern with the issue" (Rothschild, 1978, p. 60). Rothschild (1978) has made three generalizations concerning electoral race involvement:

1. National races are more involving than local races, whereas state races have the lowest level of involvement.
2. Close races are more involving than one-sided races.
3. Volatile issues and candidates tend to make races more involving. (p. 61)

Involvement by potential voters may increase when the campaigns of opponents turn away from strictly positive campaigning. Kern (1989) has argued that negative campaigns may make voters more involved and may actually increase voter turnout.

Two Cognitive Political Advertising Models

Involvement in a campaign is an important consideration in determining how political advertising affects the potential voter's choice-making process. Ray (1973) suggests that product advertising relies on a sequence of decision-making steps on the part of the consumer. The sequence begins at awareness and progresses to final choice. The cognitive steps in this sequence have been represented by the abbreviation AIDA (Attention-Interest-Desire-Action), originally developed by Strong (1925).

The AIDA model best applies to high-involvement situations (usually operationalized as a presidential or some other national campaign) with what Robertson (1976) typified as an active audience. High-involvement audiences go through a process of a change—in beliefs, then attitudes, and then action.

Ray (1973) and Krugman (1965-1966) suggest that the order of the steps differs for the low-involvement group as compared to the high-involvement audience. Rather than a change first in beliefs, then in attitudes, and finally in action, Krugman deduced that the steps were changes in beliefs, actions, and then attitudes (or Awareness-Interest-Action-Desire, AIAD). In this view, an individual's attitude(s) changes to be consistent with the person's behavior(s).

Political Advertising Effectiveness in High/Low-Involvement Political Campaigns

The effectiveness of political advertising will be strongest in low-level, local races, such as primary elections, nonpartisan races, races for state positions, and campaigns for the House of Representatives (Kitchens & Stiteler, 1979; Rothschild, 1975; Wanat, 1974).

Rothschild (1975) tested the effectiveness of political advertising for high- and low-involvement races in an experimental setting and discovered that political advertising did have a greater impact on the low-involvement races (see also Rothschild & Ray, 1974). Swinyard and Coney (1978) conducted a field experiment for high-and-low involvement races and came to the same conclusion. The evidence is convincing that political advertising is much more powerful in low-involvement races (see also Grush, McKeough, & Ahlering, 1978; Hofstetter & Buss, 1980; Hofstetter, Zukin, & Buss, 1978; McClure and Patterson, 1974). Swinyard and Coney (1978) suggest that the power of political advertising to influence low-involvement races exists because "voters in high-level races question, defend against, and otherwise counterargue against promotions, [and thus] they are able to protect themselves from much promotional influence" (p. 47).

Low/High-Visibility Races

The campaign setting has a major effect on the type of campaign that is waged. Primary elections, runoff elections, and nonparty elections are particularly influenced by political advertising because political party does not serve as a cue to the voter. Candidates must distinguish themselves from others who are similar. The task is an extraordinary positioning problem. In addition, low-visibility elections with low voter involvement are also heavily influenced by political advertising, as it is likely that very little news space will be devoted to these elections. For this reason, some political consultants have suggested that negative political advertising is a cheap, effective means of getting out the message in these situations, as these campaigns are typically low in general campaign resources and financing. Many consultants believe that it is easier and more effective to say something negative about the opposition than it is to say something positive about the sponsoring candidate (Nugent, 1987).

Cultural Variations

In addition to the type of electoral race, professional political communicators must take into consideration the political culture associated with the electoral setting. There are regional, state, and local

variations as to the public's expectations concerning appropriate election campaign behavior. For example, various political cultures exhibit greater or lesser degrees of tolerance for the introduction of
negative political advertising in a campaign (Copeland & Johnson-
Cartee, 1990; Johnson-Cartee & Copeland, 1991a; 1989a). Indeed, in
some areas, it may be necessary to run only positive spots, just as in
others, only negative political advertising should be used. Political
campaigns must be sensitive to the voters' perceptions of fair play in
their given constituencies (Johnson & Copeland, 1987; Boddewyn &
Marton, 1978).

Candidate Status

Candidate status (specifically, whether the candidate is an
incumbent or a challenger or is running in an open seat) has a significant impact on the campaign plan.   Weaver-Lariscy and Tinkham
(1987), in their survey of 1982 congressional candidates, found that
"advertising media expenditure and allocation strategies vary significantly among types of campaigns: incumbent, challenger, and open-
race" (p. 13). They recommended that incumbents spend less on newspapers, radio, and outdoor advertising because "disproportionate
spending in these media is negatively related to percentage of vote"
(p. 20), and that challengers spend more of their dollars in the broadcast media. Weaver-Lariscy and Tinkham (1987) concluded that "not
only are all campaigns not alike, but different situations call for different strategic decisions" (p. 20).

Goldenberg and Traugott (1984), in their study of congressional
elections, discerned three truisms associated with candidate status
and campaign finance: "Incumbents spend more than challengers, . . .
candidates in open races spend even more than incumbents, and . . . the
costs of campaigning have been increasing" (p. 78). In addition, Reid
and Soley (1983) found that advertising expenditures had "a more positive effect for challengers than incumbents" (p. 49).

Trent and Friedenberg (1983) and Goldenberg and Traugott (1984)
have demonstrated that incumbents and challengers view their races
in different ways. Incumbents are more sensitive to their attentive
public (those who visibly attend to politics and who participate by
making their views known through their political activities), for
they have been in contact with identified groups, individuals who fell
both into supporting and opposing camps during their term of office. In
addition, incumbents view their base of support as being much broader
than do challengers. The American political system is based on com-
promise and negotiation, and an incumbent has had the experience of
healing wounds and making friends in "enemy" camps during his or her

term of office. Thus, the incumbent's party affiliation is not the only determining factor when he or she describes the coalition of support. Incumbents view their incumbency as an advantage, and they intend to use it as such. Incumbents seek to dramatize their "incumbency status" by showing that they are "good enough for the office sought" while still possessing the office (see Trent & Friedenberg, 1983, p. 84). They do this by surrounding themselves with the symbolic trappings of the office (Trent & Friedenberg, 1983), by taking advantage of the perquisites of political office (Cover, 1977), by using the news media's willingness to report on incumbents (Robinson, 1981b), and by maximizing goodwill through constituency service (Fiorina, 1977). Since the 1940s, House of Representative incumbents have been reelected more than 90 percent of the time (Ornstein, Mann, Malbin, Schick, & Bibby, 1986). Senate incumbents have not faired as well. Return rates in the 1970s dropped to around 50 percent. However, in 1986 the return rate was 75 percent (see Goldenberg & Traugott, 1987). In 1992, despite widespread press coverage of the public's discontent with incumbent representatives and senators, despite the "throw the rascals out" mood captured in public opinion polls, despite both challengers and incumbents running on anti-Washington platforms, and despite the Republican National Committee's ads attacking the Democratic congressional members, the Congress was overwhelmingly returned.

But 1994 was a different type of election, and some researchers suggest that it was a realigning election in that the lines between the Republican and Democratic parties have been redrawn. Conventional wisdom had the Democrats doing well in '94 because the economy was strong and the nation was at peace (Steeper, 1995). But the prediction didn't pan out. No incumbent Republican governor, U.S. Senator, or Congressperson lost a bid for reelection. However, numerous incumbent Democrats were defeated, and previously held Democratic seats were lost. The Democrats lost eight Senate seats and eight governorships. And in the House of Representatives, their loses were particularly heavy, with 52 seats lost. Thirty-nine Democratic incumbents were defeated (*National Journal*, 1994). The year "1994 represents the first, deep change in the competitive situation between Republicans and Democrats in over 60 years" (Steeper, 1995, p. 6). How long lived this change will be is far from certain.

In some situations, incumbents may be forced to act like challengers, particularly when they are dropping in the polls and have worthy political opponents within their own primaries. Colford (1992b) noted that George Bush chose to air television spots in New Hampshire before the February 18th primary date. The Republican challenger, Patrick Buchanan, had mounted a vicious public relations and negative ad campaign against the president, and Bush's numbers were slipping (see Colford, 1992a, 1992b). Bush, in effect, was forced to act not as an incumbent but as a challenger. Bush's New Hampshire spots represented the second time in history that an incumbent president was forced to place ads during a primary race (Colford, 1992b). Only Jimmy Carter, when faced with Democratic challenger Ted Kennedy in 1980, had been was forced to air ads in his own party's primaries (Colford, 1992, p. 42). And, it is important to note that the Bush campaign chose to run negatives spots against Buchanan.

Because incumbents are recognized as having a formidable advantage in electoral contests, challengers must be able to convince their financial backers that the power of the campaign purse is able to nullify the advantages of incumbency (see Goldenberg & Traugott, 1984; Jacobson, 1980). Challengers stress their personal characteristics and issue positions in their campaign communications (Goldenberg & Traugott, 1984). According to Trent and Friedenberg (1983), the challenger style "can be defined as a series of communication strategies designed to persuade voters that a change is needed and that the challenger is the best person to bring about the change" (p. 105). This is accomplished in a variety of ways:

1. Attacking the record of opponents
2. Taking the offensive position on issues
3. Calling for a change
4. Emphasizing optimism for the future
5. Speaking to traditional values rather than calling for value changes
6. Appearing to represent the philosophical center of the political party
7. Delegating personal or harsh attacks in an effort to control demagogic rhetoric (Trent & Friedenberg, 1983)

Party Status

John Kingdon (1968) found that Democratic and Republican candidates differ in their campaign strategies. Democrats address labor-oriented coalitions and tend to make liberal issue appeals. Republicans address business-oriented coalitions and tend to make conservative issue appeals (see Goldenberg & Traugott, 1984; Kingdon, 1968). Although the Republicans have had control over the White House for 20 of the past 25 years, the Democrats have maintained control over the House and Senate (except for 1980-1986, when the Republicans had a Senate majority) until the 1994 election, when both houses of Congress were dominated by Republicans. Because the Republican party had viewed itself as a minority party, the party's targeted appeals tended to be more broadly based than those of the Democratic party. After the 1994 election, the Republican party enjoyed a substantial lead of eight to ten party identification points over the Democrats; however, party identification by the summer of 1995 was again virtually tied (Wirthlin, 1995).   Republican candidates traditionally spend more than their Democratic counterparts in congressional elections, and they also have been likely to emphasize television advertising (Goldenberg & Traugott, 1984; Hershey, 1974). Traditionally, Republicans have enjoyed success by taking such measures in order to reach independents and late deciders through television, which is the dominate source of news and information for these two groups.

Candidate Communication Style

A candidate's manner of presenting his or her public character to the voters is also a critical consideration in any successful development of a campaign strategy. This topic will be dealt with in depth in Chapter 4.

Political Campaign Advertising Stages

Diamond and Bates (1988) have identified four stages of political advertising in a campaign common through the 1980s: identification spots, which provide name identification for the candidate; argument spots, which identify the candidate's issue stands; attack spots, which are used to suggest the opponent's inferiority and sometimes the sponsor's superiority as well; and the "I see an America" spots, which present the candidate as a political visionary and end the campaign on a positive note (pp. 293-345;   see also Diamond & Marin, 1989; Payne, Marlier, & Baukus, 1989). Owen (1991) found that the 1984 and 1988 presidential campaigns "essentially conformed" to these timeline patterns (p. 29). Because visionary ads are primarily used by presidential campaigns, research in other political realms often fails to find a significant number of such ads.

Similarly, Peter Dailey, a Republican political consultant, has identified three levels of a political campaign: the first, where candidates "build a base of credibility"; the second, where they "offer solutions to the problems that exist"; and the third, where they "attack [their] opponent" (Devlin, 1981, p. 5). Hagstrom and Guskind (1986) offer a similar breakdown of advertising stages.

Gronbeck (1992) provides an alternative analysis:

Thus, campaigns can be charted on a timeline; we as an electorate have come to expect different sorts of political messages delivered to us at different times. We expect attention-getting messages in phase one, the rhetoric of expectations in phase two, the political myth-making and power-talk during the phase three, and the argumentative thrusts and parries as well as sloganeering of phase four. (p. 335)

Traditionally, although these campaign "timelines" differ in terminology, it becomes clear that researchers have observed that negative political advertising occurs late in a campaign. However, recently some researchers have posited a much different scenario. Kathleen Jamieson has clearly postulated in an interview with *The Washington Post* that she believes the smart candidate is one that attacks early in the game (Grove, 1988, p. A1). Similarly, Kern (1989) suggests that political consultants and their candidates began to use negative political advertising differently in the 1980s. While traditionally challengers used the majority of negative ads, these ads were usually aired late in the campaign and only after the challenger had built sufficient name recognition and had been identified with the campaign's major policy positions or issues (Kaid & Davidson, 1986). During the 1980s, challengers began using even more negative ads, and they began to use them earlier in the campaign. Perhaps most significantly, vulnerable incumbents now produce negative advertising of their own (Kern, 1989). Interestingly, Kaid and Johnston (1991), in their study of presidential races from 1960 to 1988, found that 30 percent of challengers' ads were negative as compared with 28 percent of incumbents ads (p. 58).

Kaid and Johnston (1991), in their review of presidential advertising from 1960 through 1988, found that more than one-third of all presidential ads during the 1980, 1984, and 1988 campaigns may be classified as negative. They traced the evolution of the use of negative polispots across the presidential years and found that 22 percent of the 1968 presidential campaign ads were negative, 28 percent of the 1972 presidential ads were negative, 24 percent of the 1976 presidential ads were negative, 36 percent of the 1980 presidential ads were negative, 35 percent of the 1984 ads were negative, and 37 percent of the 1988 presidential ads were negative. Clearly, negative political advertising in the presidential realm has increased.

Challengers have an important strategic reason for offering negative ads early in the campaign. Kern (1989) explains:

Early [negative] televised advertising is being used by challengers in districts in which an incumbent is potentially vulnerable for the purpose of getting news coverage that contributes to the success of fund-raising efforts and thereby helps make the race competitive. (p. 181)

Because the news media cover the use of negative ads, the challenger moves from being merely visible to being viable; Kern (1989) calls this phenomenon a "media permutation." Challengers are able to gain name recognition earlier and more easily through this process, and this translates into early money for the candidate, which has been a challenger's traditionally weak area.

In 1986, incumbent California Senator Alan Cranston became one of the first incumbents to begin a general election campaign with negative spots. In 1988, 1990, and 1992, incumbents made greater use of negative ads earlier in their campaigns, particularly when faced by a well-financed challenger or when the incumbent was recognized as being vulnerable to attack.

Negative campaigns are those in which more than 60 percent of the political advertising is negative (Tarrance, 1982). Originally, Tarrance (1982) wrote of the negative campaign in connection with the growth of independent political action committees and the use of independent campaign expenditures. Negative political advertising is the fundamental tool of PACS. However, since the early 1980s, more traditional political campaigns have also used a negative campaign approach. Some examples include: the 1986 Shelby/Denton Alabama senate race, the 1986 Cranston/Zschau California senate race, the 1988 Lautenberg/Dawkins New Jersey senate race, the 1989 Florio/Courter New Jersey gubernatorial race, the 1989 Wilder/Coleman Virginia gubernatorial contest; the 1990 Richardson/Williams Texas gubernatorial contest, the 1990 Gantt/Helms North Carolina senate race, the 1992 Abrams/D'Amato New York senate race, the 1994 Richards/Bush Texas gubernatorial contest.

IMPRESSION MANAGEMENT

In addition to lessons from traditional political science, political consultants also utilize the techniques of the modern public relations (PR) professional. PR professionals are not only concerned with actively influencing the public's evaluation of their company's character but also the evaluation of public issues likely to impact upon the company or on those issues the company is likely to affect (see Dunn, 1986; Moore & Kalupa, 1985; Newsom & Scott, 1985; Wilcox, Ault, & Agee, 1986). Strategies pursued in order to alleviate such concerns may be grouped under one heading: impression management.

Politicians are concerned with the way in which others perceive them because it is often the public's perception that determines their successes in the arena of politics (Bennett, 1988; Neustadt, 1980). For this reason, both incumbents and challengers engage in "impression management" (see Combs, 1980; Goffman, 1959; Hall, 1972; Johnson, 1984). Through public relations and advertising, the candidate attempts to define the political situation for his or her followers in the candidate's own best interests. In short, the candidate attempts to manage the public perception or impression of the situation.

Impression management involves the control of information from the campaign. This means that all information from the campaign, such as press releases, speeches, political ad-vertising, and so on, must be carefully planned and managed. Impression management entails the management of both unpaid or uncontrolled political campaign communication and paid or controlled political campaign communication. Unpaid or uncontrolled political campaign communication is communication that is not directly controlled by the candidate's campaign. Examples of uncontrolled campaign communication are news stories, public forums, interviews, and so forth. Thus the uncontrolled situations require political public relations or "the art of being believed," as veteran public relations practitioner Ivy Ledbetter Lee often quipped (Combs & Nimmo, 1993). Frequently, the communication with the news media, staff, and general public is the most difficult to manage, for it is, in public relations terms, an "uncontrolled" communication involving the participation of others who are possibly acting with goals other than to support the candidate. These goals ultimately affect the eventual message that is produced. When talking with news people, the ultimate story is determined by the reporter's perceptions, analysis, and evaluation of what the candidate has said. When communicating through others, such as campaign workers, the message frequently becomes distorted because of the very nature of the communication process. When making public appearances, even the candidate may make mistakes, and the result is the much-publicized political gaffes of the 1980s and 1990s (DeVries, 1971; Theis, 1968). During the 1988 presidential campaign, Dukakis's decision to ride in a military tank at one public appearance was ridiculed by the media, and footage of the event was used in Bush's negative ad campaign. During the 1992 presidential campaign, Hillary Clinton responded angrily to voter criticism that she was not a traditional housewife and mother. Her response that she had better things to do than bake cookies and drink tea and sit around all day did not play well with the nation's housewives. To avoid such problems, the campaign staff must be well versed as to appropriate communication strategies; they must speak with one voice to the news media. Speeches must be carefully scripted. Public performances must be carefully staged and news conferences carefully rehearsed (Whillock, 1991).

The paid or controlled political campaign communication falls under the realm of political advertising. Kaid (1981) defines political advertising as the communication process by which a source (usually a political candidate or party) purchases the opportunity to expose receivers through mass channels to political messages with the intended effect of influencing their political attitudes, beliefs, and/or behaviors. (p. 250)

Political advertising is a controlled medium in that the candidate has the ultimate control and responsibility as to what is disseminated and how or to whom it is disseminated. Accordingly, political advertising is easier to manage than political public relations communication. In addition, it serves as the more critical of the two in that how well the campaign conducts the political advertising campaign may affect how the public relations strategies are received (see Devlin, 1989; Johnson-Cartee & Copeland, 1991a). A bungled advertising campaign will lead to negative news media evaluations about the leadership of a given candidate. During a television interview, Kathleen Jamieson told NBC reporter Stan Bernard that "Michael Dukakis for two-thirds of the election forfeited the opportunity to discredit George Bush and put in place a compelling reason to vote for him. Advertising ineptitude almost unparalleled. . . . Can someone who can't manage a campaign better than this manage the government? Manage the country?" (Bernard, 1988).

In summary, candidates have a fundamental interest in impression management, in advocating their realities, in staging their own dramas, in getting their definition of the political situation out to the public in the form that they desire. Political public relations and political advertising strategies are important tools in the impression management process.

Impression Management Tactics

Consultants and researchers have pinpointed a number of techniques to ensure the consistency between news media reports, campaign communication, and political advertising. Jamieson and Campbell (1983) have created a five-point list of structured guidelines for the campaign staff:

(1) control news coverage by controlling media access, setting the media's agenda, and creating credible pseudo-events; (2) blur the distinction between news and commercials in order to increase the credibility of the commercial's message; (3) exploit the linguistic categories reflecting criteria for newsworthiness and conventions of news presentations through which journalists view campaigns; (4) insulate the candidate from attack; and (5) enlist the help of journalists in responding to attacks. (Jamieson & Campbell, 1983, p. 229)

Jamieson and Campbell (1983) recommend that the campaign staff "control news coverage by controlling media access, setting the media's agenda, and creating . . . pseudo-events" (p. 229). By limiting media access to the campaign, the staff can tightly manage the candidate's public performances; because of the limited opportunities, the news media become anxious, if not eager, to hear the candidate's messages. Thus the campaign is able to ensure that when the candidate wants intensive and extensive coverage of a particular speech or public appearance, the media will give the candidate the space or air time that he or she wants. In addition, limited access decreases the chances that the candidate will become over exposed. The problem with overexposure is twofold: one, the media may get bored with the candidate and the candidate's campaign, and two, the public may get bored with the candidate and the candidate's campaign. Both are fatal situations for the aspiring political actor, for both the media and the public will "tune out and turn off" the candidate when bored. Yet, a political campaign must set an activist stance in dramatizing its message(s) for the media. By defining issues and campaign themes in an aggressive, "newsworthy" manner, candidates are able to influence the media's campaign coverage and, by this means, control the public debate surrounding campaign issues. Thus when the paid media (advertising) state the same campaign messages, the messages are perceived as being more credible, and this restatement in another media form (e.g., news reports) works as a reinforcement. Clearly, pseudo-events or medialities can be used to create news media coverage that reinforces political advertising themes. Schwartz (1972, 1976) calls the coordination of public relations-news media themes with political advertising the process of synchronization.

Second, Jamieson and Campbell (1983) recommend that campaigns blur the distinction between news and commercials in order to increase the credibility of the commercial's message. This is done in two ways: first, the actual commercial may be designed so that it resembles a news story. The "proselytizing reporter spot" and "the person-in-the-street spot" are both examples of the news style ads that have been so popular in the 1980s and 1990s (see Johnson-Cartee & Copeland, 1991a, 1997). In 1984, James Kelly, commenting on the Reagan campaign in "Packaging the Presidency," wrote that "the managers [had] done such a seamless job of presenting their candidate this year that viewers often had trouble telling the paid political announcements from the evening news" (p. 36).

In addition to making the advertising look like television news packages, the campaign may secondarily place their news-style ads around news shows, which increases the chance that they will be misperceived as a real news piece. It is not surprising that the most frequent placement spot for a political ad is surrounding news programming (Diamond & Bates, 1988; Wilson, 1987).

In order to ensure news media coverage of campaign events, campaign consultants should "exploit the linguistic categories reflecting criteria for newsworthiness and conventions of news presentations through which journalists view campaigns" (Jamieson & Campbell, 1983, p. 229). What they mean is that successful candidates stage campaigns that utilize additional major news values, such as visual attractiveness, importance, size, proximity, brevity, negativity, and recency (Golding, 1981). The news media respond in predictable ways to such orchestrations.

The news media are frequently criticized for depicting campaigns as horse races, first-past-the-post exercises in modern democracy (Barber, 1978; Berkman & Kitch, 1986; Carey, 1976; Graber, 1980; Patterson, 1980; Semetko et al., 1991; Williams, Shapiro, & Cutbirth, 1991; Sigal, 1978), but it must be remembered that it is the interaction among the political campaign's staff and the news persons that establishes the "story of the day." Or, as Sigal (1978) has put it, "Newsmen do not write the score or play an instrument; they amplify the sounds of the music makers" (p. 465). Campaign spokespersons depict the campaigns in highly stylized ways: It is the good guys against the bad guys; it is the "right side" against the "might side." It is name calling and verbal boxing. And it is not only the political public relations messages that resemble boxing matches but the political advertising as well. For this reason, the jousting becomes a dominant theme in political news coverage of the campaign. Such news presentations are called metacampaign analysis. For the most part, it is what is known about political campaigns (Hart, 1987; Weaver, 1976).

Keeter and Zukin (1982) found that the true test of a presidential candidate rests in the media's coverage of the horse-race nature of the campaign and the media's evaluation of how well the candidate is doing in the horse race. Significantly, viability research during the 1980s found that primary voters base their voting decisions on how well a candidate is doing in the primaries and how well a candidate is likely to do on election day rather than on such things as issues, character, or ideology (Aldrich, 1980; Bartels, 1985, 1987).

Negative political advertising is frequently used as both media bait, as it attracts the attention of the news media, and as an assault against the opponent. This fits into the news values of negativity and conflict. In addition, negative political advertising is ripe for the news media's horse-race interpretations. A negative ad is like a tennis ball slammed over the net, and the news media serve as umpires who decide if it is a "fair" ball or not. Jamieson (1992) has termed the replay of such ads on television news "unpaid ads" (p. 137) or news ads

(p. 147). She found that such unpaid ads were nearly 12 times more likely to be negative than positive (Jamieson, 1992). And newspaper coverage of such ads was six times more likely to be about negative ads than positive spots (Jamieson, 1992).

In addition, because political consultants have adopted a news-style genre in their presentation of political advertising (see Johnson-Cartee & Copeland, 1991a, 1997), when the ad is discussed or reported on television, the viewer confuses the ad with the news. In other words, the viewers fail to distinguish between the report (the news account) and the reported (the ad). Cappella and Jamieson (1994) found that adwatches "adversely affected" the "interpretations of the ad by the least well-educated" (p. 342). Similarly, Pfau and Louden (1994) found that adwatches particularly adversely impacted the interpretations of the ad made by women in that adwatches actually increased the influence of the targeted ad for female viewers. Cappella and Jamieson (1994) concluded that "the adwatches affected attitudes toward the source of the ad and toward the perceived fairness and importance of the ad. Adwatches did not affect attitudes toward the object of the attack ad nor interpretation of the ad's content" (p. 342). In other words, criticism of an ad affects the voters' evaluation of the sponsor of the ad but does not apparently salvage the damaged reputation of the targeted candidate.

Political consultants believe that the news media serve as the political arbiters of fairness and honesty during a political campaign. Diamond and Bates (1988) and Hagstrom and Guskind (1986) maintain that news reporters jump on inconsistencies, untruths, or misrepresentations in political advertising. Political consultant Bradley S. O'Leary explained: "The press regulates political broadcasts every day. If we say anything that's untrue, it's on the evening news the next day. And don't forget our candidates are also punished by the voters if we say or do something wrong" (quoted in Tucker & Heller, 1987, p. 46). Similarly, Democratic media consultant David Sawyer maintained that "the marketplace works. You try to put an unsubstantiated ad on TV and in 48 hours the press will be all over your case" (Taylor, 1986, p. A7).

However, Jamieson (1992) believes that the media fail in their role to investigate political advertising abuses. She claims that while news stories emphasize the negativity of ads, they seldom analyze the truth or falsity of such advertising. Jamieson (1992) writes,

I have suggested that visually evocative, controversial, and humorous opposi-
tional ads are securing uncritical play in national news with two likely effects:
a campaign gains the benefit of unpaid access to a large audience; and false claims
in the ad segment are legitimized by airing without correction in news space and

time. More important, legitimizing misleading ads in news rewards rather than punishes the campaign that produced the material. (p. 147)

The 1988 presidential campaign provides evidence that Jamieson's (1992) claims contain a ring of truth. Bush's Furlough and Boston Harbor spots all contained political innuendo, half-truths, untruths, and misrepresentations, yet they were replayed on national news shows over and over again—not for their "dirty" campaigning tactics but for their "negativity" (see Goldman & Matthews, 1989; Jamieson, 1992). If it can be said that news reporters rarely critically examine negative political advertising, then it can be said almost as an absolute that the news media never investigate positive political advertising (Johnson-Cartee and Copeland, 1991b). Previously, we (Johnson-Cartee and Copeland 1991b) noted that because the news media do not define "positive" ads as newsworthy, the reporters rarely even review these ads. Numerous examples abound of blatant lies and distortions appearing in positive polispots (Johnson-Cartee & Copeland, 1991b).

In a closely related study, Lemert, Elliot, Bernstein, Rosenberg, and Nestvold (1991) maintained that the effectiveness of negative political advertising rests not with how the voters perceive the polispots but rather with the journalists' and other elite reactions to the polispots. In their study of the 1988 presidential campaign, they highlighted the news media's interpretation of Dukakis's failure to respond to Bush's negative advertising and the resulting critical appraisal of his leadership abilities as being far more "effective" in hurting Dukakis than any of Bush's negative ads attacking him.

Because of their negativity, negative ads serve as an important ingredient in the metacampaign epic. The metacampaign story deals with the contest or horse-race aspects of a political campaign. Reporters spin stories about who has what consultant, who is spending what, who is endorsing whom, who is attacking whom, and so on. Polispots give the spin doctors something to spin. Because news accounts emphasize negative advertising in their metacampaign stories, voters may overestimate the presence of negativity in presidential campaigns (Kaid & Johnston, 1991, p. 63).

Today, political consultants often hold press conferences where they screen ads for reporters. This promotes what has been called metacampaign news coverage (Jamieson, 1984, 2nd par.). According to Diamond and Bates (1988), this type of news coverage has become routine:

Indeed, for the indolent (or overworked) journalist, it can be easier than rolling out of bed in the morning--flip the candidate's new videotape into the home VCR and write the story of the new ads right there, or at most attend the news conference screening and file the media story. (p. 372)

According to Jamieson (1984), only those campaigns that are worried about the "ads' sins of commission and omission" fail to take advantage of this metacampaign coverage strategy (2nd par., p. xx). In other words, if the ads are truthful (taking into account both what appears in the ads and more importantly what was left out) and present a fair interpretation of the facts, then the campaigns will preview them for the news media.

The last two guidelines laid out by Jamieson and Campbell (1983) concern protecting the candidate from potential or actual negative attacks. In addition to maximizing the impact of their own negative political ads, the campaign staff should be ready to combat any negative ads that are directed at their candidate. The campaign staff should work to "insulate the candidate from attack," and if the candidate is attacked, "enlist the help of journalists in responding to attacks" (Jamieson & Campbell, 1983, p. 229).

Through careful research and analysis, the staff should know both the strengths and weaknesses of their candidate before the "public" campaign actually begins. If any potential weaknesses are found, a preemptive advertising strategy should be considered (see Chapter 5). In this way, the candidate can beat the opposition to his or her perceived weakness. An admitted weakness can be turned into a campaign virtue, for candidates who are able to admit that they have made mistakes are perceived as being more credible by the voters (Smith & Hunt, 1978). In addition, the campaign should have as its goal from the beginning the careful impression management of their candidate's campaign persona.

If, however, the candidate is attacked, the campaign should have on hand the resources and talent necessary to quickly produce refutation spots and to respond through other channels, such as the news media (see Chapter 6). The campaign should have enough research people available to quickly and efficiently provide evidence to news reporters to discredit the charges. If, however, the charges are true, the campaign staff needs to know enough about the candidate and his or her weaknesses and already have in place a contingency plan to enact when this happens. Sometimes a potentially devastating attack can be dismantled by an effective response.

In summary, the Jamieson and Campbell (1983) guidelines provide significant impression management tactics, for by using these guidelines, a campaign is more able to manage the candidate's persona. Impression management, like modern-day public relations, is "art applied to science," and it serves as an essential ingredient in the successful political campaign (Bernays, 1955).

SIMILARITIES AND DIFFERENCES IN COMMERCIAL VS. POLITICAL ADVERTISING AND MARKETING

Political consulting is the business of selling—the selling of political candidates, parties, and ideas. Political advertising, in particular, has borrowed many of its operating concepts from its commercial brother. Yet even though there are similarities, there remain fundamental differences in the two. We will now examine similarities and differences.

Similarities

Michael Kaye, a commercial and political marketing expert, believes that both forms of advertising use the same tripartite analysis steps. First, the advertiser must "know his product," then he must "look at the competition," and third, he must "understand the audience" (reported in Sabato, 1981, p. 174). Then and only then can a product be successfully positioned in the marketplace.

Positioning

This tripartite analysis leads the advertiser to the crucial stage of developing a creative strategy for positioning the product (or political candidate). Nimmo and Johnson (1980) stated,

Positioning is designed to place a product within a particular group or atmosphere as a means of distinguishing it from competing products, which, in substance, are strikingly similar to that being huckstered. The attempt is to carve out a share of the market not on the basis of distinctive traits or qualities inherent in the product, but to mold a picture of the product as distinctive because of those who buy, use or otherwise consume it. (p. 37; see also Combs, 1979; Sabato, 1981)

"Position advertising stresses *expressive* benefits associated with marketed goods, more so than material or solidary differences" (Combs & Nimmo, 1993, p. 144). According to Sabato (1981), "implication about rivals is the vital element in positioning"(p. 175). For positioning is relational, as candidates are portrayed with the opponent's image in mind; thus distinctions are made and positions are drawn based upon how they will distinguish the candidate in the eyes of specific segments of the political marketplace. "In effect, it is the logical outgrowth of image analysis in that it involves applying what you know about your brand's [candidate's] image, the competition, the market you are trying to reach, and how members of this market are motivated" (Dunn & Barban, 1986, p. 343; see also Kurtz & Boone, 1984, p. 598).

Brand Image

A brand image is the range of cognitions, affections, and behaviors associated with a product or a candidate (see Dunn & Barban, 1986; Patti & Frazer, 1988). Political consultants must consider the "brand image" not only of their own candidate but also of their opposition. Research is geared to discover what it is that the voter sees in the candidate and his or her opponent. What does the candidate mean to the voter? How do the voters evaluate the range of cognitions, affections, and behaviors associated with the candidates? According to Combs and Nimmo (1993), after the 1950s, "material differences between candidates respecting backgrounds, experience, and issues received less emphasis; the promise of solidary rewards emanating from candidates' personalities became the package in which material promises were wrapped" (p. 149).

Selling Propositions

In addition to brand imagery, a political consultant must examine the "selling propositions" associated with both the consultant's political candidate and the opposition. Selling propositions are the most persuasive arguments "that can be offered as to why prospects should buy the product" (Patti & Frazer, 1988, p. 291). In the 1960s, commercial advertisers were influenced by the concept of a "unique selling proposition" (U.S.P.). Unique selling propositions are "the differentiating qualities" of products, candidates, and/or parties (see Dunn & Barban, 1986, p. 345; Patti & Frazer, 1988, p. 294). According to the grandfather of U.S.P. and a pioneer of political consulting, Rosser Reeves (1961), the unique selling proposition must make a relational statement that draws a connection between buying a product or voting for a candidate and receiving clear benefits as a result. The U.S.P. must be drawn in such a way that competing products or candidates cannot offer the same distinction. Furthermore, the U.S.P. must be desirable enough for a large part of the target market to be favorably disposed toward this claim (pp. 47-48; see also Diamond & Bates, 1988; Patti & Frazer, 1988).

However, not all political consultants agree that U.S.P. is the strategy to use in political advertising. MacDougall believes that unlike product advertising, political advertising must have more than one selling proposition. He does not find the U.S.P. strategy a very useful one in politics for two reasons: one, there must usually be more than one persuasive reason for someone to vote for a candidate, and two, under normal situations, the campaign must appeal to more than one target group, which often means that the same candidate is being sold to widely different groups who have widely different needs and therefore require widely different selling propositions (see discussion in Diamond & Bates, 1988).

Target Marketing

A very traditional advertising/marketing concept, target marketing, is also used in political advertising. A target market is "a group of people defined by certain characteristics and focused on as the intended receivers of the advertising message" (Dunn & Barban, 1986, p. 793; see also Patti & Frazer, 1988, p. 190). In other words, a target market is a group of people who are eligible to vote or who will be eligible to vote by election day and who are likely to be predisposed toward a particular candidate and/or party because of their demographic and psychographic characteristics. The process of identifying a target market is called market segmentation. Market segmentation "identifies the wants and needs of the market for the purpose of allocating marketing resources" (Patti & Frazer, 1988, pp. 190-191).

During the 1992 presidential election, the independent political action committee Rural Americans for Fairness sponsored a direct attack ad highlighting the Bush record in rural America. The ad ended with a tag supporting the Clinton/Gore ticket. This spot was produced by Rural Americans to target rural Americans, and it contains a highly specific campaign argument.

The 1992 Rural Americans for Fairness "Neglect" Ad

Video	Audio
Newspaper headlines: "Rural Life: The Dream Goes Bust" "Jobless Picture Dreary in Rural Communities" "1990-92 worst year since depression, say economists" "As Farm Falters, Rural Homelessness Grows" "Rural America lost out under Reagan, Bush" "Rural Shortage of Physicians May Worsen" "Don't Get Sick in Rural America" "Down on the Farm: The Depression in	Sad violin music. Announcer [VO]: "They promised prosperity. They called it trickle-down economics. Maybe good news trickled down some place, but if you live in rural America, you didn't even get damp. The question you have to answer is: "Can our way of life survive another four years of neglect?"'

Rural America" "Violence Rising
in Some Rural "States" Baby
deaths four year high in rural
America" "Out of work, out of
rural welfare grants" "Rural
Crisis Takes its Toll on Teens"
"Yield New Crop of Poor, Trouble
Meeting Needs" ". . . Documents
rural poverty" "Rural Child Care
Fights for Survival" "Decline of
Rural Areas Feared" "Poverty in
America, rural children suffer"
"Rural Folk Feel Betrayed." Super:
Black and White lettering:
Clinton/Gore.

Resonance Strategy

Sound political marketing uses what Schwartz (1972, 1976) called
a "resonance" strategy. Such a strategy uses persuasive messages that
are "harmonious with the experience of the audience" (Patti & Frazer,
1988, p. 301; Schwartz, 1976). Thus, the job of a political consultant is
to create campaign messages that resonate "with information already
stored within an individual and thereby [induce] the desired learning
or behavioral effect. Resonance takes place when the stimuli put into
our communication evoke meaning in a listener or viewer" (Schwartz,
1972, pp. 24-25). This strategy doesn't create something new in the
audience rather it uses what already exists and takes advantage of
currently held information. Thus as Combs (1979) and Schwartz (1972;
1976) suggest, the political consultant works to discover the
political/cultural myths that are shared by groups of voters and that
can be evoked by mass-mediated messages (see also Nimmo & Combs,
1980). Consultants then seek to evoke the responsive chords within
voters (Schwartz, 1972). By striking these responsive chords, consultants and candidates attempt to reach the inner core of the voter's
psyche (Diamond & Bates, 1988). Democratic political consultant
Robert Squier calls these responsive chords "hot buttons" (Squier, 1987;
see also Diamond & Bates, 1988). According to Squier, "once those
buttons are pushed, I know I've got them. I've touched their emotions"
(Squier, 1987). Schwartz (1976) concludes: "Commercials which
attempt to tell the listener something are inherently not as effective
as those which attach to something that is already in him. We are
not focused on getting things across to people as much as out of people"
(p. 352). We (1997) previously provided a thorough analysis of the
responsive chords in American politics.

Packaging

In addition to the resonance/responsive chord strategy, political consultants have also adopted the packaging concept from product advertising and marketing. The package of a product has been used in a selling role since 1899, when "Uneeds biscuits appeared, not in a cracker barrel, but in a folding paperboard box" (Dunn & Barban, 1986, p. 674). "Packages communicate and promote the product while serving as containers. . . . As a communication tool, packages communicate both nonverbally and verbally. . . . The package can promote sales most successfully if it suggests some desirable qualities of the product and some product reward" (Dunn & Barban, 1986, p. 674).

The term "packaging" is also used in political advertising. In many ways, the same things said of product packaging may be said of candidate packaging. "The package" refers to the total impression-managed candidate, which is created with the thought of how the package will play on the public stage. Political consultants, then, attempt to find "what it is the public most wants to buy" and then make it available to them (Bloom, 1973). But as Theis (1968) has warned: the candidate is an unpredictable quotient in that human frailties often interfere with the best-laid strategic plans. Edmund Muskey, Gary Hart, Joe Biden, and a host of others are living proof of that statement.

The voters' awareness of candidate packaging is so elevated that in recent years political consultants have produced spots that attacked other candidates for being packaged and controlled by political consultants. In a South Dakota senate race in 1986, Democratic Congressman Thomas Daschle attacked Republican Senator James Abdnor with a polispot that showed numerous Abdnor political consultants sitting around a table deciding how to distort Daschle's political record. And in the 1988 presidential campaign, the Democratic National Committee produced about a dozen antipackaging ads that were directed against George Bush and Dan Quayle (Johnson-Cartee & Copeland, 1991a; see also Goldman & Matthews, 1989; Schram, 1991).

Hard vs. Soft Sell

Early commercial advertising was characterized by the "hard sell." The hard sell strategy was based upon "brain-pounding repetition to make its unique selling propositions" (Diamond & Bates, 1988, p. 114). Rosser Reeves (1961) is associated with the hard sell. In the late 1960s, the hard-sell strategy gave way to the "soft-sell" strategy. Soft sell uses emotional appeals that depend on the affective dimensions of the audience. Soft sell depends "on how the viewer felt about what he or she was seeing and hearing" (Diamond & Bates, 1988, p.

114). Schwartz (1972, 1976) is associated with the advent of the soft sell.

Political advertising followed the direction of commercial advertising in adopting the soft-sell approach. However, some vestiges of the old style still remain, one of which is the use of the tag line (Johnson-Cartee & Copeland, 1997). A tag line is the optional closing line that either summarizes the ad, directs the voter to do something, or asks a rhetorical question.

Comparative Advertising

We (1991a) provided an analysis of comparative product advertising literature and how these research findings relate to the study of negative political advertising. Insights from the literature include the following:

1. Challengers may benefit from producing comparative ads that show both the challenger and the incumbent in the same ad, for such an appearance increases the credibility of the challenger.
2. When a candidate discovers a weakness on the part of his opponent on matters where the candidate enjoys a comparative advantage, then the candidate should produce a comparative ad emphasizing the differences in their candidacies.
3. Candidates running in an electoral setting with large numbers of uncommitted voters benefit substantially from the use of comparative advertising.
4. Because negative information has higher recall than positive information and is considered more persuasive, candidates on a limited budget should consider comparative advertising as a cost-effective measure.
5. Candidates involved in a multicandidate primary should visually show the candidates in a comparative ad because this provides a very important tool for voters seeking to draw distinctions among candidates.
6. Candidates using comparative advertising should use primarily rational appeals rather than emotional appeals. Ads using appeals that may be evaluated through normal evidential procedures have proven to be more effective in judging task-related activities, such as judging a candidate's fitness for office.
7. Comparative political advertising that stresses one or two comparative points is far more effective than advertising that highlights more.
8. Comparative political advertising should not "offend the sensibilities of the voters, and [should] ensure that [the] negative claims are truthful and fair representation of the differences existing between the political candidates" (Johnson-Cartee & Copeland, 1991a, p. 24) in order to avoid the backlash effect that harms the sponsoring candidate.

In summary, much can be written concerning the similarities between product advertising/marketing and political advertising/marketing. Combs (1979) summarized the similarities between commercial and political advertising in the following manner:

The logic, much of the style, and the intentions of political advertising resemble its commercial ancestor. Both political and non-political advertising create a fictional fantasy world into which audiences may be transported; both utilize the full range of artistic devices to entertain and persuade; both are selling something, and they freely utilize symbols from our national mythology and primal anxieties as appeals. Both have taken on a "reality" for us to the extent that we accept these fantasy worlds as part of our environment, and they even appear to affect our perceptions of the world, political and otherwise. (pp. 338-339; see also, Henry, 1963; McGann, 1984; Nimmo, 1970)

Fundamental Differences

Although political advertising shares some of the principles of product advertising, there are some differences.

Attendance

People pay more attention to political advertising than product advertising. Patterson and McClure (1976) reported that only 20 percent of television viewers can recall specific product advertising, but 79 percent of television viewers can recall specific presidential political ads. Furthermore, 56 percent of those who can recall the presidential ads are able to give content details concerning the ads (Patterson & McClure, 1976).

Higher Persuasive Goals

The persuasive goals are much higher in political advertising than in product advertising. Bloom (1973) explained: "A commercial program can be a great success if it 'sells' 5 percent of the market. A political program will probably fail if it does not 'sell' more than 50 percent of the electoral market" (p. 29) or at least a plurality.

Shorter Advertising Season

It must be remembered that the window of opportunity for success is very narrow for a political campaign. As just noted, the political candidate must be able to mobilize over 50 percent of the voters within a 12-hour window on election day. In addition, the "advertising season" for a political campaign is very short compared to the advertising cycle of a product (Sabato, 1981; Bloom, 1973). Although the campaign season has enlarged in recent years, the fact still remains that the majority of political advertising occurs in the three to four weeks prior to election day.

Responsive Nature

The responsive nature of a political campaign changes the character of the advertising strategy. Unlike the usual long-term product advertising programs, political advertising requires responsive strategies that are able to react and respond to breaking news events, public pronouncements, and opposition advertising.

Task Orientation

Schwartz (1972, 1976) recommended a task-orientation approach to political advertising in order for it to be responsive. Task orientation involves the careful consideration of three crucial elements: (1) the refined definition of the desired campaign communication effect, (2) the identification of the appropriate responsive chords jointly held by the communicator and the audience, and (3) the evaluation of the communication environment, which includes both the media channel used and the nature of the media/message exposure. After giving thought to these considerations, and only then, should political consultants finally develop appropriate message content (see Schwartz, 1972). Thus, a task-orientation approach is a responsive approach; it deals with political situations through careful analysis of the problems, the audience, and the proposed media. Task-oriented behavior is able to deal with the needs and problems at hand. Product advertising's long-range program approach "cannot deal with these specific problems that arise on a day-to-day basis. A task-oriented campaign can create overnight a commercial which relates to a problem that has just arisen" (Schwartz, 1972, p. 356).

Image Retouching

There is one other fundamental difference between product and political advertising: the degree to which the audience is willing to accept "image-retouching" (see Jamieson, 1984, 2nd par.; Papert, 1971). A product can become "new and improved," and a candidate may alter his or her image, but there is a very fine line that candidates and consultants must walk in order to maintain credibility. It seems easy for a soap powder company to add fabric softener or bleach to its formula and have its target markets accept the change. It is quite another thing altogether for a politician to "change his stripes." Tony Schwartz, Democratic political consultant, has said that image retouching is a dangerous game to play: "You can't tell people something when they know the opposite" (as reported in Jamieson, 1984, 2nd par., p. 382). However, Richard Nixon was successful in 1968 when he presented the "new and improved Nixon" to the American voting public. In other words, one cannot go against what a large number of people know to be true. Type cannot and must not be violated (see Chapter 4). However, political consultants can offer a change in a candidate's persona if it (1) does not appear overtly inconsistent with past behavior; or (2) if they have a carefully orchestrated explanation that can effectively neutralize the overt inconsistency (see Johnson, 1984; see also Klapp, 1964).

Higher Expectations

Sabato (1981) suggested that different style vehicles may have to be utilized in political advertising because some of the traditional product advertising techniques simply will not work in the political arena. Specifically, Sabato recommended that product slice-of-life ads should not be employed in political advertising. Voters have come to expect more from political advertising than product advertising. While they may not mind watching a dramatization concerning the selection of dish detergents by two middle-aged housewives, they do not appreciate a similar dramatization comparing political candidates. Political consultants are not selling soap and they cannot advertise their candidates as if they were (Sabato, 1981). However, we (Johnson-Cartee and Copeland, 1991a) saw a more sophisticated version of the slice-of-life ad introduced at the turn of this decade, that, depending on its execution, appears to be effective.

LENGTH OF SPOT AND BUYING STRATEGY

Political advertising usually comes in 10-second, 15-second, 30-second, 60-second, and 4.5- or 5-minute lengths (Berkman & Kitch, 1986). In the 1972 presidential election, Patterson and McClure (1976b) found that only 2 percent of the television commercials were 30 seconds long. Eight years later in 1980, 55 percent of the Reagan campaign spots were 30 seconds long (Devlin, 1986). The trend had been away from the longer political ads toward shorter ones. However, during the 1988 and 1992 presidential campaigns, candidates experimented with the longer formats. In 1988 the Dukakis campaign aired several 5-minute spots 2 weeks prior to the election, and on election eve, both the Bush and Dukakis campaigns aired 30-minute ads on all three networks (Colford, 1988). In 1992, independent candidate Ross Perot adapted the infomercial to his use, a 30-minute or 60-minute "fireside chat" style ad that usually had Mr. Perot either directly addressing the audience or answering questions from an interviewer. The spots were straightforward and did not reflect any of the glitz associated with contemporary political advertising styles, but the American public watched, fascinated with this unsophisticated but real look at a national presidential candidate. Perot spent $22.8 million on network time for his infomercials during the 2 months prior to the election (Moshavi, 1992), while Bush spent $18.1 million and Clinton spent $9.4 million during their entire campaigns.

The long-form political advertisement, which runs for 5 minutes, does have its advantages. Devlin (1986) has discussed the 5-minute spot's ability to help set mood and establish character, something that both Jimmy Carter in his 1976 race for the presidency and Ronald Reagan in his 1984 reelection campaign used to good advantage. Kaid and Sanders (1978) found that 5-minute issue-oriented advertisements were superior to 60-second spots on candidate evaluation scales. Devlin (1986) also suggests that the longer spots are useful for fundraising.

Surprisingly in 1992, voters seemed to like the longer spots. In a postelection survey by the Times Mirror Center for the People & the Press, 55 percent of respondents judged that Ross Perot's infomericals were most "informative," with 20 percent saying that about Clinton's and only 8 percent saying that about Bush's polispots (Gersh, 1992). Nielsen Media Research (1993) reported that Perot's infomercials had a share ranging from 11 percent to 19 percent. During the first night of the World Series, a Perot infomercial had a 15 percent share, while the World Series only had a 23 percent share (Nielsen Media Research, 1993).

One drawback to these longer spots is that they are harder to place at television stations, most of which do not wish to alter their schedules so as to accommodate these advertisements. That is, the stations are less likely to place the spots at the times campaigns desire.

Yet another potential drawback may be that the 5-minute and longer spots are generally not as cost-effective as 30- and 60-second spots. Historically, the general consensus in academic research has been that shorter is better. Patterson and McClure (1976a) and Napolitan (1972) indicated that viewers were less willing to watch long messages than shorter ones. Swanson (1973) established that retention was about 50 percent better for short commercials versus 30-minute presentations. While it has been reported that 5-minute commercials help image scores, the same data set suggests that the 1-minute spots are better on name recognition measures (Kaid, 1981; Kaid & Sanders, 1978). However, the large audiences that tuned in to watch Perot's infomercials surprised academicians and consultants alike; it may be that the American public's tolerance for political programming is increasing.

On the other hand, political advertising has generally followed the lead of commercial advertising. If that pattern continues, there should be a move to 15-second spots. The J. Walter Thompson advertising agency's research showed that while 15-second spots are only 70 percent as effective as 30-second spots, the cost to air them is half as much (Alsop, 1987). The 1990 Helms campaign for the U.S. Senate used two 10-second spots: one on abortion and one on the death penalty. The only retarding factor in moving to the shorter commercial, according to Burt Manning of Jordan, Manning, Case, Taylor and McGrath advertising agency, may be that "agencies [have found] it next to impossible to produce patriotic and heart-warming 15s that stir an emotional response" (quoted in Alsop, 1987, p. 31).

If this problem can be overcome, it could be possible to get twice the number of spots on the air for the same amount of money. This would increase the general exposure of the candidate for no extra cost. This additional exposure could work positively for the candidate. Rothschild and Ray (1974) discovered that unaided recall of candidates was positively associated with exposure to advertising. Knowledge of candidates and their positions on issues is also positively associated with exposure to their advertising (Atkin and Heald, 1976).

Media Buys

Buying time on television stations and the networks requires a strategy. The media buy is a critical campaign decision. Political consultants "use the industry-accepted systems for dividing the country into about 200 media markets: 'areas of dominant influence' (ADIs) [for radio], developed by Arbitron Ratings Co., and 'designated 'market areas' (DMAs), grouped by the A. C. Nielsen Co. [for television]" (Hagstrom, 1992, p. 22). These rating services provide information along demographic lines. With this information in hand, the consultant then takes voter research information detailing voter turnout and public opinion polling data into account when preparing a media strategy (see Chapter 5; Hagstrom, 1992).

Media planning programs are used by consultants to develop a cost-efficient media strategy. Hagstrom (1992) writes,

In doing so, time buyers use the standard audience measure—the gross rating point—representing 1 percent of the TV-viewing audience. Theoretically, buying 100 points means that the entire viewing audience sees a commercial once. Consultants estimate that a viewer needs to see a commercial three to five times before it makes an impression, thus requiring a buy of 300 to 500 gross rating points. A buy of 500 points is considered 'saturation.'" (p. 22)

The effect of exposures on viewers is unclear. In commercial advertising research, early studies indicated that two exposures to the same commercial message within a 30-minute period are necessary for a 50 percent recall and recognition rate (Grass & Wallace, 1969). Krugman (1972) maintained that three exposures to a commercial message might be enough to create adequate recall and recognition. He also (1972) suggested that the first exposure creates a cognitive response; the second exposure creates an evaluative response; and the third exposure serves as a reinforcement of the cognitive and evaluative responses. Kamin (1978) examined the life span of television commercials. He posited that the optimal repetition level might be between 5 and 20 exposures. Kamin warned that if viewers were exposed to messages more than 20 times, it was likely that viewers would have a negative reaction to the product or brand. Heflin and Hagood (1985) found that for product commercials, "schedules which are moderately spaced (the 1-week and 3-week schedules) result in higher levels of brand recall/recognition than either highly concentrated (1-day) or highly spaced (5-week) schedules" (p. 45). This held true for immediate testing as well as for a 2-week delayed testing (Heflin & Haygood, 1985). The research on commercial advertising should hold true for political advertising, as an analysis of political advertising by Jamieson (1992) found political ads to function similarly to commercial ads.

Campaigns make media buys by working backward from those days immediately before the election. How far back from election day the campaign will buy depends on how much money the campaign has to spend. This is the case because the most important days in terms of influencing the uncommitted are those days immediately before the election (Hagstrom, 1992). Late deciders and ticket splitters often make their decision in the closing days of the campaign, and for this reason, it is important that the candidate have a strong showing going into election day. Generally, around 11 percent of the voting population remains undecided during the last week. In competitive races, a single percentage point will make the difference; therefore, in competitive races heavy media buys will occur during the closing days of the campaign. Candidates who are underfinanced may choose to place a large portion of their money during the last days of the campaign. Such a strategy bets that the party faithful will turn out regardless of media strategy, and therefore all of the candidate's meager resources should be placed on the uncommitted voters.

Candidates that cannot afford professional consultants or high-tech ad men will frequently rely on a type of program/audience analysis (Hagstrom, 1992). Programs like "Murder She Wrote" and "Sixty Minutes" are known to attract disproportionately Republican audiences, just as "Fresh Prince of Bel Aire" and "Murphy Brown" attract Democratic audiences.

In 1992, the Bush campaign made huge network television buys that were more expensive than necessary because California was included. Yet California had been identified by pollsters as a state that Bush did not have a chance of winning. While Doug Watts, a former Reagan media consultant, maintained that Bush had to do huge network buys because he was so far behind, Smith of Smith & Haroff, a Republican consultancy firm, described the Bush campaign's media network media buying strategy as "atrocious" (see Mandese, 1992, p. 52). Bush spent nearly $18 million on the three largest networks, while Clinton spent $3.8 million on the three networks. Clinton concentrated his money on buying time on stations in targeted states where he had a chance of victory (Mandese, 1992).

Sabato identified four buying schemes that campaigns have used in the past. First is the flat buy, the simplest of the four schemes. In the 3 weeks prior to an election, the campaign runs the same number of spots each week. A derivative of the flat buy is the saturation buy, which entails running the candidate's spots as often as time is available on the stations. What makes this a derivation is that any fluctuation in the amount of advertising from week to week is a function of the broadcast stations' lack of available time slots.

The second scheme is the orchestrated finish. The number of political advertisements builds over a period of 4 weeks. Sabato (1981) broke it down: 10 percent 4 weeks from the election, 20 percent 3 weeks away, 30 percent 2 weeks away, and 40 percent during the final week before election day. Increased spending during the final week of a campaign is a frequent occurrence in presidential elections. Mullen (1963a, 1963b, 1968) found that candidates for both president and the Senate will spend the majority of their advertising budgets in the last few campaign days.

The third scheme is the events schedule. The airing of political spots is contingent upon important events in the campaign. These events are usually created by the candidate's campaign, but may also be a response to events outside the direct control of the candidate's campaign.

The fourth is the stop-start scheme. This scheme consists of running ads for a period of time, stopping, and then running ads again. This strategy can be very important to nonincumbents, who may begin to run political ads in order to build name recognition and credibility long before the campaign officially begins. After a period, these spots stop and then are run again during the latter days of the campaign. This strategy can be used by a nonincumbent without a primary challenger, as the nonincumbent may want to run a series of ads during the other party's primary just to maintain name recognition while the opposition is getting extended media exposure. The Clinton campaign ran a modified stop-start scheme in 1995-1996. In the summer of 1995, his campaign ran ads in targeted states to help rebuild Clinton's favorability rating.

Since Sabato's (1981) description of political advertising buying strategies, the character of many federal campaigns has changed. Campaigns are starting earlier, more money is being raised and spent on political advertising, and negative ads are appearing early as well as late in the campaign cycle (Johnson-Cartee & Copeland, 1991a; Kern, 1989). For this reason, campaign advertising buys cover a large period of time and are frequently driven by the results of public opinion polls conducted by the campaign.

Radio/Television Consistency Buy

Edell and Keller (1989) reported that a coordinated radio-television product campaign proved as persuasive in terms of "brand name recall, the brand claims recall, the attitude toward the ad, the attitude toward the brand, or purchase intentions" as did a straight television-repetition campaign (p. 161). They concluded that the consistency between the radio and television messages yielded these results. Generally a radio/television campaign will be more cost-effective than a television campaign; for this reason, political campaigns with limited funds should give serious consideration to this media plan (Edell & Keller, 1989).

Chapter 3

Understanding the Public Opinion Process in the United States

> We hold these truths to be self-evident, that all men are created equal, that they are endowed by their Creator with certain inalienable Rights, that among these are Life, Liberty and the pursuit of Happiness. That to secure these rights, Governments are instituted among Men, deriving their just powers from the consent of the governed. That whenever any Form of Government becomes destructive of these ends, it is the Right of the People to alter or abolish it, and to institute new Government, laying its foundation on such principles and organizing its powers in such form, as to them shall seem most likely to effect their Safety and Happiness.
>
> T. Jefferson
> *American Declaration of Independence*

The term "democracy" comes from a Greek word that means rule by the people (Groth, 1971). Although it has been argued that the philosophical roots of modern democracies rest in the Judeo-Christian tradition, with its emphasis on individual worth, rationality, and freedom, generally it is recognized that the seeds of democratic thought that most influenced the founding fathers came from the Enlightenment (Christenson, Engel, Jacobs, Rejai, & Waltzer, 1981; Groth, 1971). John Locke in *The Second Treatise of Civil Government* and Jean-Jacques Rousseau in *The Social Contract* provided what has become the classical tenets of liberal democratic theory. The tenets have popularly become known as the social contract theory.

Under the social contract theory, an individual is born free with the power and capacity to regulate his or her own life and behavior (Christenson et al., 1981). In this view, every individual is unique, and despite differences in abilities, each individual merits equal political rights and opportunities. "Democracy thus is not based on individualism alone, but also on individuality—or recognition of and respect for the uniqueness of each person. The equality of democracy is an equality of differences, not of sameness" (Christenson et al., 1981, p. 176). Because individuals are born free, they are able to maximize their own potential and opportunities.

Central to the social contract theory is the concept of popular sovereignty, that is, that political power resides in each person and in society as a whole. This idea assumes that man is capable of rational choice, is motivated by principle, is aware of political issues, and is willing to participate in the governing process. It suggests that people will come together of their own accord and create a voluntary social contract with each other in order to benefit from shared resources and responsibilities. For example, individuals on an island may choose to engage in a voluntary social contract establishing a governmental system in order to develop a safe water supply, a reliable road system, or a school system. Thus individuals agree to give up some of their rights, in this case perhaps tax dollars in the form of coconuts , to enjoy a social benefit that they may not have been able to enjoy on their own. But because the contract is voluntary, members may at any time leave the group if they believe that the group is no longer representing their best interests.

The values and beliefs inherent in the social contract theory are known as liberalism (Dolbeare, 1981). Central to the core of liberal belief is the "assumption that the individual is more important than the government and that government exists for the purpose of permitting [the] individual to serve best his or her own needs and attain personal fulfillment" (Dolbeare, 1981, p. 9). (The philosophy of liberalism should be distinguished from the contemporary notion of liberalism, which has become a popular whipping post in recent election cycles. Traditional liberalism's emphasis is on individual rights, whereas contemporary liberalism focuses on group rights.) Although the majority of Americans do not recognize where their political beliefs come from, these beliefs are deeply rooted in traditional liberalism with some variations in emphasis. According to Dolbeare (1981),

The principal tension within the liberal tradition has been conflict over the assigning of priorities among the natural rights of individuals. To most property rights have been paramount, with resulting emphasis on law, contracts, procedural regularity and stability. To some human rights and equality in first political and then social and economic dimensions have been uppermost, with commensurately greater concern for participation, justice and change. (p. 5)

The first group "has continued to place its priorities on economic rights—frequently due to the conviction that this remains the best way to advance the standard of living for all in the long run, not just to advance personal self-interest—have [sic] steadily resisted government 'interference'" (Dolbeare, 1981, p. 10). And the second group sees government as a means to achieve social goals. They believe that individuals have been frustrated by external forces (e.g., poverty, lack of educational opportunities) in their attempts to achieve their potentiality and that the government should act to control or manipulate those external forces.

This fundamental tension within liberal democratic theory in America is reflected in how and in what ways the political parties campaign. Morreale (1991a) maintains that it is reflected in the political mythology of the American Dream. She notes that "there are, however, two dichotomous versions of the myth of the American Dream—the materialistic and the moralistic—that reflect different notions of America's nature and purpose" (Morreale, 1991a, p. 58). These differences are apparent in the different interpretations of the American Dream made by the two major political parties in the United States. According to Morreale (1991a),

The materialistic myth is associated with the traditional Republican position. It emphasizes individual initiative as the means to happiness and prosperity; it presupposes the value of competition, free enterprise, and individual freedom from governmental regulation and restraint. It promises that hard work will be rewarded, and presumes that individuals act on the basis of self-interest rather than concern for the social good. The moralistic myth, more characteristic of the Democratic view, emphasizes a need for community and society that may supersede individual needs; it is based upon a belief in equality, rights to liberty and pursuit of happiness, and the values of tolerance, charity, and compassion. (p. 59)

Thus fundamental tension is also reflected in the two major parties' different economic orientations. The Republican party follows the school of Austrian economics, which disapproves of governmental intervention in the economy and posits that all members of society will ultimately benefit if all members of society are allowed to pursue their economic opportunities free of government restraint. They believe that social aid throws money at the symptoms of the problem of the economic underclass but does not provide a cure for the underlying problems. The Democratic party, on the other hand, is tied to Keynesian economics, which maintains that capitalism has created gross inequalities in wealth and in order to cure these inequalities, the government should take from the wealthy and give to the poor.

MODERN BELIEF SYSTEMS

It is important to remember, however, that an awareness of or an understanding of liberal democratic theory is limited to a very few individuals who make up a political elite.   Indeed, very few Americans are able to distinguish correctly between liberal versus conservative ideological dimensions (contemporary meanings of the terms). Hennessey (1970) observed that "political attitudes are an elite phenomenon. . . . Even in modern high-energy societies most people do not have political attitudes" (p. 463).

Political Knowledge

During the past thirty years, a constant theme in political science and public opinion research has been the relative ignorance of the majority of Americans when it comes to the political issues of our times (see Bishop, Oldendick, Tuchfarber, & Bennett, 1980; Converse, 1970; Key, 1961; O'Gorman, 1975; Patterson, 1980; Tichenor, Donohue, & Olien, 1972). Superficiality in issue constructs, inattentiveness to current events, and wildly fluctuating viewpoints gave scholars reason to distrust the rationality of the average American voter (see Page & Shapiro, 1992).   In an examination of the distribution of general American political knowledge, Glenn (1972) concluded that "a large proportion of the American public can not . . . intelligently vote or participate in the democratic process" (p. 273).

Political Ideology

In 1964, Converse found that only 2.5 percent of the population used either the term "liberal" or the word "conservative" in a consistent, meaningful way. These individuals were well-educated voters who were party members, campaign contributors, and campaign rally participants. Converse observed that no more than 10 to 15 percent of the population ever considered or evaluated public affairs issues on the basis of ideological dimensions. Further, the fact that this group considered them did not mean that the evaluation was in any way meaningful, because the use of ideological dimensions tended to be inconsistent and confused. In addition, he observed that while elites were relatively stable in their evaluations of political issues, nonelites were quite changeable in how they evaluated political issues, and Converse believed this led to electoral instability.

Converse (1964) argued that 40 percent of Americans made decisions based on how they perceived a given party would benefit his or her own group, for example, social class, religious group, or ethnic group. And even more disturbing is Converse's finding that 50 percent of Americans knew so little about politics, political parties, and their own reference group that they could not tell if a victory by one party would be advantageous for them, and for this reason they focused on isolated issues when making their voting decisions. For instance, they might have wanted lower taxes; therefore, they voted for whoever promised this.

It was surprising, then, that Nie and Anderson (1974) and Nie, Verba, and Petrocik (1976), a short decade later, found that the majority of voters by this time held meaningful political beliefs by evaluating issue preferences in terms of liberal versus conservative dimensions. What had changed? How did meaningful belief systems suddenly arise from nowhere?

Carmines and Stimson (1982) provide us with the answer. They maintain that the 1960s civil rights agenda polarized Americans along ideological lines. "As the symbolic, emotionally charged issues of race took on a clear partisan complexion, they simultaneously moved to the center of mass belief systems" (Carmines & Stimson, 1982, p. 18). After controlling for race in the 1972 election data, Carmines and Stimson (1982) found the following:

1. Nearly all the increase in the structure of political beliefs reported by Nie and his collaborators can be attributed to race.
2. Controlling for race alone destroys the coherence of mass belief systems.
3. Racial matters are central to the apparent connotation of the terms of left/right discourse. (p. 18)

Similarly, Edsall and Edsall (1991) write,

Race is no longer a straightforward, morally unambiguous force in American politics; instead, considerations of race are now deeply imbedded in the strategy and tactics of politics, in competing concepts of the function and responsibility of government, and in each voter's conceptual structure of moral and partisan identity. Race helps define liberal and conservative ideologies, shapes the presidential coalitions of the Democratic and Republican parties, provides a harsh new dimension to concern over taxes and crime, drives a wedge through alliances of the working classes and the poor, and gives both momentum and vitality to the drive to establish a national majority inclined by income and demography to support policies benefiting the affluent and the upper-middle class. (p. 53; see also Brady & Sniderman, 1985)

In short, according to Edsall and Edsall (1991), "When the official subject is presidential politics, taxes, welfare, crime, rights, or values . . . the real subject is race" (p. 53).

A disturbing picture of the American electorate emerges. A very small elite group is capable of evaluating political issues in a meaningful way, that is, (1) they are able to define in an accurate way what the issue is, (2) they are able to articulate the main viewpoints on the issue, (3) they are able to identify political leaders and/or political groups who support the various viewpoints, (4) they are able to correctly identify where support of this issue places them on an ideological continuum, and (5) they demonstrate a stable opinion concerning the issue. Roughly 10 to 15 percent believe that they are meaningfully evaluating political issues along ideological lines, but in reality, these same individuals are very inconsistent and confused in dealing with ideological dimensions. Most significantly, the average voter is woefully unprepared to evaluate political issues in any meaningful way. And therefore, voters are open to persuasive appeals from political campaigns that may tap deep-seated beliefs, stereotypes, or even prejudices.

THE AMERICAN PUBLIC OPINION PROCESS

The Structure of Public Opinion

If by and large, Americans do not have meaningful belief systems, what is public opinion? How do political candidates evaluate what could and should be included in their platforms? The answer rests in the four phases of opinion construction. If one considers the American population as a whole, one sees that individuals differ on any political issue in terms of interest, motivation, and activity (Sego, 1977). And depending on the differences observed in interest, motivation, and activity, they can be classified into four groups. The American population can be viewed as a pyramid.

On the bottom of the pyramid is a group of individuals that political scientists call the chronic know-nothings. They are apolitical. Because they are not interested in political issues, they do not seek information concerning them. Thus the name "chronic know-nothings"—they do not know anything about public issues. Chronic know-nothings make up about 4 percent of the American population (Sego, 1977).

The next group above the chronic know-nothings on the pyramid is the largest group of citizens, the general public (Sego, 1977). Members of the general public do not hold meaningful beliefs about public issues. They are not able to assess public issues along ideological lines. They have very little interest in politics, and for this reason, they do not actively seek information about the political process. However, they may attend to the mass media, and thus they may passively acquire information in this manner. These individuals may or may not vote. They make up about 70-75 percent of the American population.

However, on occasion, members of the general public may ardently care about a public issue, and they may then choose to seek information and to get involved in the political process. For example, many of the members of the right-to-life movement have no prior experience with political issues, and, importantly, even as they become involved in the right-to-life cause, they do not branch out into other political issues. They remain one-issue activists. And only for this one issue may they be considered members of the attentive public (Sego, 1977). Such individuals are led by dramatic arguments and stereotypical reasoning processes.

Some members of the general public respond similarly to public issues in that they take a populist stance on political matters (Axelrod, 1967). While truly not ideological, it is a predictable means of behavior. These individuals are against foreign aid, oppose U.S. involvement overseas, favor tax cuts, and favor domestic reform programs that guarantee full employment and medical health care. They are more likely to be nonvoters and poorly educated.

The attentive public is made up of individuals who are interested in political issues. They seek information about politics. They talk about politics with their colleagues and friends, and they participate in politics by joining social and political groups where such matters are discussed. Members of the attentive public may give money to political campaigns or volunteer as campaign workers. Because members of the general public may temporarily join the attentive pubic on selected issues, it is difficult to pinpoint exactly what percentage of the population makes up the attentive public. On most political issues, the attentive public is between 10 and 17 percent of the population. However, on occasion, when a subject becomes unusually controversial and volatile, the attentive public may swell to between 20 and 40 percent of the population. An example of such an issue would be abortion (Oskamp, 1991).

The fourth major group of American citizens and the one we are most familiar with is the opinion-making public (Sego, 1977). The members of the opinion-making public have the same general characteristics as the attentive public, but they are actively engaged in the day-to-day world of political negotiations. These individuals are the political players in America. They may run for political office or they may be successful officeholders. They're the lobbyists, political consultants, and news reporters who are actively engaged with other members of the opinion-making public. These are the individuals who establish the parameters of the political process in that they structure, define, and determine the limits of political debate. What we often know of public issues is in reality the voice of a very few activists. Thus in the final analysis, public opinion "is not opinion *of* the public or of publics, but opinion *made* [emphasis in original] public" (Vatz, 1976, p. 206; see Nimmo, 1978; Sego, 1977).

Consequences of Pyramidal Structure

One very important conclusion must be drawn from this discussion. The vast majority of Americans are either not interested in politics or are turned off by it. Part of this group may be open to demagogic appeals that feed on their stereotypical information base and take advantage of their unsophisticated decision-making processes. Because these individuals do not have group contacts to mitigate mass media influences and because they have not developed clearly defined, strong core political beliefs, they are more open to mass-communicated messages than those individuals who belong to groups and often discuss politics with their family, friends, and co-workers.

This view of the American public and of our future is quite distressing. Recently, another approach to the study of American political behavior that is not so pessimistic has emerged. Page and Shapiro (1992) have argued that despite evidence that the public has little political information and that political opinions widely fluctuate among the masses, political science should reexamine its depiction of the average American citizen. Page and Shapiro (1992) contend that "the American public, as a collectivity, holds a number of real, stable, and sensible opinions about public policy and that these opinions develop and change in a reasonable fashion, responding to changing circumstances and to new information" (p. 1). Page and Shapiro (1992) argue that "*collective* [emphasis in the original] public opinion has properties quite different from those of the opinions of individual citizens, taken one at a time" (p. 1). They suggest that individual citizens use shortcuts in understanding and processing political reality. They turn to opinion leaders, people they trust and respect for guidance. They seek direction from their elected representatives, and they attend to the mass media for criticism and analysis. In other words, the average individual citizen counts on others "to do political reasoning for them and to provide guidance" (Page & Shapiro, 1992, p. 17). They argue that, over time, the collectivity maintains stable and rather consensual opinions on public issues. While Page and Shapiro find reassurance in these observations that the average citizen does in fact behave in a rational manner when confronted with political policy decision making, we find their analysis less than comforting. It places the average citizen at the mercy of their elected officials and news media figures. While the average individual may find it useful

to rely on others and useful to take shortcuts in understanding the political process, following such a behavior pattern short-circuits the
democratic process. Although Page and Shapiro (1992) appear to be
saying something completely different from our previous discussion on
public opinion, they are observing the same political behavior phenomenon yet drawing very dissimilar conclusions about the desirability of such social and political behavior.

Recently, Steeper (1995) has argued that the 1994 election was
the first meaningful election in 60 years in that the election could be
considered a "policy election" where voters voted either for a conservative direction or a liberal direction for the country to take. In the
past, changes in our competitive party system have been brought about
by unresolved issues that voters found to be highly significant in their
consideration of party identification. Steeper (1995) suggests that the
election turned on cultural conservatism—a term used to describe a belief system that supports "a belief in God, hard work, patriotism, fru-
gality, personal and family responsibility, and self-reliance" (p. 6).
Supporters of cultural conservatism are not limited to fundamentalist
Christians, for their ranks are quite huge. A majority of Americans
favor cultural conservatism, while the religious right is still a small
minority. There are those who would suggest that such cultural conservatism may be viewed as a backlash against the multiculturalism
of the 1980s and 1990s. Indeed, Carmines and Stimson (1982) and
Edsall and Edsall (1991) argue well that the observed "cultural
conservatism" is actually a backlash on the race issue in American
politics.

Party Identification

Measurement of party identification "does not involve official
party membership, registration, or campaign activity, but depends en-
tirely on the respondent's self-classification as a strong or not-so-
strong Republican or Democrat or as an Independent" (Oskamp, 1991,
p. 317). "Strong partisans (particularly strong Republican partisans)
are more likely to vote than weak ('not so strong') partisans, who vote
more than Independents" (Erikson, Luttbeg, & Tedin, 1991, p. 12).
Traditionally, party identification has been a relatively stable personal characteristic. Usually when change was observed, it took place
when an Independent moved into either the Democratic or the
Republican camp. It was rare for a Democrat to become a Republican or
vise versa. However, in recent years this has become a bit more complicated. Researchers have observed a decrease in the determination
of voting behavior by party identification (Declercq, Hurley, &
Luttbeg, 1975; Wattenberg, 1986). Many voters during the 1980s would

consistently vote for Democratic candidates for state offices and even congressional races, but they would vote for a Republican presidential candidate. Because of this, pollsters were forced to ask voters if they considered themselves to be Republican, Democratic, or Independent in voting for state-elected offices and also what they considered themselves to be when considering presidential candidates. In 1984, for example, 44 percent of U.S. congressional districts elected a representative from the opposite party of their presidential vote (Wattenberg, 1986). In 1994, the voters threw out large numbers of Democrats in state and federal offices. And in 1994 and 1995, an unprecedented number of Democrats began to switch parties. U.S. Senator Richard Shelby of Alabama and U.S. Senator Ben Nighthorse Campbell of Colorado became some of the first Democrats to make the jump.

In 1988, the Democratic and Republican parties were virtually tied in terms of party identification, with each party maintaining a steady 33 percent of the voters (Gilligan, 1988). But after the fall 1994 Republican landslide, national political polls showed the Republicans with 53 percent and the Democrats with 41 percent (Moore, 1994). By the summer of 1995, however, the two parties were roughly equal again in terms of party identification (Wirthlin, 1995).

Sociographics

Until recently, it was fairly easy to predict the dominant political party by the region of the country. But with dramatic shifts in party loyalty during the 1980s and 1990s that is no longer true. However, on most social issues involving religious, moral, or racial attitudes, it is safe to assume that the South is between 10 and 20 percent more conservative than the rest of the country (*Public Opinion*, 1988).

Recent research has indicated an increase in class-based politics in the United States. Middle-income and upper-income groups have become strongly Republican (Petrocik & Steeper, 1987). According to Erikson, Luttbeg, and Tedin (1991), "As one goes from poor to affluent, one does in fact see a decline in the percentage of people holding liberal positions on . . . economic issues" (p. 170) such as policies promoting full employment and funding social programs. "On noneconomic issues, liberalism tends to increase rather than decrease as one goes up the status ladder. Typical are the relationships between social class and opinions on women's rights, the rights of accused criminals, abortion, and nondiscrimination against homosexuals" (Erikson, et al., 1991, p. 170). High-status voters exhibit 'ess racial prejudice than do low status voters and are more tolerant of atheists, communists, and socialists. "Educational achievement promotes political tolerance and political [social issues] liberalism" (Erikson, et al., 1991, p. 171). However, "on economic issues, high income is negatively related to liberalism while education is not" (Erikson, et al., 1991, p. 172).

African-Americans differ markedly from white Americans in their political party affiliation. In 1988, 62 percent of blacks identified themselves as Democrats, 32 percent as Independents, and 6 percent as Republican. During that same year, 30 percent of whites identified themselves as Democrats, 38 percent as Independents, and 31 percent as Republicans (Erikson, et al., 1991). Since World War II, Lyndon Johnson has been the only Democratic president to win a majority of the white vote.

In the 1980s and 1990s, religious fundamentalism became a force to be reckoned with on election day. "Members of evangelical churches now make up about 25 percent of the population and about 40 percent of all Protestants. Comparatively speaking, they tend to be rural, southern, less affluent, and less well educated than the rest of the population" (Erikson, et al., 1991, pp. 192-193). Such fundamentalists are usually "traditional on social issues, strongly anti-Communist, and libertarian on economic questions" (Erikson, et al., 1991, p. 193). "Black vs. white differences are particularly strong on economic issues such as the pace of domestic spending, and whether the government should guarantee everyone a good standard of living" (Erikson, et al., 1991, p. 179). Blacks are more likely to support civil rights and affirmative action, and they are less likely to support abortion rights (Erikson, et al., 1991).

During the past 15 years, researchers have observed a gender gap in American politics; that is, that men and women differ as a group on how they are politically aligned. "In 1980 women were 3 percent more Democratic than men; in 1984 they were 8 percent more Democratic, and in 1988 they were 10 percent more Democratic (1980, 1984, 1988 NES surveys). This Democratic tendency is most notable among unmarried and well-educated women (Erikson, et al., 1991). Research has shown that women are opposed to aggression and therefore are less likely to support defense spending. And, they support "compassion issues relating to jobs, education, income redistribution, and protection for the vulnerable in society" (Erikson, et al., 1991, p. 200).

Voting Turnout

Voters are more likely to go to the polls during presidential election years than in off-year elections. Since World War II, presidential election turnout has ranged from 49 to 63 percent, and during off-year elections the turnout has ranged from 36 to 45 percent (Oskamp, 1991). Those voting in off-year elections have strong party identifications and tend to be more politically oriented than those who do not (Campbell, 1964). Greater fluctuations in outcome have been observed during presidential election years, because of the political instability of those choosing to vote. "For the 1988 presidential election, approximately 89 million citizens voted (48 million for Bush and 41 million for Dukakis), approximately 25 million were registered to vote but did not, and approximately 48 million adults never registered" (Lavrakas, Holley, & Miller, 1991, p. 173).

Timetable for the Voting Decision

Generally speaking, 80 percent of the voters have their minds made up by the August before the November election day (Oskamp, 1991). However, under certain conditions, such as a highly controversial race, a highly negative campaign, or an explosive political debate, some voters who habitually are not late deciders will under these conditions wait to make up their minds until the last week before the election day. This may also be true when a campaign has been overshadowed by other electoral contests during the campaign season or when the political communication from the opposing camps has been unusually lackluster. Voters will delay deciding because they do not know enough to make what they consider to be an informed judgment. It is possible to find up to 35 percent of the voters making their decision during that last week before the election (Oskamp, 1991). Flanigan (1972) points out that while the majority of voters may have determined whom they will vote for before the political campaign actually begins, in most competitive election situations, it is the undecided that determine the election. And therefore, political media become all-important to the success of the campaign. These late-deciding voters tend to be the least interested, least knowledgeable, least partisan of the voters who ultimately cast their ballots. However, some knowledgeable Independents also wait until the end to make their voting decisions.

Because of the power of the mass media in political elections, a review of the political media consumption of voters and an analysis of the public opinion process must go hand in hand. It is important, therefore, that one have an understanding of the American news media in order to understand public opinion.

THE DRAMATIZATION OF NEWS

In 1976, Kraus and Davis (1976) succinctly stated the power of the news media:

The mass media create common reality by shaping the conceptual environment in which humans communicate.... Political reality is formed by mass communication reports which are talked about altered, and interpreted by citizens in a society. The totality of this process constitutes reality. (p. 211; for a similar analysis, see Brody & Page, 1975)

Nimmo and Combs (1983) call this reality a mass mediated reality. They maintain that "the vast bulk of political reality that most of us take for granted (whether we are private citizens or public officials) consists of a combination of fantasies created and evoked by group and mass communication" (1983, p. 6; see also Lippmann, 1965). Nimmo and Combs (1983) define fantasy as

a credible picture of the world that is created when one interprets mediated experiences as the way things are and takes for granted the authenticity of the mediated reality without checking against alternative, perhaps contradictory, realities so long as the fantasy offers dramatic proof for one's expectations. (p. 8)

Much like Fisher (1984) or Bormann (1972), Nimmo and Combs (1983) believe that human communication, whether interpersonal, group, or mass communication, may be characterized as storytelling. "When something happens that is ambiguous in meaning, provokes people's interest, and raises doubts demanding resolution, the popular urge is to represent *what really happened* [emphasis in original] in dramatic ways" (Nimmo & Combs, 1983, p. 14; see also Bennett & Edelman, 1985; Darnton, 1975; Knight & Dean, 1982; Schudson, 1982; Tuchman, 1976). Nimmo and Combs (1983), like Weaver (1976) before them, believe that there is a "melodramatic imperative" in the process of news creation. In literary criticism, melodrama refers to plays

based on a romantic plot and developed sensationally, with little regard for convincing motivation and with an excessive appeal to the emotions of the audience. The object is to keep the audience thrilled by the awakening, no matter how, of strong feelings of pity or horror or joy. Poetic justice is superficially secured, the characters (who are either very good or very bad) being rewarded or punished according to their deeds. Though typically a melodrama has a happy ending, tragedies which use much of the same technique are sometimes referred to as melodramatic. (Holman, 1972, p. 312)

Today people are most familiar with this genre in the form of soap operas. However, Nimmo and Combs (1983) and Bennett (1988) believe that the melodramatic imperative is evident in political news. "Dramatized news is more melodrama than serious theatre, more soap opera than Shakespeare" (Bennett, 1988, p. 40). However, there are dangers in such dramatized news.

Because dramas are simple, easy to grasp, and offer a semblance of insight into the individual motives behind an action, they may give people a misguided sense of understanding the politics of a situation. People may think they understand an issue when, in fact, their understanding is based on a mixture of fantasy, fiction, and myth. (Bennett, 1988, p. 40)

People live in a state of pluralistic ignorance—"a situation in which individuals hold unwarranted assumptions about the thoughts, feelings, and behavior of other people" (O'Gorman, 1975, p. 314; see also Nimmo & Combs, 1983). Because people hold a false understanding of the problems and opportunities in today's society, they are not able to effectively solve problems or to maximize their opportunities. According to Bennett (1988), melodramatic news has severe consequences:

1. Distraction from potentially important causes of problems
2. Creation of a false sense of understanding rooted in individualistic explanations
3. The promotion of dramatically satisfying but practically unworkable solutions. (p. 44)

In today's world, "mediated, secondhand reality is one's politics" (Nimmo & Combs, 1983, p. 18). Yet that secondhand reality, in its dramatic form, is often more negative than many observers are aware.

Negativity

In the early 1970s, Wamsley and Pride (1972) and Robinson (1976) warned that an emphasis on the negative aspects of politics and governmental processes in news media accounts could denigrate the political system. Graber (1989), in her discussion of the criteria for news selection, establishes negativity or "natural or man-made *violence, conflict, disaster,* or *scandal* [emphasis in original]" as one of the more important ingredients in verifying newsworthiness (p. 84-86).

One veteran campaign manager put it this way:

"Newsworthy" means featuring disagreement, conflict and contrast. It means painting campaign participants as heroes and villains. It means making one's point briefly, at the start of a speech, and using popular, emotionally stirring symbols. It means tailoring one's speech to the needs of the moment and capturing the audience's fancy. (Lorenz, 1978)

Analysis of the dramatic nature of news content has led researchers to conclude that an emphasis on conflict is a requirement. Four types of dramatic conflict are used in news stories: man versus man, man versus himself, man versus fate, and man versus nature (Johnson, 1984). Political leaders are pictured as "Davids" fighting the mighty "Goliaths" of inflation, unemployment, or AIDS. However, the story rarely has a happy ending. Inflation isn't killed, and unemployment doesn't fall to the ground. AIDS lives on to kill another day. It often seems that there are no happy endings. The result is that, in many instances, political leaders are portrayed as ineffectual (Schram, 1991).

Sabato (1991) documented a growing negativism on the part of the American news media. He posits that the news media's emphasis on the sensational, the dramatic, the titillating, and the trivial has led to increased negativity in the nation's news content. Competitive pressures and the nature of pack journalism then exacerbate this problem. After Watergate, according to Sabato (1991), a whole generation of reporters raised on the interrogation style popularized by the political coverage of that time entered the news business. This led to a mode of investigative journalism that emphasizes the character issue and the subtext in American politics. Sabato (1991) explained,

Frequently, a near consensus (accurate or not) forms around a politician's personality and faults, and each pol is typecast with shorthand labeling of various sorts. This set of preconceived images and stereotypes becomes the candidate's sub-text--that is, the between-the-lines character sketch that guides and sets the tone for press coverage. Journalists are always on the lookout for circumstances that fit the common perceptions and preconceptions about a candidate, especially his or her shortcomings. A major incident that validates the sub-text (and therefore the press's own judgment) has a good chance of being magnified and becoming a feeding frenzy. (p. 71)

Sabato (1991) used Joe Biden as an example of the operation of the subtext. Biden was a 1988 Democratic presidential candidate whom reporters had pegged as an intellectual lightweight who was good at giving speeches. When reporters finally discovered that Biden had "cribbed" certain speech passages from a British pol, they immediately went on a feeding frenzy (Sabato, 1991).

Kumar and Grossman (1981) had this to say of the nation's news media:

What might be said of them is that they strive to become the arbiters of the political system. They legitimize and delegitimize individuals, points of view on issues, and even institutions such as the presidency itself. Collectively and individually, news enterprises act as if they set the ethical norms for candidates and the criteria by which policies should be evaluated. In sum, these organizations attempt to establish the criteria of rectitude for political operations in the United States. It is no wonder that the other actors, including the President, resent them. (pp. 106-107)

Media themes, whether negative or positive, are very important in the process of shaping the public's political reality. This mediated political reality is essential for understanding the American political process.

According to Haight and Brody (1977), there is "repeated evidence of a relationship between the public's response to day-to-day news and approval of the President, which is in turn related to his ability to govern" (p. 58; for a similar election year analysis, see Shapiro et al., 1991). Entman (1989) found that the public's evaluation of news is also related to how they feel about interest groups, public policies, and political leaders. Similarly, Graber (1976) stresses that "the correspondence of mass media images to images held by mass and elite publics makes constant themes in news stories important social indicators" (p. 173). Thus, the presidential dominance of news has ramifications not only for a president's attempts at impression management but for the American political system as well.

Campaign News

In the presidential arena, Matthews (1978) observes that the impact of campaign news "can be felt either on the *process* or the *outcome* [emphasis in the original] of presidential nominations" (p. 56). This observation holds true for lower-level offices as well. Obviously, the news media are influential in determining who drops out before the primary, who wins the primary, and ultimately who is the victor in the general election. But not so obvious is the day-to-day impact on how political campaigns present their candidates to the public. "Political campaigns have become little more than a series of performances calculated to attract the attention of television news cameras and their audiences" (Matthews, 1978, p. 55).

Research has shown that presidential campaign news stories emphasize the conflictual nature of the political campaign, with particular emphasis on the horse-race aspects of the campaign and the political strategies and tactics used by various candidates and their consultants to win the horse race (Arterton, 1978, 1984; Marshall, 1983; Patterson, 1980; Robinson & Sheehan, 1984). News stories during political campaigns are said to prime the voters. "That is, presenting certain topics in campaign news stories make[s] those topics more accessible in viewers' thinking (primes them), and as a result these topics assume more weight in viewer's judgments about the candidates"

(Oskamp, 1991, p. 294). Williams, Shapiro, and Cutbirth (1991) found that campaign news—those stories that had been framed as "campaign" news—had far greater impact on audience agendas than did other political stories that had not been framed.

Although research has found that newspaper coverage is particularly critical in the early stages of a campaign in determining the audience's agenda, television becomes increasingly important as the election day draws near (Shaw & McCombs, 1977; Williams et al., 1991). Page, Shapiro, and Dempsey (1985) have demonstrated that a single news commentary on national network television may create as much as 4 percentage points of opinion change. Ivengar and Kinder (1986) have demonstrated that television viewers exposed to repeated stories concerning a national problem then used that problem as a means by which they assessed how well a president was doing. In the 1992 presidential race, the press's repetition of stories about the economy made that the main issue of the election. President Bush was judged by many on how well he was handling the economy.

Zucker (1978) found that the news media were more likely to have influence with voters on issues that they could not personally experience, such as foreign relations. Palmgreen and Clarke (1991) found that the "agenda-setting impact of the media . . . is generally weaker at the local level" (p. 116), because voters have an opportunity to have firsthand knowledge of the issues. On the other hand, in local elections, newspaper editorials and endorsements have been found to have a critical influence on election outcomes (Coombs, 1981; Erikson, 1976; Mason, 1973; Scarrow & Borman, 1979).

Semetko et al., (1991) found that American newspapers were far more biased than network coverage of the 1984 presidential election. "Political philosophies were apparent in front-page story selection, amount of directly quoted material used, the quantity and nature of the contextualizing remarks appearing in coverage (even in straight news stories), and in the themes embedded in stories, editorials, and columns" (p. 83). The authors observed that,

Because most U.S. newspapers do not have direct competition, and because nearly all newspapers are locally rather than nationally oriented, this means that they can be more partisan in their approach to election coverage if the bulk of their readers are similarly partisan. (Semetko et al., 1991, p. 84)

However, the newspaper and television agendas were highly similar in subject content. The reliance on wire services and central campaign news sources as well as the pack mentality of the national press corps worked to create similar media agendas. And interestingly, the research documented significant differences between candidate and media agendas. The media concentrate on the horse-race aspects of the election with particular emphasis on the "behind-the-scenes conduct of the campaign" and on the public opinion polls (Semetko et al. 1991). Differences between candidate agendas and media agendas were far more apparent in the network coverage, suggesting that television reporters have greater flexibility in how they handle campaign news stories (Semetko et al., 1991).

Reporting Public Opinion Polls

The reporting of public opinion polls either establishes momentum for a candidate or destroys it. Hickman (1991) argues that polls are particularly crucial during primary contests, because they help distinguish similar candidates from each other. He also suggests that in contests where little information is available about the candidates or when interest in the election is low, political polls may help establish voter preference. "Evidence shows that perceptions of the candidate's likelihood of winning a nomination contest directly, indirectly, and interactively affect candidate's chances of gaining popularity and winning votes" (Hickman, 1991, p. 103; see also Bartels, 1988; Brady & Johnston, 1987).

In a study of the 1988 presidential election, Lavrakas, Holley, and Miller (1991) found that 71 percent of Americans were aware of public opinion polls that were predicting the election outcome. Ninety-five percent of those aware of the polls were able to correctly identify George Bush as the candidate leading in the polls. "Those Americans most likely to be aware of these opinion polls were more educated, older adults with the greatest daily exposure to the news media, those who were employed, people who defined themselves as politically conservative, and people who identified with a political party" (Lavrakas et al., 1991, pp. 159-160). Individuals with the greatest daily news exposure and those who were Republicans were more likely to closely follow poll stories. Sixty-nine percent of respondents said that they were very interested or somewhat interested in polling stories. But after the election, 66 percent of respondents said that there were too many polling stories. People with more education and older adults were more likely to be critical of the frequency of polling stories. A plurality of respondents felt that "the media's reporting of the horse race aspect of these polls did more harm than good to the presidential election process" (Lavrakas et al., 1991, p. 162).

Interestingly, Lavrakas and associates (1991) detected both an underdog effect and a bandwagon effect of public opinion polls during the 1988 election. The underdog effect is observed where after an individual is told that a candidate is losing in the polls, the individual switches his or her previously self-reported intention to vote for a candidate to the candidate's opposition. It could be viewed as a sympathy vote or support for the under dog. The bandwagon effect is observed where after an individual is told that a candidate is winning in the polls, he or she switches his or her previously self-reported intention to vote for a candidate to the opposition in order to be on the perceived winning side. Under experimental conditions, about one in five respondents demonstrated the underdog effect and one out of ten respondents demonstrated the bandwagon effect. The authors were able to establish demographic profiles for those individuals most likely to exhibit the bandwagon and underdog effects:

Younger adults, those who did not identify with the Democratic party, and employed persons were most likely to demonstrate the bandwagon effect. In contrast, "Reagan Democrats" and those without a political party affiliation, women, liberals, and unemployed and lower-income persons were most likely to demonstrate the "underdog effect." (Lavrakas et al., 1991, p. 172)

About one in five registered nonvoters reported that knowledge of Bush's lead in the polls influenced them or may have influenced them to stay home (Lavrakas et al., 1991). This is probably an "*underestimate* [emphasis in the original] of the proportion of nonvoters who were so influenced, as it would be 'socially desirable' for some respondents to deny that these expectations were instrumental in leading them not to vote" (p. 174). The evidence from research consistently shows that turnout is higher when voters perceive the race as being close. When polls indicate otherwise, people choose to stay home because they believe that their vote won't matter (Traugott, 1992a).

Lavrakas, Holley, and Miller (1991) were able to show that the fears of a generation of researchers concerned with the widespread dissemination of public opinion poll results were well grounded. Boorstin (1961) has argued that the American news media have gone far beyond "news gathering" to "news making" in that they routinely produce "pseudo-events." One such example of a pseudo-event is the use of public opinion polls by newspapers and broadcast networks. For Gollin (1980), the pseudo-event is something created by the news organization "specifically in order to be reported, whose ambiguity of meaning is intrinsic to its interest, and that often has the character of a self-fulfilling prophecy" (p. 449). Crespi maintains that this self-fulfilling prophecy is a feedback loop in which "(1) definitions of what is news, (2) determine the content of polling, (3) affect the political process, (4) which then becomes news" (Crespi, 1980, p. 466). Similarly, Broh (1980) writes that "a poll suggests an issue to which there is a political response, which is then reported, and another poll is taken to determine the response to the action, beginning a sort of chain reaction" (pp. 527-528).

Often findings from political polls provide a mere superficial acquaintance with the expressed views of those sampled and questioned. This leads to broad, sweeping generalizations, often exploited as political tools of persuasion, rather than dispassionate reports. Traugott (1992a) points out that

polls can influence political elites as well. Most financial contributors, for example, want to back a winner. Results from media polls, as well as private polls paid for by a campaign, are commonly used by candidates to encourage support for their efforts or to discourage contributions to an opponent who, they would argue, has little chance of winning. These effects can be especially pronounced early in the campaign, when candidates are often not well known and not rated highly in polls. (p. 128; see also Dexter, 1954)

In addition to encouraging or discouraging financial contributors, early poll reports can influence political activists such as political consultants, paid campaign workers, and volunteers. Traugott observes,

Professional campaign staff workers who are trying to decide which campaign to join, and whose careers are often based on their record of working for successful campaigns, use the results to evaluate candidate's chances. . . . A poor showing in the polls can devastate a nascent candidacy, especially of someone who is qualified but relatively unknown, if it limits fund-raising possibilities and campaign staffing. (1992a, p. 129; see also Dionne, 1980; Hickman, 1991)

The Debate Expectation Game

Another pseudo-event used by the American news media is the political campaign debate. While it is true that American political debates are as old as our republic, it has also been true that debates have primarily taken place not for their audiences but for the news media that cover them. This was true for two very important reasons: (1) voters watching the debates tend to be more knowledgeable and therefore more likely to have already made up their minds prior to the debate, and (2) debates tend to reinforce those already predisposed to vote for a given candidate. Traditionally, campaign debating has been regarded as a risky enterprise, not because of how it affects the voters watching the debate but because of how the media might cover the debate. Still, despite candidates' fears of making political blunders that will later be used against them in campaign ads and news stories, the majority of candidates are willing to debate. Around 75 percent of incumbents in the House of Representatives do engage in debates with their opponents (Martel, 1983). According to Martel (1983), the reason for this high rate of debate participation rests with the decline of political parties. Incumbents must generate their own active support coalition, for they can no longer rely on the party to get out the vote for them. Particularly in this modern age of instant media campaigns, the incumbent must be forever watchful against a well-financed opponent who is able to buy instant name awareness. Thus, the incumbent is forced into an aggressive stance of eagerly seeking opportunities to dramatize his or her leadership style, voting record, and the public's acceptance of his or her candidacy.

Recent research suggests that debating may be the way to go for both incumbents and challengers. Even if a candidate is ahead in the polls, he or she should still debate. Favored candidates are usually perceived as the winner in campaign debate, and this can work to increase the margin of victory, which in turn leads to an increased ability to raise campaign funds in the future and possibly to consideration by party activists for a higher office (Leuthold & Valentine, 1981; Martel, 1983). But most important, recent research indicates that the news media expect candidates to debate, and if they do not, they will often suffer the criticism of the news media (Sears & Chaffee, 1979). "Refusing to debate may generate damaging negative publicity" (Martel, 1983, p. 45). According to the 1980 Congressional Debate Survey, constituents now expect their political leaders to debate; political debates have become an important part of the campaign ritual (Martel, 1983). The candidate who refuses to debate will often be perceived as being cowardly or having something sinister to hide. In addition, a candidate who first refuses to debate and then later decides to do so may also be at a disadvantage. The public may have already developed negative expectations about the hesitant candidate that may contaminate any evaluation that the voter might make concerning the candidate's performance in the debate (Scott, 1981).

In planning for a political debate, political consultants must consider not only their candidates' performances but also how they manage the news coverage of that debate. The sum process of how they manage the debate expectation game is called metadebating. In terms of the performance itself, consultants concentrate on the physical attractiveness and attire of the candidate, extemporaneous speaking ability, personality projection, stage management, knowledge about issues, and rehearsed comments that capture the audience's imagination by triggering underlying beliefs or emotions (Jamieson & Birdsell, 1988; Martel, 1983). However, in addition to the actual debate, consultants must also prepare tactics that assess how well a candidate is likely to do without establishing unrealistic expectations. In the first Reagan versus Mondale debate in 1984, Reagan was perceived as the loser more for what he didn't do than for what he did do during the debate. Because the "Great Communicator" didn't give a spectacular performance, the media labeled Mondale the winner—he had performed better than expected. The public opinion polls conducted immediately after the debate had Mondale winning by between one and nine percentage points. But one night after the news media's coverage of the debate, an ABC News/*Washington Post* poll found Mondale winning by 55 percent to 19 percent. And one night later, the gap got even wider. A *New York Times*/CBS News poll showed Mondale the winner, with 66 percent to Reagan's 17 percent (Erikson et al., 1991).

While debate preparations and predebate expectations are important, the postdebate expectation games are just as important. The news media give the debate its public character by telling voters who won and who lost (Sears & Chaffee, 1979). Therefore, the political consultant must use all of his or her political savvy to manage the media's take on the debate. If problems arise during the debate, the consultant must be prepared to downplay the mistakes or gaffes while highlighting the positive aspects of the performance. In 1976 during the Ford-Carter debate, Ford misspoke himself by insisting that Poland was not under the political domination of the Soviet Union. This mistake received prominent play in the subsequent press coverage of the debate. While opinion polls immediately afterward showed no consensus as to the victor in the debate, the polls taken after the news coverage of the debate showed Carter the clear victor (Erikson et al., 1991). As we have mentioned previously, it is the consultant's job to spin-doctor. James Carville explained it this way: "When you're spinning a reporter, you're telling them how to look at a story. Or you're telling them they're covering it wrong" (Matalin & Carville, 1994, p. 431).

Failure to Manage the News

The failure to manage the news is every bit as lethal to a political campaign as an incompetent advertising campaign. The failed 1992 Bush presidential campaign is a perfect example of poor spin doctoring losing an election. No matter how improved the economy became, the Clinton campaign kept telling the media that the economy was in the dumpster, and the news media reported that. Bush was labeled a "foreign policy president" who was out of touch on domestic issues and who had allowed the economy not only to stall but to take a nose dive (see Matalin & Carville, 1994). The Bush strategy was to link foreign policy to successes to economic prosperity at home. Matalin explained their three-point strategy:

1. that there was an electorate awareness of our domestic policies and past achievements;
2. that the President would get credit for foreign-policy achievements;
3. that there would be an economic recovery. (Matalin & Carville, 1994, p. 81)

The Bush team was dead wrong on point one, right on point two, and one-half wrong on part three: there was a recovery, but the voters either didn't know about it or didn't believe it when they were told. The Bush team never prepared an effective, credible response to the Clinton accusations. And the tale played out, leaving Bush the loser.

In conclusion, the power of the American news media to direct voter attention to various aspects of political campaigns creates a situation where political consultants have to be equally adept at handling the media and producing campaign advertising. Any understanding of the American public opinion process must take into account the influence of the mass media on that process.

Chapter 4

Understanding Political Leadership

"Leadership" as a phenomenon and an art is highly dramatic.
J. Combs
Dimensions of political drama
(1980, p. 77)

Leadership, then, is not to be understood as something an individual does or does not have, at all times and places. It is always
defined by a specific situation and is recognized in the response of
followers to individual acts and speeches. If they respond
favorably and follow, there is leadership; if they do not, there is
not.
M. Edelman
The symbolic uses of politics
(1964, p. 75)

The nature of leadership is "always temporary and uneasy" (Edelman,
1964, p. 91). Leadeship is a dynamic relationship between the leader
and his or her followers. It is constantly changing and evolving as it is
being renegotiated and redefined based on the events that transpire.
The process of going about this negotiation process is quite simply, talk
(see Hall, 1972). "Talk . . . involves a competitive exchange of
symbols, referential, evocative, through which values are shared and
assigned and coexistence attained" (Edelman, 1964, p. 114). "Talk is a
largely irreplaceable means of defining situations, exigencies, and the
way the world is" (Brummett, 1980, p. 293). Leadership is a function of
communication and is only demonstrated through communicative
behaviors.

Much has been written upon how and by what means political leaders use to "talk" with voters. We will present a brief review of the literature in this area.

COMMUNICATION STYLE

A candidate's style is the "manner or method of enacting or expressing a public character" (Combs, 1980, p. 15). According to Trent and Friedenberg (1983),

In election campaigns, style can be seen as a blend of what candidates say in speeches, news conferences, interviews, advertisements, brochures, and so on, as well as their nonverbal political acts or behavior, such as kissing babies, wearing funny hats, shaking hands at rallies, waving at crowds from the motor-cade, as well as their facial expressions and gestures while answering a question. (p. 71)

In recent years, greater attention has been given to the voters' evaluations of candidates' style and the significance of said evaluations on voting decisions. Husson, Stephen, Harrison, and Fehr (1988) have noted that subjects' ratings of presidential candidates' interpersonal communication style were predictive of their preferences for president (even when controlling for political party preference). Two perspectives can be identified. One group suggests that individuals choose candidates that they find most like themselves. A second group suggests that while voters want someone like themselves, they also want someone a little better than themselves in some noticeable way. This illustrates one of the many paradoxes associated with American politics: voters may want someone of the people yet above the people (Johnson, 1984).

Lane (1978) suggests that as society has become more and more autonomous, as individuals have distanced themselves from traditional group commitments such as church, family, class, and party memberships, individuals have become more "on their own" when evaluating political candidates. Indeed, he suggests that as they no longer have group pressures influencing their voting decisions, they turn to their own evaluations of interpersonal style and behavior when evaluating political candidates. Lane explores the interrelationships of friendship (interpersonal) and leadership selection processes and maintains that for the most part, the character properties that people value in friendships are the same character properties that they value in political leaders. In modern society, he argues, there are certain cross-pressures operating that work to ultimately provide individuals with the type of friendships or leaders they desire. Particularly authoritarian-type individuals seek out others who are willing to establish in-groups and out-groups as they survey the world. Others have developed a "cold" personality, in that they seek others who show dimensions of coldness, shrewdness, ruthlessness, and self-centeredness. Individuals seek others who share the same moral values and incorporate shared visions of equity and justice in interpersonal relationships. As society has become increasingly structured around the workplace, individuals have sought those who share their own levels of competence, status, and willingness to work. Finally, people seek those who desire and who are willing to give a specified level of warmth, love, or emotional support. Thus, for Lane (1978), it is the interaction of these values that ultimately determines who we choose as friends and leaders.

However, other scholars have taken a different approach. They emphasize that while voters want political leaders whom they can identify with, voters still want their leaders to have certain valued characteristics to a greater degree than they themselves do. We have termed this tension the Everyman/Heroic Conflict, and it is one of the many paradoxes of political leadership in the United States (Johnson-Cartee & Copeland, 1997). Indeed, others have argued that in recent years politicians, in their efforts to gain supremacy on television, have created a starlike atmosphere around themselves. Tim Luke (1986-1987) argues that Americans live in a televisual democracy that encourages the cult of charisma. Luke adopts Weber's (1978) conceptualization of charisma. Charisma is defined, then, as that

certain quality of an individual personality by virtue of which he is considered extraordinary and treated as endowed with supernatural, superhuman, or at least specifically exceptional powers or qualities. . . . What is alone important is how the individual is actually regarded by those subject to charismatic authority, by his "followers" or "disciples." (Weber, 1978, pp. 241-242).

What is interesting is that many of the qualities associated with charismatic leaders would make them popular dinner guests, in that they would be warm, energetic, enthusiastic, witty, and intelligent, yet receptive and open (see Riggio, 1987). Luke (1986-1987) points out that these individuals, while taking on star like qualities, are just "spectacular representations of a living human being" (p. 68). He explains the complexity that the modern-day presidential candidate must face when dealing with the televisual democracy during an election:

The symbolic struggle for charismatic authority increasingly emphasizes nuances in style, symbol-management and image-cultivation, usually independent from any objective measure of effectiveness. In turn, hard or soft, strong or weak, warm or cold, open or closed, aloof or affable variations in the candi-

date's style are daily coded and decoded in the news media as their relative political sign values. They become indicators of the candidate's leadership cal-
iber, concern for the people, and approach to the problems. And, the range of
voters' popular devotion and enthusiasm for candidates often rests on the
politico's skillful or hapless effectiveness at simultaneously seeming warm,
hard, strong, open, and affable in several different demographic markets. (pp.
67-68)

Clearly Lane (1978) and Luke (1986-1987) differ as to the degree
of similarity between the voter and a chosen leader. For Lane (1978),
the leader is of the people. For Luke (1986-1987), the leader is of the
people but simultaneously above them in that he or she has
maximized the agreed-upon most approved characteristics. Notice
that both scholars place a premium on interpersonal communication
skills, particularly those related to relational communication.

Relational Messages

In 1967, Watzlawick, Beavin, and Jackson suggested that communicated messages contain two parts: the content of what was communicated and the relational dimensions. The relational portion of
the message provides meaning to the content portion. Clearly, relational communication is an important ingredient in political communication discourse. According to Burgoon and Hale (1984), relational
messages "are those verbal and nonverbal expressions that indicate
how two or more people regard each other, regard their relationship,
or regard themselves within the context of the relationship" (p. 193).
Burgoon and Hale's work revealed seven categories of communication
behavior: immediacy/affection, similarity/depth, receptivity/trust,
composure, formality, dominance, and equality (1987, p. 36).

Burgoon et al. (1987) found that messages that rate higher in
terms of positive relational meanings, that is, those emphasizing sim-
ilarity/depth, equality, immediacy/affection, composure, and recep-
tivity/trust and those deemphasizing or ignoring dominance and formality are judged as far more satisfying and influential by subjects (see
also Pfau, 1990). Thus para-interpersonal skills are a critical component in candidate evaluations, and those interpersonal styles that reflect high ratings of relational communication components are most
likely to be judged positively. The term "para-interpersonal" refers to
the candidate appearing to be interpersonally communicating; the
candidate adopts the appearance of interpersonal style, that is, the
style of talking to two or three people, when in fact the candidate is
addressing a public or mass audience.

Television emphasizes interpersonal communication skills, such
as nonverbal cues (primarily facial expressions, paralinguals, and

body language) that indicate warmth and composure (Jamieson, 1988; Pfau, 1990). According to Pfau and Kang (1991), relational messages are intrinsic to this new, connected style. "Relational messages play an important role in television communication because this context features the perception of direct contact between source and receivers" (Pfau & Kang, 1991, p. 116). The parasocial relationship involving the source and the receiver, in effect, resembles the interpersonal communication context (Beniger, 1987; Pfau & Kang, 1991).

Pfau (1990) found that relational messages contributed far more to persuasiveness than did content when evaluating television contexts. In their study of televised presidential debates, Pfau and Kang (1991) further narrowed the field of significant relational dimensions, and they concluded that candidates who seek to maximize their persuasiveness through the use of television should "use relational messages that feature more similarity and involvement and, to a lesser degree, more composure" (p. 124). Thus Pfau and Kang join others who maintain that television is a unique political communication modality (see Kern, 1989; Meyrowitz, 1985; Ranney, 1983) where "candidates accomplish political influence . . . through higher levels of intimacy and expressiveness" (Pfau & Kang, 1991, p. 124). Ronald Reagan and Bill Clinton provide examples of two individuals with widely varying public personas who have been able to conquer and personalize the connected style.

TALK, POWER, AND IMPRESSION MANAGEMENT

Simply put, talk is the essence of power and power is

control or influence over the actions of others to promote one's goals without their consent, against their will or without their knowledge or understanding (for example by control of the physical, psychological, or sociocultural environment within which others must act). (Buckley 1967, p. 186)

Hall (1977) defines power as simply the ability to define the situation for others.

Impression management means that control over the conduct of others for one's own interest is achieved by influencing the definition of the situation in which all are involved. This is accomplished by acting in such a way that an image is created of the actor (and related objects) that lead[s] others to voluntarily act as the actor wishes them to act. (Hall, 1977, p. 2)

As mentioned in Chapter 2, impression management has two dimensions. First, the "impression manager" uses the power of information flow control (Hall, 1972). The information presented to the audience (e.g., media personnel, crowd, staff) is the choice of the impression manager. And, second, the impression manager uses a variety of symbolic devices to mobilize support in defining the situation (see Combs, 1980). Persona is the term used for what the "impression manager" wishes to portray (see Lee, Johnson, & Beld, 1979).

It is important to remember, however, that the ultimate "definition of the situation" is the joint action or intersubjective reality of the participants, for example, citizens, the mass media, and other governmental actors. Impression management techniques are simply the means used by political leaders to enter and engage in the negotiation process, the drama known as politics.

Consistency

Despite Ralph Waldo Emerson's claim that "A foolish consistency is the hobgoblin of little minds," a primary consideration for any leader interested in managing his or her public persona is the necessity of consistency. "Every leadership role carries with it the burden of consistency and performance. For an audience to relate to an actor, the actor must foster an impression of authenticity" (Combs, 1980, p. 98; see also Jamieson, 1984; Johnson, 1984). Thus, "public relations and advertising should be completely coordinated" (Fisher, 1976, p. 85) so that the campaign is presenting a consistent picture of the desired persona. Kaid, Leland, and Whitney (1992) attributed Bush's 1988 presidential campaign's success to consistency in the campaign's political communication strategies and tactics.

Consistent behavior, in addition to aiding political actors in their relationships with the public, also aids them in their relationships with the mass media. According to Kumar and Grossman (1981), "Just as power tends to adhere to those [political actors] who sense what it is made of, favorable publicity comes to those . . . who have a sense for dramatizing and personalizing issues and policies" (p. 105). If a political actor is consistent, then it is easier to stereotype him or her. Stereotyping is "basically a process of definition based upon past experience" (O'Hara, 1961, p. 170). O'Hara explains that

we first, define, and then we "see," that is we "see" things not as they are but as what our definition tells us they should be. And our definition reflects the sum total of our experiences with the thing being defined, which is brought to bear at the moment of perception. (1961, p. 170)

Stereotyping "enables the mass communicator to frame his message with the least amount of lost motion, and it enables the receiver to

comprehend what is being communicated with equal speed and facility" (O'Hara, 1961, p. 194; see also Gans, 1979; Lippmann, 1965).

According to Jamieson and Campbell (1983), consistency "is one of
the categories reporters use to test a candidate and a campaign" (p.
253). Indeed, media a ttention accorded to political gaffes and flip-
flops (inconsistencies on issue positions) provide ample evidence for
such a test. Johnson (1984) found evidence that president-elects who
maintained a consistent communication strategy received far better
treatment in the major news magazines and national newspapers than
those who did not.

Similarly, Smith and Golden (1988) provide evidence that Jesse
Helms's consistent use of what they term "a Soap Opera anecdote"
proved far superior to James Hunt's rather "random, one shot, style of
storytelling" (p. 247) in the 1984 North Carolina senate race. In other
words, Helms's political advertising created a story line where an
identifiable group of characters were advanced across a series of scenes
or political ads.

The Helms story line, for example, introduced the audience to the heroes, villains, and fools to be portrayed across a variety of scenes that depicted states of
victimage, the presence of scape-goats, and the idiocy of fools. Hence, once the
Helms' story line was established viewers could easily follow the flow of
events from segment to segment. (Smith and Golden, 1988, p. 247)

Hunt, on the other hand, provided little or no thematic continuity
within his political advertising. Rather, the political advertising
campaign appeared as disjointed snapshots of political issues or
themes. For this reason, the news media and the voters were not able
to draw linkages between the various issues that Hunt raised.
Although he consistently portrayed Helms as a villain, Hunt's ads
were not able to provide a believable and convincing version of reality.
Indeed, Hunt's depictions of Helms's villainous acts were so disjointed
and unrelated that the news media and the voters began to question
the veracity of the messenger (Smith & Golden, 1988, p. 248).

Consistency, then, is one of the supreme tests used by modern-day
arbiters of the political system. By seeking the inconsistencies in the
candidate's political record, public relations, and advertising, the
news media provide ammunition for opponents. A candidate's
political ads must be consistent—with what a candidate has said or
done in the past, with what a candidate is currently doing or saying,
with what a candidate is expected to do and say personally, and with
what a candidate is expected to do and say as an American political
leader. A number of examples come to mind. After facing political
opposition, President Clinton has taken different positions on the same

issue. These inconsistencies have damaged his credibility during his administration. His vacillation on the issue of gays and lesbians in the military and the issue of affirmative action has brought severe criticism from the media. Political leaders, like most people, may change their minds on issues, and their political philosophy may evolve over time. This is a natural process. However, these changes in spoken policy positions or voting records are viewed negatively by the news media. Such flip-flops make for important news and advertising copy.

By adapting or altering existing images associated with their public personae, candidates may inadvertently create a violation of type. A violation of type is "almost any public conduct that contradicts an image important to people" (Klapp, 1964, p. 124). Shyles (1988) points out that John Glenn's ad team in his 1984 presidential bid tried to transform Glenn's image from one of an astronaut to one of a statesman. They did this because voters perceived Glenn as being highly qualified as a pilot and as an astronaut, but they failed to see Glenn as a qualified leader even though he had performed extraordinarily well as a U.S. Senator. For Glenn, the astronaut persona was his central role. A candidate's central role is the "thing for which people admire him or that they expect from him" (Klapp, 1964, p. 138). Once such a central role is fixed in the mind of the public, it becomes very difficult to transform the candidate's central role. Unfortunately, Glenn's ad strategy failed to provide the voters with a compelling reason to alter or adapt their images of Glenn's central role. Instead, the ads produced a dissonant message by emphasizing the personal characteristics associated with the heroic figure (Glenn's astronaut role) while at the same time positioning Glenn as a modern-day statesman. The way in which the ads were constructed created a violation of type.

Shyles (1988) contends, "The most important speculation is the extent to which a perception of unreality by voters, *even when composed of factual and true accomplishments conveyed accurately,* [emphasis in original] can damage a presidential candidate" (p. 24). Alterations in portraying candidate image must be artfully and skillfully developed and managed. Failure to do so results in the political death of a candidate. Shyles writes: "It remains of the utmost concern for candidates to convey at the very least a convincing appearance of reality, a semblance of truth, even if the account or portrayal of the candidate is less accurate than another which, while more accurate, may be less desirable to report" (1988, p. 18).

Political candidates can also get into trouble when they violate the public trust. For example, candidates should not make false charges in a political ad, because the news media may hop on that "inconsistent behavior"; such behavior does not satisfy the news media's definition of the correct conduct for the American political arena. The news media are frequently called upon by other political actors to investigate false political advertising and to explore the lies within. In summary, political spots must be consistent with the public image that the candidate wishes to convey.

As with most rules, there is an exception. If a candidate knows that an ad will create a discrepancy between his or her past record and present statements, a candidate may choose to first inoculate the audience to such a change. If such an inoculation strategy is used, the candidate would call attention to the discrepancy and explain why it exists before the opposition could do so. In this way, the opposition cannot effectively use it against the candidate once the "new position" ad appears. By first bringing the discrepancy to the public's and media's attention, the political actor gains control over how the perceived discrepancy will be discussed.

The Dramatization of Candidate Imagery

Political Schemas

Miller, Wattenberg and Malanchuk (1986) maintained that voters develop a political schema that is used in their evaluations of political candidates. They wrote that

the cognitive process underlying the evaluation of candidates . . . is clearly a dynamic one involving an interaction between the individual and the political environment. Voters abstract from their experience of past presidents those features and behaviors they associate with political success, and then evaluate other candidates with respect to these same characteristics. During the campaign the candidates no doubt emphasize certain characteristics in ways that reflect on or cue judgments of their competence, integrity, and reliability, because they believe these are relevant to the conduct of the office. Voters in turn respond to these campaign messages not only because they are relevant to their schema for presidential candidates, but also because these are the terms in which the political dialogue is conducted. (Miller et al., 1986, p. 535)

Clearly, voters construct their evaluations of political candidates though a dynamic process that assesses the political messages presented by the mass media. How one feels about what one knows and how one acts based upon what one knows and feels is based on a number of intervening variables—mostly tied to the psychological makeup and sociological background of the individual. The resulting image of the candidate has cognitive (knowledge or information), affective (emotions), and behavioral (action) dimensions.

Choi and Becker (1987) maintained that voters evaluate opposing candidates in comparison with each other before they decide who to support:

They develop a more-or-less distinctive picture of a candidate, which may or may not be an accurate one, and, to the extent that they do this, they can discriminate among or between candidates. . . . Issue (or image) discrimination is operationalized as the perception of absolute difference between candidate's issue positions (or images). (p. 269)

Clearly, voters use a comparative analysis in deciding whom to vote against or whom to vote for on election day.

A voter's image of a candidate includes "thoughts about a candidate's issue positions, political philosophy, family or background, personality and leadership, or even campaign style" (Trent & Friedenberg, 1983, p. 74). And, as previously discussed, the voter views candidates in terms of their political and stylistic roles. A body of research suggests that voters perceive a candidate through frames of reference that utilize "evaluative," "potency," and "activity" meanings (Osgood, 1957). "Put in simple terms, voters respond to a candidate by evaluating him as good or bad, and by assessing his strength and his capacity for action" (Nimmo & Savage, 1976, p. 47).

Glass (1985) and Miller, Wattenberg, and Malanchuk (1986) found that respondents with higher education levels were more likely to focus on "personality characteristics than on issue concerns or partisan group connections" (p. 521). Because of differences in research methodology, Glass (1985) and Miller et al. (1986) report slightly different findings. Personality characteristics most often emphasized reflected "performance-relevant criteria such as competence, integrity, and reliability" (p. 521). Voters emphasize the candidates' personal qualities in order to gain insight into the candidates' potential performance in office (see also Keeter, 1987; Kinder & Ableson, 1981; Popkin, Gorman, Phillips & Smith, 1976). Moreover, it is the contention of Miller et al. "that a presidential prototype, or schema, as we shall label it, can and will be evoked during the actual campaign period when people receive the appropriate stimuli to trigger these preexisting cognitions" (1986, p. 523). Although the relative importance of individual categories have changed over time, the schema has remained fairly stable. Competence was the primary dimension for candidate evaluation from 1952 to 1984; however, integrity and reliability became more important after 1964 (Miller et al., 1986). Glass (1985) provided a slightly different evaluation. His data analysis revealed more emphasis on personal character evaluations such as strength, educational attainment, or honesty over competence evaluations.

Ideal Candidate

Research has shown that voters have an ideal candidate in their heads—or an ideal candidate image (Hellweg, 1979; Nimmo & Savage, 1976). During the decision-making process known as the voting decision, voters compare their ideal candidate image with the real candidate image associated with the various contestants. Research has indicated that voters perceive their "ideal candidate" in terms of source valence criteria, composed of three primary dimensions:

The first is credibility, in such qualities as high ability, good character, and energy. The second is interpersonal attraction, which can be thought of as a candidate's social and physical attractiveness, and the third is homophyly, the similarities in personality, social class, educational background, or beliefs voters believe they share with the candidate. (Trent & Friedenberg, 1983, pp. 75-76; see also Bowes & Strentz, 1978; Kendall & Yum, 1984; Lashbrook, 1975; Wakshlag & Edison, 1979)

According to Trent and Friedenberg (1983), two critical campaign activities center around discovering the ideal candidate image and the successful portrayal of the candidate's image:

First, one of the most crucial tasks facing candidates, especially during the surfacing stage, is to determine just what attributes voters believe are ideal for the office sought. Second, campaign activities in later stages are designed to attempt to illustrate that the candidate possess[es] these qualities. (p. 74)

And that the opposition does not.

Negative Candidate Evaluations

Studies that show voters are more likely to cast their vote against a candidate than for a candidate (Fiorina & Shepsle, 1990; Johnson-Cartee & Copeland, 1991a; Kernell, 1977). Miller et al. (1986) found that among the more educated voters, negative evaluations of candidates' competence and reliability increased significantly, while comments "regarding integrity, charisma, and personal characteristics revealed little systematic rise in negative judgments" (p. 534). This finding emphasizes the dissatisfaction with presidential candidates as "real leaders," a point earlier demonstrated by the work of Denton (1982) and Schram (1991). Less educated respondents did not show such a high increase in negativity in candidate evaluations except for grade-school-educated respondents, who appeared more negative on personal characteristic evaluations (Miller et al., 1986).

It is important to note, however, that Klein (1991) found that the perceived character weaknesses on the part of presidential candidates were "more predictive of overall evaluations and voting than characteristics judged to represent strength" (p. 412). He concluded: "These results suggest that there is now ample evidence that perceptions of negative characteristics have a more powerful impact on voters than perceptions of character strengths" (Klein, 1991, p. 417; see Johnson-Cartee & Copeland, 1991a, 1997).

The Importance of the Image Debate

Political scientists often discount the average voter's so-called rational method of arriving at a voting decision, a method by which candidates are evaluated on the basis of personal attributes. However, there may be one overwhelming reason why voters use personal attributes as their primary means of evaluation. The news media use dramatic evaluations of political candidates as the central part of election news stories (Barber, 1974, 1978; Bennett, 1988; Dahlgreen, 1981; Entman, 1981; 1989; Gans, 1979; Golding, 1981; Graber, 1989; Nimmo & Combs, 1983; Semetko et al., 1991; Tuchman, 1981). Because of this, the public views issues in terms of "personalistic encapsulations" (Pool, 1965). Schwartz (1976) explained it this way: "All our research reveals that people are consumed with issues. The point . . . is that when it comes time to choose the person to be elected, voters are looking for the man best capable of dealing with the issues" (pp. 355-356). Democratic consultant Charles Guggenheim says: "I can't separate issues from personality. Candidates are in the business of issues. It's like trying to judge a lawyer who won't address himself to the law" (quoted in Agranoff, 1976, p. 302).

Yet if this is true, why then is political advertising, which contains some issue references, more effective in creating a positive candidate image than spots that contain only assertions as to the candidate's integrity, trustworthiness, and so forth? (Kaid & Sanders, 1978; see also Denton, 1982; Dybvig, 1970). The answer seems clear. Perhaps a story will suffice to illustrate the point. As a child, one of the authors was told a story in Bible school that contained this gem of wisdom: "Don't tell others that you're good; show others that you're good through word and deed." Applying this to the political situation at hand, the following axiom remains: dramatize your leadership style through appropriate political issues. It hardly seems surprising that "research indicates that the best way to make a positive image

impression on the voter is to use issues" (Devlin, 1986, p. 26). As
Democratic Senator Joe Biden has said, " Issues give you a chance to
articulate your intellectual capacity. Issues are a vehicle by which
voters determine your honesty and candor" (quoted in Agranoff, 1976,
p. 301). In short, issues serve as "convenient mechanisms for projecting
an appropriate image" (Kaid & Davidson, 1986, p. 185; see also
Denton, 1982; Dybvig, 1970; and for the consultant perspective, see also
Napolitan, 1972; Sabato, 1981; Schwartz, 1972, 1976; Wyckoff, 1968).

Republican consultant Robert Goodman has concluded, "I think
people have always voted for people. According to surveys, they
have always voted on honesty, competence and charisma, in that order. Many times issues are only used as a foil to express personal
virtue" (quoted in Agranoff, 1976, p. 301).

Imagery in the Drama of Politics

There is a danger in any attempt to discuss imagery, because there
are as many definitions of the term "image" as there are people trying
to define it. Practitioners in the fields of advertising, marketing, and
public relations have bantered the term about for years. Yet there is
not a consensus as to what "image" actually means. Some view images
as external attributes of objects, while others see it as an individual's
internal subjective reality. A student of popular culture, Daniel
Boorstin (1962), in his work *The Image: Or What Happened to the
American Dream*, suggests that an image is a creation of the advertising specialist in that the image is the collection of attributes
that the practitioner assigns to his or her product in order to create an
impression. Political campaign observers have used the term "image"
similarly in their discussions of candidate packaging (McGinnis, 1969;
Napolitan, 1972; Wyckoff, 1968). Others have a much different view
of "image," seeing it as an internal construct. For instance, public
relations expert Albert Sullivan suggests that images are internal re-
flections of the world, and he warns against a simplistic view of imagery. Sullivan (1965) observes that people do not accept into their
images all the campaign or product attributes that practitioners are
trying to project.

Social scientists appear to agree that images are internal subjective realities, but they do not agree as to the origination of these internal realities. There are three main views explaining the source of
images: the image projection thesis, the perceptual balance principle,
and the transactional imagery principle (Nimmo & Savage, 1976).

The image projection thesis can best be understood as a hypo-
dermic-needle theory of images. An image emanates from a political
candidate, and people attend to the stimuli and accept the projected

image (Goffman, 1959). O'Keefe and Sheinkopf (1974) have suggested that television campaign advertisements supply the voter with images. This thesis implies that the candidate has control over the audience's interpretation of the campaign messages, and it assumes that all people respond similarly to like stimuli (Nimmo & Savage, 1976).

The perceptual balance principle argues that voters have beliefs and attitudes that determine whom their electoral choice will be. Voters either seek a candidate with similar views, or they exercise selective perception and impose these views on a candidate (Donohue, 1973; McGrath & McGrath, 1962; Meyer & Donohue, 1973).   An individual's image is viewed as practically static.   This principle implies that people with like ideologies will perceive candidates in the same way and will respond to candidates in the same way (Nimmo & Savage, 1976).

In 1971, Brownstein tested the stimulus- and perceiver-determined views, and he found that

candidate image . . . proved a better predictor of voter choice than shared, candidate-to-voter attitudes on issues, although the latter was a good indicator. When combined, vote prediction was virtually perfect. The results thus suggest that homeostatic [perceptual balance principle] and image [projection thesis] theories of electoral decision making are properly thought of as complementary rather than competitive or exclusive. (pp. 48-49)

Consequently, in 1976, Nimmo and Savage proposed a transactional perspective of imagery in which they suggested that "a candidate's image is a function of both the characteristics people project on him and the qualities he tries to project to them" (p. 89). This perspective grew out of the work of the early symbolic interactionists, who theorized that through social interaction an individual develops an internal picture of the world, a subjective reality (Baldwin, 1897; Cooley, 1902, 1909; Dewey, 1925; Mead, 1934).

In 1959, Boulding pursued the early symbolic interactionists' line of thought in his book *The Image*. In this work, he uses the word "image" to indicate a "subjective knowledge of the world . . . that is built up as a result of all past experience of the possessor of the image" (pp. 5-6). An individual believes his or her image to be true and bases behaviors on the perceived image. However, an individual's image is "a reflection of reality, not definitive knowledge of it" (Nimmo & Savage, 1976, p. 8). The image is formed and modified through the process of social interaction. Following the symbolic interactionist's belief that meaning is created through an evolving interpretative process, Boulding (1959) suggests, "The meaning of a message is the change which it produces in the image" (p. 7). It is still important to remember that "each communication depends on past communications in which participants have been involved" (Ivey & Hurst, 1971, p. 207). The image is the photogray glasses with which an individual views the world, but as the glasses' lenses pick up messages from the sun, the lenses "adapt" to these messages and alter their tinting, changing to some degree how an individual perceives the world.

In his classic work *Public Opinion*, Walter Lippmann (1965) suggests that "the analyst of public opinion must begin . . . by recognizing the triangular relationship between the scene of action, the human picture of that scene, and the human response to the picture working i tself out upon the scene of action" (p. 11). Lippmann was writing about a construct now called the transactional image. Nimmo and Savage (1976) have defined the transactional image as "(1) a subjective, mental construct (2) affecting how things are perceived but also (3) influenced by projected images" (p. 8).

Candidate Imagery

Applied in a campaign setting, it can be said that a candidate's imagery is based on "reciprocal relationships reflecting continuing exchanges between leaders and followers, in which the former not only project selected a ttributes but must also imagine how followers perceive them; the latter perceive leaders and imagine how leaders perceive them" (Nimmo & Savage, 1976, p. 89). The content of a candidate's image has three dimensions: cognitive, affective, and behavioral (see discussion, Nimmo & Savage, 1976, p. 9; see also Bostrom, 1970). The cognitive aspect deals with what is known about the candidate's stands on the issues, voting record, experience, personality, and so forth. The affective dimension deals with how the individual then feels about what he or she knows. Does the individual feel positively or negatively about that he or she knows? And finally, how the individual then acts upon what the person knows and feels about the candidate is the behavioral aspect. Will the individual contribute money to a campaign? Will the individual volunteer his or her time to stuff envelopes? Will the individual vote for the candidate or vote against the candidate?

IMAGE TRIVIALIZATION

Unfortunately, a majority of the academic and professional consulting literature has trivialized the image construct. Repeatedly, the term has been used to refer to the character and physical attributes of political candidates (see critical discussion, Shyles, 1986, p.

114).   However, the term "image" denotes much more than just whether a candidate has a pretty face or a nice personality. When researchers (both academicians and professional consultants) use the term "image" to refer to character and physical attributes and "issues" to refer to political policy statements, they do a disservice to their readers. By coding and characterizing media and political presentations in terms of images and issues, they are (1) misusing the construct "image," (2) providing a naive picture of our perceptual screens, (3) setting up a false dichotomy between the two terms, and (4) constructing an operant-biased rating schema.

These so-called character/physical attributes (images) and these so-called voter concerns (issues) are intertwined in a person's perceptual framework. While it may be useful to code them separately, researchers must not kid themselves that voters, viewers, listeners, readers, and so forth actually perceive them as separate. People experience a Gestalt of multichannel, multipatterned messages in the totality of their perceptions. The distinction between the two are artificial constructs used to facilitate operationalization in traditional social science research.

In addition, much of the academic research laments the "sorry state" of both mass-mediated news reports and political advertising for concentrating on image (character/physical attributes) rather than issues (specific political policy statements).   Thus, researchers find themselves in the position of addressing images pejoratively and issues superlatively. It is just not that simple. Such an analysis demonstrates intellectual bias that misleads a reader into believing that the typical discussion of issues in some way imparts significant amounts of critical information to the voter.   In truth, it does not.   Park (1940) maintained that news provides people with "acquaintance with information," not "knowledge about" things.   The so-called issues of the day are little more than buzz words that have been couched in "personalistic encapsulations" (Pool, 1965, p. 177).   What can be said of mass-mediated news reports can certainly be said of political advertising.

A simple solution to this confusing image/issue quagmire might be to use phrases borrowed from the political/social psychology literature. Candidate images are composed of multiple dimensions of understanding. Studies have shown that voters perceive candidates in terms of the roles they appear to fill. These roles have been termed the political role and the stylistic role (Nimmo & Savage, 1976; for similar categories, see Kjeldahl, Carmichael, & Mertz, 1971; Roberts, 1973). The political role of a candidate is composed of those acts that are germane to the candidate's position as a community leader. This involves the candidate's perceived qualifications—past, present, and future (Nimmo & Savage, 1976). Qualifications would include such items as retrospective policy stands, prospective policy stands, experience, and so forth. The stylistic role of a candidate refers to acts that are not directly political but involve personal qualities such as physical appearance, bearing, integrity, speech patterns, and personality projection (Nimmo & Savage, 1976).

In order to avoid the oversimplification of the perceptual process, researchers should remember to ask themselves the cognitive image question, What is it that we know? The answer: both political and stylistic roles. That—and how we feel about what we know, and how we act upon what we know and feel—is the sum totality of our image.

Chapter 5

Political Communication Effects

Descriptions of how political communication and political advertising functions (how and why people respond to it) have been of great interest to political leaders, campaign consultants, academicians, media practitioners, and others. The process of explaining how communication functions in society is an area called communication theory. Over time, as information and evidence accumulate about relationships between and among various concepts, theories have evolved. Since theory is a "representation of the state of affairs at a given time" (Littlejohn, 1989, p. 2), theory is in a constant state of change, as we continue to build our knowledge base about how people respond. What follows is a snapshot of what we think we know, now.

LIMITED EFFECTS

In 1960 Joseph Klapper wrote the classic *The Effects of Mass Communication,* which explained his view that the mass media were not the usual cause of attitudinal or behavioral change but rather served to reinforce preexisting dispositions. Klapper believed, for example, that if a person was conservative, the media could reinforce that conservatism or even accentuate it, but the media by themselves could not usually cause a liberal to become a conservative. Klapper maintained that the media operated within a nexus of influences and that most of these influences—for example, family, religion, friends, education—were far more important in creating attitudes, beliefs, and behaviors than the media.

Klapper did believe that if these other influences were nonexistent or sufficiently weak, then the media could play a role in creating attitudes. As we have already discussed in chapter 2, political advertising is most effective when people don't have an existing predisposition. Reinforcement theory predicts that will be the case and that for people who have already selected a candidate, the media will serve to reinforce that selection. The mechanisms that explain this process of reinforcement are selective exposure, perception, and retention.

These three processes—selective exposure, perception, and retention—form the cognitive basis for reinforcement and most other limited effects perspectives. Because of its centrality to much of earlier mass media research, a clear understanding of these concepts is useful.

People are viewed as having predispositions that they do not like to have challenged. People attempt to keep the attitudes and orientations that currently exist through a process called homeostasis. To maintain homeostasis, people exhibit a tendency to expose themselves only to messages that agree with their currently held beliefs (Cooper & Jahoda, 1947). This process is called selective exposure. In order to cope with information or messages that challenge existing predispositions, it was hypothesized, people simply change their perception of the event so that what they think they see is congruent with what they want to see (Cooper & Jahoda, 1947) in a process dubbed selective perception. The final process, selective retention, is very close to selective perception. It is claimed that people remember only those items that are in agreement with their predispositions. The result of these three processes, it is believed, is a resistance to ideas or behaviors with which the person disagrees.

Selective perception and selective exposure are key concepts in understanding reinforcement theory in political communication. Selective perception suggests that people will perceive information in a way that is consonant with their previously held views. For example, Katz and Feldman's (1962) review of studies of the Nixon-Kennedy debates found that television viewers more often found the candidate they were supporting to be the winner of the debate than their candidate's opponent.

Selective exposure suggests that people will attend to or seek messages that are in accordance—usually called consonance—with their held views. For example, Schramm and Carter (1959), discovered that twice as many Republicans viewed a Republican gubernatorial candidate's telethon as had Democrats. In a local school election, voters who thought their side would win the election exposed themselves to more information about the election than those who thought their side would lose (Greenberg, 1965). Faber and Storey (1984) showed that respondents could recall more information from the political ads of those they supported than those they opposed.

The limited effects view of the media is summarized by McCombs (1972), who wrote that "reinforcement has been adjudged the dominant effect of political mass communication. And selective exposure and selective perception are the concepts commonly used to explain this outcome" (p. 174).

As seen in the discussion above, the media, and specifically television, is viewed as having some type of effect on some people, although no one can be precise as to whom or what is being affected. Berelson may have provided the ultimate definition of limited effects in 1948 when he wrote of limited effects, "Some kinds of communication on some kinds of issues, brought to the attention of some kinds of people under some kinds of conditions, have some kinds of effects" (172). An approach as nebulous as this lacks parsimony, and so theorists again began to rethink the effects of the mass media. In addition, many researchers, guided by what some called common sense or "gut instinct," critically examined the basic conceptualizations of the early effects research.

One reaction to limited effects was that some theorists focused their research not on a powerful media but on an active audience. This perspective came to be called uses and gratifications. These researchers view people as being instrumental in how they use the media, rather than as passive receivers of mediated messages.

USES AND GRATIFICATIONS

One reaction to the limited effects tradition was to reverse the direction of control in the relationship between media and audiences. Effects research views the media as doing something to the audience. The reverse, that the audience does something to the media or that audiences uses the media to fulfill their needs, provided the basis for the uses and gratifications approach. This approach

views the members of the audience as actively utilizing media contents, rather than being passively acted upon by the media. Thus, it does not assume a direct relationship between messages and effects, but postulates instead that members of the audience put messages to use, and that such usages act as intervening variables in the process of effect. (Katz, Blumler, & Gurevitch, 1974, p. 20)

Summarized succinctly, effects theories envisage media content doing something to people; uses and gratifications approaches envisage people doing something to media content.

The uses and gratifications approach examines how certain psychological and sociological attributes of an individual are related to the individual's communication use. Researchers attempted to find generalizations about the kinds of gratifications sought through the media. However, this research has proven elusive as the gratifications sought vary a great deal even within similar demographic groups (McQuail, 1969).

Katz et al. (1974) have summarized four basic assumptions of the uses and gratifications approach. First, the audience is active and goal directed; that is, people actively select the mediated messages to which they wish to be exposed. Second, the selection of media to fulfill felt needs lies with the individual. Third, the media compete with other possible of sources, such as interpersonal communication, in fulfilling the needs of the audience. Fourth, audience members are sufficiently self-aware, so they can describe their needs, goals, and uses of the media directly without the need to "trick" the information from the them in an experimental sense.

Some of the earliest evidence in this tradition was generated from a series of studies conducted by Lazarsfeld and Stanton in the 1940s (1942, 1944, 1949). These studies attempted to define the functions of the media, primarily of radio, for the individual. Similarly, Lasswell (1948) identifies three functions that the mass media fulfills for an audience: surveillance of the environment (an awareness of what is going on), correlation (an editorializing or coordinating process that puts information into perspective), and cultural transmission (disseminate values that are common to the culture). Wright (1960) added entertainment as a fourth function.

Theorists and researchers in the uses and gratifications tradition have continued to expand and refine the four functions suggested by Lasswell and Wright (cf. Blumler & Katz, 1974; *Communication Research*, 1979). In addition, researchers have attempted to measure how successful people are at attaining the gratifications they seek from the media.

As with the general study of mass communication, the study of the relationship between politics and the mass media has also used the uses and gratifications approach. Blumler and McQuail (1969) found that in Britain television served a number of functions for prospective voters. Their research was guided by the idea that the effects of media on an individual are dependent on the reasons a person exposes her- or himself to political messages. Mendelsohn and O'Keefe (1975) found that the difficulty of selecting the candidate for whom to vote, when the decision was made, and the amount of attention paid to the campaign directly affected the functions of the media for the people studied.

The expanding number of functions of the mass media combined with a growing corpus of other research indicated that perhaps television and the other media were more influential than current theory suggested. The mounting evidence implied to some that limited effects and uses and gratifications were not telling the whole story.

CONDITIONAL POWERFUL EFFECTS

Reaction by some researchers to the restrictions of the limited effects tradition was to formulate a view of the media as, once again, a powerful influence on viewers. Noelle-Neumann (1981; 1983) argued that the limited effects viewpoint had outlived it usefulness. According to Noelle-Neumann, the limited effects model is based on research that was completed before television became such a dominant and ubiquitous influence in people's lives. Television is viewed as being a more powerful medium than print, and therefore the effects from television viewing are much more powerful and uniform than the limited effects tradition suggests. Based on this new perspective, she calls for a reassessment of the limited effects model.

From her research in Germany, Noelle-Neumann concluded that under certain conditions the mass media have real and powerful effects. These conditions—ubiquity, consonance, and cumulation of mass communicated messages—are met in a modern industrialized society. Ubiquity means that the mass mediated messages give the appearance of being omnipresent (Noelle-Neumann, 1973). Consonance, as Noelle-Neumann uses the term, means that the messages from mass media news sources provide a similar picture of the world for the viewer. Cumulation speaks to the repetition of similar messages over an extended period of time. Noelle-Neumann views cumulation and consonance as "unanimous illumination, unanimous argumentation with regard to events, people, and problems" (Noelle-Neumann, 1981, p. 138).

Noelle-Neumann envisions the power of the media to be a product of people's need to know. As the world becomes more complex, people's need for news, information, and entertainment finds succor in the media. Though Noelle-Neumann never says so explicitly, her reasoning about the renewed power of the media comes from the media's ability to provide the information that people want. She notes (1981) that in then West Germany the increase in television penetration into homes has been accompanied by an increased interest by the population in politics. She views this increased interest as a result of the focus of television on political issues.

One power that the media have is the ability to focus people's attention on specific issues or stories. This ability to direct public opinion is called agenda setting. The first study of agenda setting was performed by McCombs and Shaw (1972) during a presidential election campaign, though Lazarsfeld, Berelson, and Gaudet (1948) had observed the phenomenon almost a quarter of a decade earlier. McCombs and Shaw (1972) found that those issues given prominent attention by the media were the same issues that people said were important to them (cf., McLeod, Becker, & Byrnes, 1974). Many researchers (e.g., Atkin, 1980; Baus & Ross, 1968; Rudd, 1986) have commented on attempts in political campaigns to determine the agenda for the media and ultimately the electorate.

Other researchers began to rethink their position on the power of television in politics, viewing television as a very real force. Rothschild (1978) capsulated the situation when he wrote: "A growing set of data indicates that a major shift in communications and communications effects may be occurring" (p. 64). Television is powerful "because it instantly and vividly reaches the most persuadable voters, who ignore, or fail to be exposed to, political information presented in other media" (McClure & Patterson, 1974, p. 3).

As an indicator of the high impact level of televised political advertising, Atkin (1980) notes that the rate of penetration of political messages through television is higher than for any other medium. With the continued insinuation of television into our daily lives have come a number of theorists, who are adopting the powerful effects perspective in terms of political communication (e.g., DeVries & Tarrance, 1972; Lang & Lang 1968; Mendelsohn & Crespi, 1970; Noelle-Neumann, 1981; Wyckoff, 1968).

Such heavy use of television has caused some researchers to rethink the potential effects of the mass media on political behaviors, beliefs, and attitudes. Kaid (1981) provides a summary of the limitations inherent in the limited effects approach from the political perspective as discussed by Kraus and Davis (1976):

1. Such studies [of the effect of the mass media on politics] fail to treat the mass media as serious variables
2. Most studies predate the domination of television in politics
3. Audience predispositions such as party identification seem to be weakening (Kaid, 1981, p. 251)

As discussed earlier, partisan predisposition, often operationalized as party identification, had been found to be the central organizing variable for political decision making. Mounting evidence (e.g., Converse, 1962; DeVries & Tarrance, 1972) and our own analysis suggest an erosion in this central organizing variable, though Joslyn (1981) found it to be the best predictor as late as 1981.

Earlier research (Converse, 1962) had found a growing trend for voters to vacillate between parties in their voting. This vacillation has continued to the extent that party identification falls behind the personality characteristics of the candidate and the issues as factors in decision making (DeVries & Tarrance, 1972). Graber (1980) concludes that this reduction in party influence has led to an elevation of the power of the media and particularly of television in influencing elections.

Dependency Theory

Working in the United States independently of Noelle-Neumann during roughly the same time, Ball-Rokeach and DeFleur (1976) proposed a similar theory, the dependency model of mass communication.

The dependency model takes a systems perspective, with audiences, media, and society as three transactional elements. Systems perspective is meant to indicate an approach that views a whole as an interrelated group of objects (see Monge, 1977). DeFleur and Ball-Rokeach (1976) view mass communication as "involv[ing] complex relationships between large sets of interacting variables that are only crudely designated by the terms 'media,' 'audiences' and 'society'" (p. 5). The transactional nature of the model points to the interrelationships that exist between the three identified elements.

Dependency theory posits that for any one of the three elements (audiences, the media, society) to attain its goals, it must depend upon the other two. For example, audiences become dependent on the media to provide information about society. The increasing complexity of society, coinciding with expanding media technologies, leads to the audience's need for the media to provide news, social norms, entertainment, and other functions to individuals. The more important a particular function served by the media is to an individual, the more dependent the individual becomes on the media, and consequently, the more affected the individual will be by the media.

Dependency theory discusses three types of individual effects: cognitive, affective, and behavioral. In other words: what we know (cognitive), how we feel about what we know (affective), and how we act based on what we know and feel (behavioral). Once again, how strong any one of these affects will be on an individual is in direct relation to how dependent the individual is on the media. Five types of cognitive effects are specified by DeFleur and Ball-Rokeach (1976): (1) creation and resolution of ambiguity, (2) attitude formation, (3) agenda setting, (4) expansion of an individual's belief system, and (5) values. Behavioral effects are generally divided into activation, the creation of new behaviors, and deactivation, the extinguishing of old behaviors.

Within the dependency model, one can observe macro and micro effects. Macro-effects are those that occur at the societal level. Usually macro effects can be viewed as those that support the existing ideology or those that are seen as catalysts that foment change in society. Micro-effects are those that happen at the individual level. One of the advantages of the dependency model is that it allows examination of both macro and micro effects within the framework of a single model. Some attempts have been made to create a synthesis of the dependency and the uses and gratifications approaches. Rubin and Windahl (1986) have called their new perspective the Uses and Dependency Theory. As with any hybrid, they view their new theory as having strengths not found in the theories from which it spawned and as having fewer weaknesses. They assert that "uses and gratifications, then, adds a voluntaristic element to dependency, just as dependency adds a more deterministic flavor to uses and gratifications" (1986, p. 279).

POLITICAL REALITY

In *Public Opinion*, Walter Lippmann (1965) suggests that people respond to realities created in their minds rather than to some objective outside world. Lippmann called this world in our minds the pseudo-environment. These "pictures in our heads," or images, are usually created through contact with the media rather than through direct experience. Kessel (1965) describes this as an individualized cognitive map of the world. This concept has come to be known as the social construction of reality.

Social Construction of Reality

Reality is created through the social process of communication (cf. Berger & Luckmann, 1966; Schutz, 1970; Watzlawick, 1976). What one knows and what one thinks one knows is shaped by the communication process. Shotter (1984) has linked all human experience to communication. As such, reality is no longer objective but subjective (Gergen, 1985). A culture's language constricts what can be known (Whorf, 1956). This linguistic relativity is known as the Sapir-Whorf hypothesis. As Sapir notes:

It is quite an illusion to imagine that one adjusts to reality essentially without the use of language and that language is merely an incidental means of solving specific problems of communication or reflection. The fact of the matter is that the "real world" is to a large extent unconsciously built up on the language habits of the group. (Whorf, 1956, p. 134)

Nimmo and Combs (1983) have interpreted the work of Watzlawick and others who view reality as being created through communication to mean "(1) our everyday, taken-for-granted reality is a delusion; (2) reality is created, constructed, through communication not expressed by it; (3) for any situation there is no single reality, no one objective truth, but multiple subjectively derived realities" (p. 3).

For most people, almost all political knowledge is constructed through the mass media. Relatively few people have actually met and talked with a U.S. senator, or a Supreme Court justice, or possibly even a city council member, but no one doubts their existence. What is known of them and their deeds comes predominantly from the media, and if it was necessary to prove the existence of, say, a U.S. Supreme Court justice without reference to any mediated information, few could do so. What is important is that people believe they exist and behave as if they exist. Thus the mass media provide the political mosaics from which we build our own personal reality (McCombs, 1979).

Negative Information

Information that often makes the most impact on people's view of reality is negative information. Negative information seems to make a greater impression on people than does positive information (Taylor, 1986). This greater impact of negative information over positive information is called the negativity effect. Kellermann (1984) describes the effect as "the tendency for negative information to be weighted more heavily than positive information when forming evaluations of social stimuli. Across widely varying events, setting, and persons, positive experiences or positive aspects of stimuli have been found to be less influential in the formation of judgments than are negative experiences or negative aspects of stimuli" (p. 37; see also, Anderson, 1965; Hamilton & Huffman, 1971; Hamilton & Zanna, 1972; Hodges, 1974; Jordan, 1965; Levin & Schmidt, 1969; Miller & Rowe, 1967; Warr & Jackson, 1976; Wyer, 1970).

Negative information appears to be immensely powerful, as it is given more weight than positive information; is able to change existing attitudes more than positive, and is easier to retrieve than positive (Briscoe, Woodyard, & Shaw, 1967; Cusumano & Richey, 1970; Feldman, 1966; Freedman & Steinbruner, 1964; Gray-Little, 1973; Kellermann, 1984; Lau, 1980, 1982, 1985; Leventhal & Singer, 1964; Mayo & Crockett, 1964; Reeves, Thorson, & Schleuder, 1986; Richey, Koenigs, Richey, & Fortin, 1975). In addition, Richey and colleagues demonstrated that negative first impressions are much more difficult to change than positive first impressions (Cusumano and Richey, 1970; Richey, McClelland, & Shimkunas, 1967) .

The power of negative information reinforces the choice of many consultants and candidates to "go negative" in their political advertising. "Voters will tell you in focus groups that they don't like negative ads, but they retain the information so much better than the positive ones" says Republican consultant Roger Stone ("Negative Advertising," 1986, p. 104). It is unlikely that political consultants and candidates will give up this powerful tool soon.

ATTITUDES

Perhaps the most popular definition of attitude has been that provided by Katz (1960): "*Attitude* is the predisposition of the individual to evaluate some symbol or object or aspect of his world in a favorable or unfavorable manner [emphasis in original]" (p. 168). The central concept is that an attitude is a "predisposition" or a readiness to respond to an object or symbol. Viewing attitudes as a readiness to respond has been a key feature of attitude definitions since the first peak of attitude research in the 1920s and 1930s (Allport, 1935; McGuire, 1985). Readiness to respond suggests that an attitude is not equivalent to behavior; rather, it is an inclination to react in a particular way.

Katz (1960) also suggests that attitudes are composed of two parts, "Attitudes include the affective, or feeling core of liking or disliking, and the cognitive, or belief, elements which describe the effect of the attitude, its characteristics, and its relation to other objects" (p. 168). Katz is suggesting that an attitude is a single whole that is comprised of two elements. The cognitive element of attitude is composed of ideas or beliefs. McGuire (1985) characterizes these attitudes as "distinguishing properties" (p. 242) of an object. Examples might be "Corvettes have only two seats" or "Democrats are liberals." The second element identified by Katz was the affective dimension. Affect refers to emotions. McGuire (1985) characterizes this component as "how much the person likes the object" (p. 242). Examples might be "Corvettes are beautiful" or "Republicans make me sick."

Others added a third part to attitude, the dimension of behavior, or the conative component. These are the inclinations to actions with which some object may be linked. McGuire (1985) viewed this as the "person's gross behavior" (p. 242). Examples of behavioral attitudes might be "I always vote for the Democrats" or "If I owned a Corvette, I'd drive it all the time."

This *triumvirate in uno* has been controversial. Some support the tripartite nature of attitudes (Bagozzi, 1978; Krech, Crutchfield, & Ballachey, 1962; Ostrom, 1969), while there are others, like McGuire (1969), who have rejected these divisions. Ajzen and Fishbein (1975) have suggested that these three components should be seen as distinct entities. Within this view attitudes would designate the affective dimension, beliefs would be the old cognitive dimension, and behavioral intentions would not change. For the purposes of this book, it is unnecessary to decide whether an attitude has three components or whether these are three distinct entities. The view taken here is that there are three components—whether unified or separate—consisting of cognitive, affective, and behavioral, which are useful in organizing and understanding political communication research.

This brief definition of attitude may not have cleared up the meaning for you. Don't feel disheartened. Dawes and Smith (1985) candidly assessed the situation, "It is not uncommon for psychologists and other social scientists to investigate a phenomenon at great length without knowing what they are talking about. So it is with *attitude* [emphasis in the original]" (p. 509).

Attitude Formation

The formation of an attitude means that a person has a predisposition to respond where previously there had been none. There are a number of factors that may interplay in order to create an attitude. Since the topic matter of this book is political advertising, the greatest attention is given to those communication-related factors. However, the reader should be aware that such factors as transient physiological factors, direct experience, and social institutions, among others, may influence the attitude formation process (McGuire, 1985).

Direct Exposure

Direct exposure to an object will create favorable disposition toward the object (Zajonc, 1968; Zajonc, Shaver, Tavris, & Van Kreveld, 1972), a phenomenon sometimes referred to as mere exposure. McGuire's (1985) review of the literature on exposure leads him to conclude that with few exceptions, "exposure results in monotonically increasing liking for the object, even when occurring to exhausting lengths" (p. 255), which means that the greater the contact, the greater the liking, unless the original exposure was originally negatively evaluated (Perlman & Oskamp, 1971). This has been generally supported in field studies of name exposure in political campaigns (Grush, 1980; Schaffner, Wandersman, & Stang, 1981).

Social Institutions

Social institutions and group identification such as family, peers, school, church, and demographic grouping have traditionally been viewed as important in the formation of attitudes. Some of the traditionally important institutions and groups will be mentioned here.

For most children, the family serves as the most influential power in attitude formation. The influence of the family may be seen in children's orientations toward gender roles (Hoffman, 1977; Vogel, Broverman, Broverman, Clarkson, & Rosenkrantz, 1970), religion (Jennings & Niemi, 1968), race relations (Ashmore & Del Boca, 1976), and other matters. In terms of politics, children usually form political attitudes similar to those they perceive as being similar to their parents' attitudes (Abramson, 1983; Berger, 1980; Himmelweit, Humphreys, Jaegers, & Katz, 1981; Kinder & Sears, 1985; Sears, 1975), and the children usually align themselves with their parents' political party preference (Jennings & Niemi, 1974).

Party identification, once selected, is better at influencing candidate preferences than influencing policy stands. Researchers who have attempted to study why people show a particular preference for a candidate in the 1970s invariably found party membership important (Nygren & Jones, 1977; Rusk & Weisberg, 1972). For those who do factor analysis, party identification is one of the most consistent of all factors to emerge (Kinder & Sears, 1985). But while party is important for candidate preference, the distinction between rank-and-file members of the two parties on public policy issues is in a process of fading (Bishop & Frankovic, 1981; Miller, Miller, & Schneider, 1980).

Traditionally, membership in a political party was based, in large measure, on the economic class to which the person belonged (Glenn, 1973). Working class and the poor were destined to become Democrats, and the upper class and wealthy were foreordained to join the Republicans. Petrovick and Steeper (1987) have shown the wealthier members of society shifting to the Republican party from 1952 to 1986.

Predictably, membership in an economic class continues to influence a person's attitude formation. Members of the working and lower classes tend to line up on one side of social policies, while members of the middle and upper classes queue on the other side of the line (e.g., Vannenman & Pampel, 1977). While class may make a difference in attitude formation, Kinder and Sears (1985) rejected labeling these differences as indications of a class struggle. We are not so sure the conclusion they reached is correct.

The geographical location in which people live may influence the attitudes they form. Survey research reveals that in matters of moral, religious, racial, occupational, and other similar attitudes, where a person lives does matter. For example, the South is often 10 to

20 percent more conservative than the rest of the nation (Oskamp, 1991).

In short, affiliation with family or group does serve to guide a person's attitude formation. These affiliations serve as the primary crucible for attitude formation. The importance of these groups by far outstrips the influence that the media play in attitude formation (McGuire, 1985; Klapper, 1960).

Communication

Attitudes are often created through communication. McGuire (1985) has divided the various sources of communication from which one may obtain a new attitude as hypnotic suggestion (Sarbin & Coe, 1972), conformity (Allen, 1975), groups such as peers (Smith, 1983), indoctrination (McEwen, 1980; Melton & Moore, 1982), and the mass media.

Klapper (1960) and, a quarter century after him, McGuire (1985) maintain that the mass media are one of the *least* influential of those forces that are active in attitude formation or, as we will note later, change. Both men agree that television, the most popular of the mass media, is most likely to have an effect on attitude formation where the other socializing forces on the individual are weak. However, that is not to say that television never shapes the creation of an attitude. Television will often expose viewers to new situations, objects, and people about which the viewer will form some attitude. This is particularly true in politics; during a campaign, a person's vote is often solicited by people with whom the viewer has little or no familiarity. But, this attitude is subject to change by the other socializing forces just mentioned.

ATTITUDE CHANGE

Attitude change, goal-seeking behaviors, and persuasion are differing terms for generally the same concept. Researchers from many fields have studied how a predisposition to respond might be changed. Researchers in attitude change have viewed attitude change as the dependent variable—that which is influenced by some other variable(s)—and the causes of attitude change as independent variables. Oskamp (1991) has reviewed the independent variables frequently studied and has lumped these variables into five categories: source, message, medium, audience, and target variables. Within these five categories, he identifies over 60 variables. For those interested in a thorough review, we recommend McGuire (1985) for your reading.

Source Variables

Those studies interested in source variables focus on the characteristics of the point of origin for the information. Those source variables most commonly studied are credibility, attractiveness, and power.

Credibility

The first of the source variables to receive systematic study was credibility; that is, the perceived truthfulness, trustworthiness, and expertness of the person communicating. Hovland, Janis, and Kelley (1953), as well as others, found credibility to be positively related to the amount of attitude change in the audience. People are more likely to believe and change their attitudes on the basis of testimony by someone they find credible than from a person they find incredible. There are constraints on this positive relationship. For example, a person may be perceived as too expert or superior to the receiver. Research has shown that people are most willing to accept information from those they consider slightly but not vastly superior to themselves (cf. Deaux, 1972; Huston, 1973). The source will be viewed as less credible when the person is perceived as self-involved or very interested in the outcome (Harmon & Coney, 1982; Wheeless & Grotz, 1977).

Attractiveness

Communicators who are perceived as familiar, likable, and similar to the receiver will have the most impact. These three areas have been the traditional social science operationalizations of attractiveness As discussed above, the greater the familiarity from exposure, usually the greater the persuasive appeal of the communicator. Not surprising that people we find likable are more likely to be persuasive than people we dislike (Sampson & Insko, 1964). Similarly, it is not surprising that people are more persuaded by physically attractive communicators than physically unattractive people (Chaiken, 1979; Dion & Stein, 1978).

Communicators who are perceived as being similar are also considered more attractive. Usually similarity has been handled in terms of demographic and ideological similarity. Demographic similarity is primarily important for "behavioral acceptance," while ideological similarity is more important for "abstract acceptance" (McGuire, 1985, p. 266). In terms of political decision making, ideological similarity is more powerful.

Power

McGuire (1985) writes: "Persuasion occurs through the compliance process when the receiver wants to get a reward or avoid a punishment from a powerful source" (p. 266). The power of the successful political candidate derives from the candidate's ability to provide for the commonweal of those who elected the candidate. This may be concrete, in terms of appropriations for the home district, or more abstract, in the form of legislation that reflects the concerns of those who elected the candidate.

Message Variables

Communication content is the most often thought of influence in changing attitudes. As such, message variables have received the strongest research scrutiny. Message studies may be categorized into those that study types of arguments, message style, selection of evidence and arguments, quantity of evidence and arguments, and extremity of arguments.

Types of Arguments

Typologies of effective arguments date back centuries. The most commonly cited historical list of arguments is Aristotle's *ethos*, *pathos*, and *logos*. McBurney and Mills (1964) defines argument as "a line of reasoning, or an inference from premises, offered to support a conclusion, and . . . several types of reasoning that can be so employed" (p. 115). Andreñ (1980) offers propositional and nonpropositional arguments as a means of understanding arguments used in advertising. Propositional arguments are rational arguments, and nonpropositional are antirational arguments. Reynolds and Burgoon (1983) provide a much more extensive list of argument types available to the communicator. Arguments that are positive or negative may be made.

Message Style

The stylistic devices of delivery and word choice generally constitute the stylistic areas for study. The use of paralinguistic elements influences the receiver's responses, as does the choice of words used to convey the message. We have argued that candidates need to adopt a more interpersonal style of presentation. The television setting, in fact, has forced the more intimate style.

In formal speech-giving settings, research shows that the style used in delivering the message (loudness, pitch, and other paralingual devices) interacts with other variables. McGuire (1985) writes,

With a high trust (Miller & Basehart, 1969) or a high prestige (Pearce and Brommel, 1972) source or a low involved receiver (Mehrley & McCroskey, 1970), the more dynamic style has greater effect; but with a low-trust or low-prestige source or highly involved receiver, an appropriately modest, subdued style produces more persuasion. (p. 270)

The choice of words that a candidate uses will also affect the persuasiveness of a message. Carmichael and Cronkhite (1965) have, not surprisingly, shown that speakers should use language that is prevalent to the audience, shying away from words that are not commonly used by the audience. The candidate, in part, demonstrates unity with an audience through the language of the speech. Thus, obscure words makes the speech less persuasive as the speaker appears more distant. Analogies (McCroskey & Combs, 1969) and metaphors (Johnson & Taylor, 1981), when not done to excess, all heighten the persuasiveness of the message.

Selection of Evidence and Arguments

The content of communication is composed of arguments and evidence to support arguments. The general rule is that a speech should have three or five major points. Evidence suggests that the most persuasive arguments should be placed at the first and last of the speech as they will be the most influential, because they are remembered. This placement is called primacy and recency.

Quantity of Evidence and Arguments

General areas of inquiry have covered the optimum quantity of information to provide, the most effective number of arguments to use, and the effects of repetition of information.

As anyone who has been forced to sit through a long-winded speech knows, shorter is better. Research verifies that shorter messages increase receiver's retention of the main arguments (Reder & Anderson, 1980). This seems to be particularly true for people watching at home, as studies indicate that for those people who are more easily distracted shorter is better (Harkins & Petty, 1981).

However, shorter messages do not necessarily indicate fewer arguments. In commercial advertising research findings suggests that the greater the number of different arguments, the greater the recall of the advertisement by the viewer. However, a greater number of arguments by itself is insufficient to affect attitude change (Strong, 1974).

Extremity of Arguments

Generally people prefer to hear arguments with which they agree. That is not to say that people expose themselves only to consonant information, because the evidence is clear that there are any number of occasions when people will seek or at least not avoid dissonant information (cf., Ball-Rokeach, Grube, & Rokeach, 1981; Frey, 1982; Wyer & Frey, 1983). In general, there are cognitive theories that attempt to explain which arguments will be accepted and which rejected based on how closely those arguments align with some already existent attitudes. The two areas to be briefly covered all fall within the general area of consistency theory and have played a major role in attitude research: dissonance theories and social judgment theory.

Consistency Theories

The primary feature of consistency theory is that people attempt to keep attitudes, beliefs, and behaviors in agreement with one another. When people perceive that any one of these three are not consistent, they experience an uncomfortable state. People don't like to be uncomfortable, so they act to remove the inconsistency. Generally, psychologists have talked of people maintaining a state of homeostasis.

Festinger's (1957) cognitive dissonance theory has been the most influential of all the consistency theories. Festinger argued that one of three types of relationships exist for any two cognitive or behavioral elements: irrelevant, consonant or dissonant. Irrelevant relationships are not of concern to people, but the other two, consonant and dissonant, are. People try to maintain consonant relationships; when there is not a consonant relationship but instead a dissonant relationship people become uncomfortable and actively work to remove the discomfort. How hard people will work to remove the dissonance depends on the intensity of the dissonance. Festinger posits a positive linear relationship between the amount of dissonance experienced and the amount of effort expended to remove the dissonance.

One of the times when people experience dissonance, according to Festinger, is when they must make a decision. So selecting the candidate for whom to vote can be a dissonance-producing experience. To relieve this dissonance, a voter can seek information that reinforces the selected choice, for example, paying attention to the campaign commercials of the chosen candidate. The person with dissonance might shield him- or herself from information that would question the decision; for example, the person could ignore campaign materials from the candidate who will not be receiving the person's vote. The person may distort, misinterpret, or argue with the dissonant information that supports the candidate not selected. For example, one might respond to a newspaper endorsement of the other candidate by telling oneself that the newspaper has long been known as a tool of the candidate's party.

Social judgment theory predicts which arguments will be accepted by an individual and which arguments will be rejected. Sherif, Sherif, and Nebergall (1965) proposed that people make a decision based on anchor points that are created by existing dispositions and environmental factors. The social judgment theory posits that there are latitudes of acceptance, rejection, and noncommitment. Latitude of acceptance maps the range of arguments similar to a person's already held attitudes that the individual will internalize, and leading to attitude change. Arguments that fall outside the person's range of acceptance will be rejected and do not affect attitude change. On any topic, the "width" of a latitude—either acceptance or rejection—depends upon the amount of ego involvement a person has in the topic. The greater the ego involvement on a given topic, the narrower is the person's latitude of acceptance and the wider the person's latitude of rejection.

A person may support a candidate because the candidate is perceived to have views similar to the voter's. If the voter has worked in the campaign of the candidate, there will be greater ego involvement in whether that candidate wins the election than if the voter took no part in the candidate's campaign. This increased ego involvement means that the arguments against the candidate must fall within a much narrower latitude of acceptance than for the person who has very little ego involvement in the campaign. To fall within the voter's latitude of acceptance, the argument must be perceived to be similar to those already held by the voter.

Audience Variables

People are different, and so any given message will affect a group of people in different ways. Individual differences among receivers play an important part in how attitudes are changed. Usually these differences are seen as being personality or demographically based. The four discussed here are age, intelligence, sex, and self-esteem. However, Cronkhite (1969) finds these variables to be of limited utility to people who are planning their messages for a large audience. This is particularly true in the mass media with its mass audience. The general characteristics of the audience who will view political commercials are not so homogenous that one may know precisely who will see and hear the message.

Age

Changing a person's attitude becomes more difficult as the person matures (Janis & Rife, 1959). After about the age of 9 (Eron, Huesmann, Brice, Fischer, & Mermelstein, 1983; Ward & McGinnies, 1974), people become less prone to persuasion.

Intelligence

As with many of the receiver variables, the relationship between intelligence and persuasibility is not a linear one. Indeed, the relationship may not even exist. The evidence is suggestive of no relationship (Pence & Scheidel, 1956, cited in Cronkhite, 1969). McGuire (1985) argues that higher intelligence may create an enhanced resistance to persuasion, but that is offset by greater comprehension and inference drawing, which leads to decreased resistance to persuasion.

Sex

The effect of sex on susceptibility to persuasion lacks a definitive answer. It was long thought that women could be persuaded more easily than men (for example, Furbay, 1965; Janis & Field, 1959; King, 1959; Scheidel, 1963). By the mid-1970s, the weight of opinion seemingly had swung to the side of no difference between men and women (Eagley, 1978; Maccoby & Jacklin, 1974; Sohn, 1980). However, there continues to be evidence suggesting that, taken as a whole, women are more persuasible than are men (Eagley & Carli, 1981; McGuire, 1985).

Self-esteem

The relationship between self-esteem and persuasibility is not linear (Cox & Bauer, 1964). While there is evidence that supports a linear relationship—higher self-esteem, lower persuasibility (Janis & Field, 1959; Linton & Graham, 1959)—more recent evidence reveals the relationship to be more complex (see McGuire, 1985, for his suggested mediating factors, and Lehmann, 1970; Nisbett & Gordon, 1967; and Zellner, 1970 , for supporting studies).

Applied Attitude Change

The principles of attitude change have been simplified and applied specifically to the campaign setting. Nimmo (1970) has summarized attitude change into reinforcement, crystallization, activation, and neutralization.

The ability to reinforce a previously held disposition, for example, a choice on for whom to cast a ballot, has been discussed at several points in this chapter. Nimmo adopts the term from Klapper (1960) and believes that it is the most powerful effect of television.

When the undecided voter makes a decision, the process of crystallization takes place, as Nimmo puts it. The media are seen as actually instigating attitude change rather than reinforcing a disposition. Crystallization is a decision point. Nimmo makes a distinction between reaching a decision and voting. Activation is the act of voting for those people who have experienced crystallization.

The exposure to political advertising may cause some people to reduce their positive evaluation of their preferred candidate. Nimmo calls this neutralization. Of the four processes Nimmo discusses, he rightly points out that this is the least frequently occurring one. While some may waver during a campaign, the majority return to their preferred candidate when it is time to vote.

RECEIVER'S RESISTANCE TO PERSUASION

A discussion of attitude change would be incomplete without mention of those factors that have been found to offer some resistance to persuasion. A number of approaches have been employed, the most relevant here are commitment, anchoring, and inoculation.

Commitment

A commitment that requires a person to state his or her beliefs in public generally confers resistance to change for those beliefs (Bennett, 1955). A person who must actively defend her or his held beliefs will have even greater resistance to change than one who makes a simple public commitment (Halverson & Pallak, 1978).

Behavioral commitment to an attitude makes it more difficult for an individual to disavow the attitude or more colloquially, change her or his mind. Behavioral commitment, according to McGuire (1964), "makes changing belief dangerous, costly, awkward, or at least harmful to self-esteem, it strengthens the believer's tendency to resist social influence attempts aimed at the belief" (p. 198). McGuire posits three methods by which an individual may demonstrate a behavioral commitment to an attitude, "(1) internally thinking about his belief, (2) verbally stating his belief and becoming publicly identified with it, or (3) acting overtly in some irreversible way on the basis of his belief" (McGuire, 1969, p. 261).

Political campaigns are one of the most obvious places for the use of behavioral commitment. Campaigns are designed to draw in people in order to have them commit to the support of a candidate using one of the three methods outlined by McGuire. The campaign—especially political advertising—is designed to make the prospective voter think about the candidate the voter is supporting. When a news story, ad, or a piece of campaign literature induces the recipient to think once again about the candidate, that process creates a stronger commitment to that candidate. If an individual announces support for a candidate and that support becomes known, it is difficult for the person to then change to another candidate. The placement of a bumper sticker on one's car or placement of a yard sign in front of the voter's home invokes both the second and third methods for increasing the commitment to an attitude. For those who have committed, it is generally only necessary for the candidate to avoid making a major gaffe or having some unfavorable information revealed about the candidate. Even if these unfavorable situations happen, some supporters will still find it impossible to abandon the candidate for whom they have made such a strong mental commitment.

Anchoring

This technique for resisting attitude change requires that initial attitudes be connected to other attitudes. Anchoring attempts to link a given attitude to other cognitions in such a fashion that one could not change the attitude without rethinking all the linked cognitions. The connection to deeply felt attitudes makes change difficult, as all attitudes would have to change. McGuire (1985) says one of the most effective methods is to link new attitudes to beliefs. Beliefs may also be anchored to other people who are important to the person (Tannenbaum, 1967).

Inoculation

This method of resisting attitude change seems to hold the greatest utility for political candidates. In situations where the campaign may suspect the use of an attack against the candidate, inoculation strategy provides a method of dealing with potential charges or attacks. This strategy is particularly useful to use for those voters who might be subject to switching their vote if the preferred candidate is attacked by the opposition.

McGuire and his associates (Anderson & McGuire, 1965; McGuire, 1961a, 1961b, 1962, 1964; McGuire & Papageorgis, 1961, 1962; Papageorgis & McGuire, 1961) view the attack of undefended attitudes as analogous to the introduction of a disease into the body of an immune-deficient patient. Researchers analogized that attitudes would be strengthened by exposing individuals to a relatively weak counter-attitudinal message while providing the refutation to that counterat-titudinal message at the same time. This is similar to physicians in-troducing a weakened virus into the body so that the body can produce a defense for the real disease.

McGuire (1964) believed that for inoculation to successfully function, a person must first have sufficient knowledge to defend the preexisting attitude, must have the opportunity to practice the de-fense, and must be motivated to use the defense. McGuire (1961a) found that messages with additional supporting information (e.g., evidence) as an adjunct to defense building counterarguments create a more effec-tive defense than messages that just contain defense-building counter-arguments. The combination of defense building counterarguments and supporting information was the strongest for maintaining attitudes when the person was faced with a new or novel attack against a held attitude.

McGuire (1962) also discovered that the inoculation effect in-creases as the passage of time increases between exposure to the de-fense-building counterargument and exposure to an attack. It was thought that as the time between inoculation and exposure to attack increased the amount of practice dealing with counterattitudinal mes-sages also increased. The practice of defending against counterattitu-dinal ideas works to strengthen the resistance to subsequent nonconso-nant messages. This would suggest that inoculation ads would be most effective if introduced early in the campaign.

Pfau and Burgoon (1988) applied inoculation concepts to political communication. They concluded that inoculation is effective in three specific fashions: "[1] undermining the potential influence of the source of political attacks, [2] deflecting the specific content of politi-cal attacks, and [3] reducing the likelihood that political attacks will influence receiver voting intention" (Pfau & Burgoon, 1988, 105-106).

Chapter 6

Political Communication Research Methods and Applications

Political communication research has been slow to gain acceptance among many traditional party politicians. Political leaders often appear uncomfortable with the idea that research could tell them how to strategically create and evaluate the appropriate communication campaign plan. And many politicians simply feel uncomfortable with the resulting implication: that he or she is a political product for public consumption. In both 1952 and 1956, Democratic presidential candidate Adlai Stevenson was very reluctant to use modern political marketing and advertising techniques (Diamond & Bates, 1988; Jamieson, 1984, 2nd par.). His words reflect the attitudes of an entire generation of American politicians. In 1952, Stevenson told America,

I don't think the American people want politics and their presidency to become the plaything of the high-pressure men, of the ghostwriters, of the public relations men. I think they will be shocked by such contempt for the intelligence of the American people. This isn't soap opera, this isn't Ivory Soap versus Palmolive. (Diamond & Bates, 1988, p. 60)

The same refrain was heard in his acceptance speech at the 1956 Democratic convention:

The men who run the Eisenhower administration evidently believe that the minds of Americans can be manipulated by shows, slogans, and the arts of advertising. This idea that you can merchandise candidates for high office like breakfast cereal—that you can gather votes like breakfast cereal—that you can gather votes like box tops—is I think the ultimate indignity to the democratic process. (Diamond & Bates, 1988, p. 78)

In America, at least on the presidential level, Stevenson was the last of his kind (Jamieson, 1984, 2nd par.).

An anecdote from Great Britain illustrates the differences between our political media cultures and shows how widely accepted "cornflake" candidates have become in America (Johnson & Elebash, 1986). During the 1979 general election campaign, British Labour leader James Callaghan said, "I don't intend to end this campaign packaged like cornflakes. I shall continue to be myself" (*Time*, 1979, p. 42). A knowing American reporter from *Time* magazine commented: "Margaret Thatcher, apparently, would rather be prime minister" (*Time*, 1979, p. 42).

On the national political scene, campaigns were quick to use polling data to make choices concerning traditional campaign issues. Campaigns also immediately recognized the advantage of media-buying data to make sophisticated and well-targeted use of their campaign dollar. However, the same political campaigns have been slow to fund or appreciate sophisticated quantitative and qualitative analysis for developmenting political communication strategies and tactics (see Devlin, 1981). Frequently, political communication research is rejected "because it doesn't fit the judgment level of people running the campaign" (Republican political consultant Peter Dailey, quoted in Devlin, 1981, p. 4). Republican consultant Michael Murphy has complained,

In House campaigns you still have arguments between media people and the door knockers who ask whether they really need TV. People win for sewer commissioner because they mailed out 25,000 potholders. They think the way to win for Congress is to mail out 50,000 potholders. ("Technology, Strategy," 1985, p. 2564)

Even today political consultants find House and senatorial candidates who are suspicious of modern political research techniques. However, most will fund public opinion polling, because they need the survey reports to show prospective contributors that their candidacy is viable for fund raising purposes. Otherwise it is difficult to get money for communication research even though much could be piggybacked to more traditional campaign research activities. All too frequently, some federal and many state and local political candidates tell consultants that "party determines the vote" or that "we only advertise because it's expected." Or worse: "That's not the way we do things around here" or "All that numbers stuff is just junk." Democratic political consultant Charles Guggenheim (quoted in Wolfson, 1972b, p. 14) says that these "old tribal rituals" are appalling.

As all political consultants know, research saves time, money, and effort. Due to insufficient research, campaigns often find themselves plagued by costly, ineffective ads, or worse, ads that harm the candidate's standing. Improper use of valuable campaign advertising dollars is just one potential reason why an otherwise successful campaign loses on election day. While campaigns try to save money by doing only the minimum amount of research, they often find the lack of information is even more expensive.

For our purposes, political communication research will be defined as the systematic gathering of information for the development of a consistent communication strategy and its subsequent communication tactics. A political communication research plan must examine five critical areas: voter research, candidate research, message research, channel research, and campaign-setting research.

VOTER RESEARCH

The first principle of waging an effective campaign is to know and understand the voters. A maxim of modern political consulting is that one must know what the voters want and then package the candidate so that he or she fits the image of the successful officeholder that people maintain in their minds. While this may seem rather manipulative or cynical, this has become a standard axiom in political campaign management. A candidate can never know too much about those the candidate desires to persuade.

A thorough analysis of the "geographic and political subunits, their population patterns and its growth, education levels, racial distributions, occupational patterns . . . , and its voting habits" (Agranoff, 1976, p. 159) should be conducted. A clear picture as to what is on the voters' minds is necessary for the campaign to effectively craft messages that will persuade the voters. The key to persuasion may be summarized in a phrase that we often use with clients in a mantra-like fashion: specific messages designed for specific audiences for specific results. The only way to fulfill this persuasion axiom is to conduct an intensive and extensive research program into the potential voters' political psyche.

Since it is usually difficult to pinpoint who will compose the exact list of those who will go to the polls and vote, researchers often must seek to identify information about a more diverse group of people than the candidate or the campaign may first imagine as the candidate's targeted voters. Voter research will often attempt to isolate likely voters. It is these likely voters who should serve as the principal target for the candidate. The goal of voter research must be to locate and query those people who have a probability of exercising their franchise on election day.

CANDIDATE RESEARCH

Candidate research involves much more than simply "knowing" your own candidate. Although it is important to understand how your candidate views himself or herself, the race or campaign experience, and the political office that the candidate is seeking, it is far more important to have an objective evaluation of your candidate and your candidate's record. An thorough evaluation involves a careful, complete, objective analysis of your candidate, your candidate's likely opponents, and the potential voter's conception of the ideal candidate for the office sought. As you may remember, "the ideal candidate" is the voter's description of that composite of qualities, traits, and issue positions that the voter would most like a candidate to possess for a particular office. Keep in mind that a careful candidate analysis involves identifying associated issues, political affiliations, leadership traits, and so on for each candidate, both real and "ideal," in the race. This detailed analysis should be conducted before a candidate ever announces her or his candidacy. Such an analysis involves asking the following types of questions when designing a survey instrument:

1. How do the voters describe the ideal candidate for political position X? (See Nimmo & Savage, 1976)
2. What are the strengths and weaknesses associated with your candidate?
3. What are the strengths and weaknesses associated with the likely opponents?
4. How does each potential candidate compare with the traits, qualities, and issues associated with the ideal candidate for office X?

In addition to identifying the voters' perceptions of potential candidates prior to the election season, the campaign must take the proactive stance of seeking out all available information that is likely to impact on the campaign but may or may not be part of the public consciousness. Clearly, a detailed examination of the political record of all candidates—including the one for whom the consultant is working—should be conducted. This includes political affiliations, financial donors, voting records, past and present position statements, and the success and failures of the candidate's past performances in political offices. This information is essential to the development and creation of positive, negative, inoculation, and responsive advertising. In addition, a close, honest examination of the candidate's personal life should be conducted. Are there any vulnerabilities located there? Is the candidate a person who filed for bankruptcy but now wants to hold an office involving responsibility for taxpayer money, such as the office of state treasurer? Is the candidate planning on using "family values" as a campaign theme though the candidate is two years behind on child payments to a former family? Has the opponent been convicted of tax evasion or drunken driving? Is there a criminal record? Are there any embarrassing personal situations for either candidate that if publicly aired might prove damaging to the campaigns? Such as the candidate we once had who forgot to mention that he had remarried before divorcing his previous wife—twice. These questions should be answered for all candidates in the race.

A thorough analysis of candidate style should also be conducted. Does the candidate tend to be effect modeling—inviting the people to be more like the candidate—or effect contrasting, pointing out the superior differences between the candidate and the average person? What about the rest of the candidates in the race? Which candidates have an open style and which candidates have a closed style? Is it possible to characterize the candidates as "hot" or "cold"? Is there some potential political gain that can be produced through the manipulation of candidate style variables, that is, is your candidate likely to be at an advantage or a disadvantage because of his or her style of communicating? Which communication situation best suits the communication style of your candidate? For example, is your candidate most comfortable with one-on-one discussions, speaking extemporaneously before a group, delivering a memorized speech, or answering impromptu questions from reporters? These same questions should be asked about the opponent.

Business executives and would-be executives have acknowledged the role of both personal appearance and personal speech performance in the successful climbing of corporate ladders. However, politicians, the very group most frequently accused of being packaged, often have problems dealing with presentation of self. Candidate dress, interview performance, speech training, and television training have become important components in modern elections. National consultants such as Michael Sheehan, Associates, provide valuable services to clients who need help with their impression management. In addition, many college professors, who are experienced in persuasion and impression management consult with state and local clients. Unfortunately, many politicians resist candidate training. Campaign managers must assess how receptive the candidate is to new ideas dealing with public performances. In other words, how open is the candidate to criticism and retraining? And perhaps most important, is the communication style of the candidate likely to improve through participation in a public speaking and media presentation training experience?

In developing a campaign strategy, candidate status, that is, whether a candidate is an incumbent or a challenger or is running for an open seat, makes a difference in the conduct of the campaign. In addition, party status factors—whether the candidate is of the majority or minority party, whether the candidate is a Democrat or a Republican—and whether it is a truly competitive election make a difference in how the campaign is waged.

A detailed analysis of the possible winning coalition of voters that realistically could be created to support a candidate should be identified. A winning coalition will be made up of different types of groups and individuals. Republicans have traditionally formed business-oriented coalitions, while Democrats have formed labor-oriented coalitions. While those party stereotypes do have their basis in fact, it is also important to remember that it takes a broad base of support in order to win and that traditional coalitions are in a state of flux. A candidate cannot rely on tired party truisms when planning a campaign. All realistic potential avenues should be explored. Political activists, party leaders, traditional financial resource bases, supportive organizations, and so on should be contacted and evaluated as to their potential support.

In addition, a thoughtful evaluation as to the problems and potentials associated with the planned campaign organization should be considered. Will the campaign contain sufficient grassroots volunteer support, financial support, and leadership to survive the rigors of the campaign season? Are there sufficient legal and accounting professionals represented in the organization? Does the candidate have a strong volunteer base? Does the campaign organization represent a wide cross section of the constituency? Are there any campaign veterans who are able to lend their expertise to newcomers in the campaign?

MESSAGE RESEARCH

As in product advertising, a great deal of attention should be placed on advertising message research. In product advertising, message recall has traditionally meant a study of the recognition and recall of various advertising messages (see Fletcher & Bowers, 1988). However, in political advertising, message research also involves a careful testing of political mythical appeals and their appropriateness for various target groups (see Johnson-Cartee & Copeland, 1997). An examination should be made of the "electorate's political norms, expectations, and the political styles and tactics they are likely to approve" (Agranoff, 1976, p. 160) in order to create appropriate advertising messages. This means that a thorough understanding of the political mythical constructs of the electorate should be an essential part of this analysis. While a great deal of attention has been focused on national political mythical appeals, it should not be forgotten that there are also regional and local myths that may be used by the astute candidate. Resonance strategy, which uses persuasive messages that are "harmonious with the experience of the audience" (Patti & Frazer, 1988, p. 301), must by necessity utilize the appropriate mythical constructs for a given constituency. As we've discussed elsewhere, these mythical constructs serve as responsive chords within the voter (Schwartz, 1972).

The campaign should ask itself a series of message-oriented questions. What persuasive styles are most likely to impact members of your winning coalition? What types of persuasive appeals are most likely to serve as "hot buttons" for your target groups? What package of advertising content and presentation styles is best suited to your candidate and campaign goals?

The campaign must also be aware that it will need to have the ability to construct print and electronic ads that will engender a positive attitude about the advertisement itself. Research into attitudes toward the advertisement has demonstrated significant impact on attitude toward the object of the advertisement. MacKenzie and Lutz (1989) suggest that all advertisers create ads high in positive affect and containing some entertainment value for the audience. Careful study of political advertising has also shown that poorly produced political advertisements reflect on the sponsoring candidate. People will negatively judge a candidate on the quality of the advertising (Kaid & Davidson, 1986; Owen, 1991; Shyles, 1986). Viewers do notice bad production; as Keating and Letané (1976) noted of television, "The audience is more aware of the flaws in the technical use of this most familiar medium" (p. 120).

CHANNEL RESEARCH

The campaign should conduct a scientific analysis of the media habits of the proposed winning coalition. The allocation of the campaign's advertising dollar should be based on this analysis. The campaign should be aware of how the audience in turn evaluates messages received from the various media channels in terms of credibility. For example, does the expected audience use the various media differently for political messages (Johnson-Cartee & Copeland, 1997)?

Obviously, the campaign's financial picture will also influence the selection and frequency of use of the mass media channels. A secondary analysis of rating services' data allows for informed buying decisions that encourage the efficient and effective use of campaign dollars. Often the services of a consultant or media specialist is necessary in developing an overall media buying plan, particularly if the office spans several media markets. The ability to formulate a media buying plan that produces the largest exposure of the message through the media with the most efficient use of money is both an art and a science.

CAMPAIGN SETTING

It is necessary to approach campaign-setting research from a variety of angles, because different campaign settings necessitate different campaign strategies. Campaign settings are a complex, interrelated series of relationships that are often very difficult to define. Agranoff (1976, p. 160) suggests that such variables as the following be considered: the political mood or climate (national, state, local) at the time of the election, other political or economic situations that may have a bearing on the election (for example, war, high unemployment, an economic depression, ethical scandals), the election level of the particular contest (federal, state, local), the electoral system of the particular contest (partisan, nonpartisan), and the type of election (primary, runoff, general election). Analysis of such wide-ranging factors often involves informal research methods rather than the more rigorous methods of social science.

In short, in order to mount an effective campaign the strategist must be aware of at least five elements of the campaign setting. Voter research, candidate research, message research, channel research, and campaign setting must be taken into account when developing a consistent communication strategy that involves an appropriate positioning of a candidate in relationship to other electoral actors and when creating political advertising.

INFORMAL RESEARCH METHODS

We make a distinction between informal and formal research methods. Informal methods do not involve the rigorous application of scientific standards associated with modern social science research methods. Informal methods do not begin to explain or predict people's political behavior with any type of scientific validity or reliability. Rather, these methods are simply exploratory in nature. They serve as guideposts for directing the more formal and rigorous scientific procedures. Informal research methods provide subjective information. It is from this subjective information that a campaign consultant, manager, or advertising strategist begins to develop a "feel" for the important actors, organizations, issues, political factions, and so on that are likely to impact on an election. Four of these informal research procedures will be considered. We view informal research methods as a starting point for the campaign. While there are plenty of old-timers who are happy to talk about the victorious seat-of-the-pants campaigns of which they have been a part, informal research methods prove insufficient for candidates seeking the more prestigious offices.

Talking with Voters

One of the most time-honored procedures in planning or running a political campaign is the candidate's deliberate interaction with a wide variety of potential constituents. Candidates frequently appear at malls, main streets, churches, plant gates, and civic festivities in order to meet as many voters as possible. From this experience, candidates get to hear what is on the voters' minds. And while this is only impressionistic, it helps the candidate and the campaign in preparing for speeches and in designing campaign strategies. In short, when candidates talk with voters, the candidate is creating a series of shared experiences that both the candidate and the voter may call upon in order to make decisions within the context of the electoral campaign.

Obviously, voter contact is not only an important informal research method but it is also an important persuasive device (see Agranoff, 1976; Berrigan, 1982; Blydenburgh, 1971; Eldersveld, 1956). Voters who have personally spoken with a candidate come to feel that they in fact have a type of personal relationship with the candidate and therefore have a personal stake in the candidate's political future. Candidates often attend public meetings or community forums in order to express their views on issues, make contact with the politically active, and attract media coverage of their candidacy.

Key Informants

Candidates spend a great deal of time soliciting political advice from people who have traditionally been identified by such terms as key informants, opinion leaders, significant informants, influentials, political insiders, experts, or even power brokers. These individuals have one thing in common: experience and expertise in a given area that the candidate desires to use.

Candidates will talk with a wide variety of individuals, from the head of a local union to a former governor of the state. Party leaders will be invited to give their opinions. Political journalists and other prominent news figures will be asked to discuss the upcoming race with the candidate. University professors who are experts in foreign policy, economics, political science, health care, and other social issues may be called upon for advice. Prominent business, civic, and cultural leaders should be contacted. This process has a twofold purpose: to identify current and emerging trends that key informants believe to be significant, and to show the appropriate respect to the movers and shakers in society. By seeking the advice and support of these key informants, the candidate flatters these people as to their own importance, not only within the candidate's campaign but also within the political setting. It is a form of political stroking.

In some situations, candidates actually create advisory boards that frequently meet with the candidate to share ideas and to explore changes in the political currents of the campaign. Appointments to these boards is considered to be prestigious. Such appointments both improve a candidate's information base and flatter the political notables in a given race.

In addition, candidates and their campaign managers frequently participate in candidate clinics sponsored by their political party or by private organizations wishing to see candidates aligned with their political interests. These clinics are at the state and federal level. Often political action committees provide free campaign know-how to candidates whom they support. During these clinics, key informants present the latest in campaign and fund-raising techniques and advice. These clinics account for some of the increased sophistication among American political campaigns, and they also help account for some of the striking similarities between the campaigns of candidates from widely different geographical areas.

Field Reports

Campaign organizations may still be characterized as military organizations in terms of grassroots support staff or volunteers. Field officers represent the campaign organization, either as volunteers or paid partisans who serve within each designated geographical unit. These field officers report either to a geographic unit manager, the campaign manager, or the candidate. Field officers usually report to the campaign at least once a week, with increasing frequency as election day draws near, until the officer is reporting at least once a day. Field officers have a variety of duties. They are responsible for maintaining contact with key opinion leaders, scheduling candidate appearances, participating in campaign fund-raising, recruiting volunteers, and monitoring currents of opinion in the local citizenry.

Field reports offer the candidate the opportunity to receive impressionistic but potentially important political information and advice from informed supporters. Through these field reports, the candidate may be alerted to significant changes among the constituency which he or she might otherwise miss. The reporting process also gives the field officers an opportunity to communicate with the candidate, which usually improves their morale and increases their enthusiasm.

Campaign Organizational Research Techniques

As anyone who has been involved in a political campaign knows, campaign committee meetings frequently have little or no direction and can be wasteful in terms of time, money, and effort.   Recently researchers have developed several procedures to help the candidate or campaign manager structure meetings with campaign officers so that goals for the meeting are achieved. Fishel (1985a, 1985b) identified three possible small-group techniques that may be used to improve the quality of the decision making necessary in all political campaign organizations: the Nominal Group Technique, Idea Writing, and Structured Brainstorming. All three techniques have their origins in organizational communication research (Fishel, 1985a).

Nominal Group Technique (NGT) is beneficial at the very beginning of the campaign. First developed by Delbecq, Van de Van, and Gustafson (1975), the nominal group technique places 6 to 12 key campaign officers together in order to generate lists that can later be used to develop political communication strategies. According to Fishel (1985a),

The NGT is most helpful in producing information on the following topics: candidate strengths and weaknesses; opponent strengths and weaknesses; issues; messages; appropriate environments for TV commercials; fundraising events; media events; polling questions; potential volunteer leaders; finance committee members, and the like. (p. 18)

Group participants individually develop lists, share them, discuss them, and reach a consensus as to what should be contained on the final versions of these lists.   This process increases campaign solidarity by creating a desirable feeling of group ownership of the campaign (see Fishel, 1985a).

Idea Writing is frequently used among the campaign's creative people—specifically, the public relations and advertising specialists. Participants are given a stimulus to which they individually react, such as a photograph or phrase. Ideas are shared, critiqued, and reworked. These ideas are then converted into external campaign messages. This process is beneficial in all phases of the campaign's creative strategy: ad content, ad layout, media events, press releases, synchronization techniques, and so on (see Fishel, 1985a).

Structured Brainstorming uses participants who are key members of the campaign. These campaign members are asked to give detailed information concerning the topics, ideas, opportunities, weaknesses, and so on already identified by the Nominal Group Technique and the Idea Writing technique. In other words, structured brainstorming fleshes out previously generated ideas by adding views from a larger number of campaign workers (see Fishel, 1985a). It also helps build morale by including workers in decision-making situations.

FORMAL RESEARCH METHODS

Formal research methods are "designed to provide more objective and systematic data" (Cutlip, Center, & Broom, 1985, p. 216). Remember, formal research methods answer questions about situations that simply cannot be answered objectively using informal approaches. Formal research methods can be separated into those methods that provide information about what was and is and those that predict what may be in the future.

Quantitative and Qualitative Research Approaches

Formal research methods may use approaches that are quantitative, qualitative or the two combined. Quantitative research methods involve the assignment of numerical values to identifiable political variables using the laws of probability and the procedures of scientific observation. Quantitative analysis is considered to be more objective than qualitative research and therefore more generalizable. Quantitative research is used for description, exploration, and prediction. Questions whose answers require information about how people in the aggregate react are generally the province of quantitative methods.

Qualitative research, on the other hand, emphasizes the richness of data that may be lost with a reduction of experience to easily managed arithmetic. Qualitative research methods serve to maintain the uniqueness of the individual experience by not attempting to compress it into a numeric value. Qualitative research is primarily used for descriptive or critical purposes. Qualitative results are not meant to generalize to the public at large.

By associating significance of observation with only numerical frequency, the quantitative researcher may be losing equally important political information (see Johnson, 1985). For example, a quantitative researcher in the year 2000 may look back on the events of our times—the economic, cultural, and political events that shaped American politics in the twentieth century—and never corsider seriously the impact of political assassinations in creating our world. On the other hand, a qualitative researcher might suggest that the assassinations of such political leaders as John F. Kennedy, Martin Luther King, Jr., and Robert Kennedy were very significant factors in shaping American politics for years to come (for a discussion of qualitative methods, see Marshall & Rossman, 1989; for a discussion of quantitative methods, see Babbie, 1986).

Of course, rigorous scientific procedures and informed evaluation of the data are necessary for proper utilization of both of these techniques. The task of interpretation usually falls to the political consultants and other appropriate specialists who may be brought in to assist with the campaign. Political consultants serve as "interpreters of data, they become strategists and tacticians" (Berkman & Kitch, 1986, p. 150).

Formal research methods may use data that are collected specifically for the campaign, in primary analysis, or data that have been collected for some other reason but can still be used by the campaign, in secondary analysis.

Primary analysis uses data specifically collected for the campaign. The data collected are designed to answer specific questions that are important to campaign strategists. Primary data analysis is superior to secondary data analysis because the information collected is specifically tailored to campaign needs. Since primary analysis requires the campaign to collect and analyze the data, it is more expensive than secondary analysis.

Secondary analysis does not require the collection of new data; rather, it is an analysis of previously collected data. Before we examine primary means of data collection, we will first turn to secondary analysis.

SECONDARY ANALYSIS: OPPONENT AND CANDIDATE ANALYSIS

As the name suggests, secondary analysis utilizes information collected by others for some other, often unrelated, purpose. Campaign researchers often seek political data for secondary analysis from such sources as federal, state, and local governments, regional and nationally published polling material, party-produced materials, and library and information services. As noted above, secondary analysis is cheaper than primary analysis because the original data don't have to be generated. However, because the data were collected for other purposes, the questions asked of it are limited by what information is available to the researchers. Two primary uses of secondary analysis will be considered: opponent and candidate analysis and voting behavior analysis.

Library Research and the Creation of Databases

Reagan speech writer Ken Khachigian has said that political campaigns are won and lost on the bookshelves of American libraries (discussed in Bayer & Rodota, 1985). In 1984, the Republican National Committee formed the Opposition Research Group with an initial budget of $1.1 million. The task of the Opposition Research Group was to amass every "possible piece of information on all eight Democratic candidates then running for president" (Bayer & Rodota, 1985, p. 26). Staff members content analyzed such items as: *Congressional Record* speeches, newspaper and magazine clippings, broadcast news transcripts, campaign literature, previous campaign advertising, and so on. "In order of priority, readers/coders looked for (1) direct quotes by the candidates; (2) quotes attributed to the candidates; and (3) quotes about the candidates by other individuals. (Bayer & Rodota, 1985, p. 26). All material was stored in a computer for easy access. Each day, material was coded and stored in order to keep an up-to-date record.

In this way, the Republican incumbent, Ronald Reagan, was able to know if the Democratic candidates were inconsistent in their public statements. Such inconsistencies made for important negative attacks in political speeches and advertising messages. The key to a successful opposition resource base is access. The Republican National Committee provided yet another innovation.

An electronic communications system was developed to link 50 state party headquarters, 50 state campaign headquarters and spokesmen in all 208 ADIs (Areas of Dominant Influence—broadcast rating markets) with Opposition Research, the Republican National Committee and Reagan-Bush '84 headquarters. Party and campaign spokesmen had instant access to up-to-the-minute talking points, issue papers and draft speeches for use in discussions with local media. The database itself was accessible to key campaign and party officials—even on board Air Force One and Air Force Two. (Bayer & Rodota, 1985, p. 27)

The Opposition Research Group was able to provide a detailed analysis of the Mondale-Ferraro platform, policy positions, speeches, and so on. The group was invaluable in preparing Reagan and Bush for the debates. The Opposition Research Group in the 1992 election became much better known when candidate Ross Perot accused it of creating lies about his background. Opponent research is not unique to the Republican party as the Democrats now create their own similar research group.

Producing the research or ideas necessary for ads directed at the opposition can be done well in advance of the actual election. For example, *U.S. News and World Report* ("Nasty Ads," 1991) created three potential negative ads that could be used against candidates the magazine considered the front-runners in January of 1991: George Bush for the Republicans and Governor Mario Cuomo and Senator Sam Nunn for the Democrats. While the magazine's ability to pick Democratic presidential candidates may not be too good, the article does illustrate the ease with which one can organize a campaign strategy from an analysis of a candidate's record well in advance of an actual campaign.

On-line Databases

Congressional strategists no longer have to gather their own material for candidate and opponent analysis. On-line computer databases such as the *Washington Post*'s Legi-Slate, *Congressional Quarterly*'s Washington Alert Service, and the McClatchey newspaper chain's Washington On-Line provide comprehensive "information on votes, bills introduced [U. S. House of Representatives and the U.S. Senate], and attendance records" (Anders & Marlowe, 1987, p. 61). In addition, "all three systems have analytical capabilities that allow you to perform sophisticated research" (Anders & Marlowe, 1987, p. 64). According to Anders and Marlowe (1987), these databases provide an invaluable resource: "Opposition-research techniques that can help launch an attack on an incumbent also can help protect an incumbent from attack. Legislative research can find an incumbent's weak spot and help find ways to shield it—or turn it into a strength" (p. 61).

Mead Data's Nexis information retrieval system provides computer access to large daily American newspapers, National Public Radio, Cable News Network, and other media outlets. Business and governmental sources are also available on this continually expanding data base. The Nexis search program allows the user to do an in-text word search through millions of articles and documents. Nexis can be very useful in learning about individuals, groups, or specific issues. The Nexis system is frequently used by media outlets for their own research. Some larger community, college, and university libraries offer free or low cost Nexis access.

Campaigns that find Nexis unavailable or too expensive may be able to find additional information through resources available as part of the World Wide Web on the internet. Access to the internet is becoming easier to find and cheaper everyday. Many community libraries are now offering patrons free access to the services available on the web. While the information is not as easily searched as with Nexis and other commercial information services, much information is available. Those wishing to use the web should begin by using one of the search engines such as Infoseek, Alta Vista, or Yahoo for starting points.

Self-Directed Roll-Call Analysis

Great care should be given to voting analysis, both for the candidate and the opponents. Voting analysis is a highly complicated procedure. Anderson, Watts, and Wilcox (1966) have produced a *Legislative Roll-Call Analysis* that guides the researcher through a maze of indices and scales. At all costs, a political candidate must avoid the appearance of using falsehoods or making unfair charges against his or her opponent (see Agranoff, 1976; Johnson-Cartee & Copeland, 1991a; 1997).

SECONDARY ANALYSIS: VOTING BEHAVIOR ANALYSIS

Robbin (1980) suggests that the "efficiency of a campaign depends on *accurate* delivery of *effective* [emphasis in the original] communications" (p. 25). Researchers attempt to ensure that specifically created political communication messages reach specifically targeted individuals for specifically defined results through an analysis of voting behavior. This ability is made possible from an understanding of the characteristics of potential message receivers

According to Hughes (1984) there are three main types of secondary data relevant to voting behavior analysis: political or partisan data, voter-specific demographics, and geodemographic data. Partisan data indicates the party affiliation of voters. This party affiliation has been recognized as being very important to some voters in making their voting decisions. Partisan data may be obtained either from government office records detailing precincts' voting patterns for particular races over time or from voter registration information, such as party affiliation or participation record. Voter-specific demographics are the personal demographics located on the voter registration cards at registration headquarters (for example, race, occupation, address). The third type of data is geodemographic and is obtained through census records. As the name implies, these data are concerned with the voter makeup of specific locations. Government census records, available in almost every county library, provide a wealth of information. Census reports present summarized data by residential block, block groups, zip codes, town, county, state, and so forth. (see Hughes, 1984). "Key census variables usually include race and ethnicity, age, income, renter- vs. owner-occupied, level of education, family size, total voter age population, government employees, median value of housing, median rent, and median income" (Hughes, 1984, p. 28). Geodemographic data are very useful in targeting messages to specific groups.

Demographic Targeting

"Demographic targeting generates population characteristics within election districts and is particularly helpful in determining which areas in the district may be receptive to specific campaign messages" (Fishel, 1983, p. 11). Demographic targeting primarily utilizes the voter-specific demographics for analysis. From this analysis, campaigns develop highly specific database techniques (see Getter & Titus, 1984; Tobe, 1984). Computers can sort through data bases which may contain thousands of constituent files by various demographic characteristics such as occupation, income, and race, which allows campaigns to target and contact voters that they identify as likely contributors or supporters. Demographic targeting "attacks the problem of effectively allocating communication resources through aggregation and inference" (Robbin, 1980, p. 27).

Geodemographic Targeting

Candidates gain access to census data either by purchasing data directly from the Census Bureau, hiring private data companies to provide the appropriate information (see discussion in Magill, 1982), or sending volunteers to government publication depositories to search for the needed information. One such private data company is the Claritas Corporation formed in 1971 (Magill, 1982).

Jonathan Robbin created the Claritas Cluster system for the Claritas Corporation. The system is a voter-targeting methodology based on geodemographics. According to geodemographic theory, like people live together in small communities. By the word "like," we mean similar in demographic characteristics. A "cluster represents a number of small geographic areas containing populations which are homogeneous along a very substantial series of socioeconomic and demographic indicators" (Robbin, 1980, pp. 28-29). The Claritas Cluster system assumes that

the determinants and consequences of human grouping can be used to explain and predict individual behavior as it varies over different types of neighborhoods. The Claritas Cluster system uses this principle for creating estimates of neighborhood characteristics not measured by, but related to, the underlying Census data. Included among these characteristics are political variables key to winning elections. (Robbin, 1980, p. 29)

According to Robbin (1980), decisions based on Claritas Cluster Analysis are "better informed than traditionally targeted efforts, and correlate better not only with observed poll findings but also with election results" (p. 34). In the 1982 elections, geodemographics became the rage. Not only Claritas, but two other similar systems, PRIZM and ACORN, were used during the campaign (Schneider, 1983). Schneider (1983) suggests that geopolitical data should be combined with census data for more valuable cluster analysis. Such items as neighborhood partisanship or religious affiliation would strengthen the explanatory powers of cluster analysis.

Brace and Jaede (1984) have demonstrated the usefulness of computerized graphics and mappings in presenting geodemographic and geopolitical data for the purpose of campaign strategy development. The use of graphics and maps provide a visual presentation easier for the nonexpert to use. Information to be useful must be usable.

Electoral Targeting

Electoral targeting is an examination of the "historical voting patterns within an election district" (Fishel, 1983, p. 11). By using electoral targeting before the campaign actually begins, campaign researchers are able to identify key geographical areas on which to concentrate their time and resources. "It can aid us to schedule candidate and volunteer time wisely; similarly, it can help determine areas for literature distribution, direct mail, telephoning, yard sign placement, voter registration, and get-out-the vote activities" (Fishel, 1983, p. 12). In effect, researchers are able to prioritize precincts according to each precinct's voting histories through the creation of a composite index. This allows for more efficient use of campaign resources.

The electoral targeting approach utilizes partisan data that can be obtained from the county board of elections (or similar body). Electoral targeting is time-consuming but very inexpensive. It takes no more than several volunteers, several pocket calculators, and some notepads. It is possible for a single person to perform the electoral targeting if the election area isn't too large. Volunteers or campaign staff workers collect and analyze information for high-visibility, low-visibility, and representative races. A high-visibility election is associated with high voter turnout and is usually an executive race such as one for president, governor, or mayor. A low-visibility race is the election contest that can be identified as receiving the lowest percentage of partisan voting in electoral contests. Normally these are for positions such as tax collector or county clerk. A representative race is a past electoral contest for the same position as the current candidate. The race should have been conducted under similar electoral circumstances, which usually translates into the race having occurred in recent voting history (see Fishel, 1983). Simple calculations involving frequencies, rankings, and percentages are used to determine the average party turnout (average number of people likely to vote in a given precinct), average party vote (average partisan vote in a given precinct), average party falloff (difference between the partisan vote in a high- and low-visibility elections). Only competitive elections are considered. Electoral targeting yields a great deal of important information for relatively little cost (for an excellent step-by-step guide, see Fishel, 1983).

PRIMARY ANALYSIS

When information cannot be located from another source, then the campaign must generate its own needed data through original research. Primary analysis is both time-consuming and costly, but it may produce rich rewards. Primary analysis uses a variety of techniques to fulfill the specific information needs of the campaign.

Survey Research

Survey research is the solicitation of voters' self-reported opinions through mail, telephone, or personal interviews. In the context of a campaign, survey research is more commonly known as polling, and has become a standard of most federal and statewide campaigns.

Weaver-Lariscy, Tinkham, and Nordstrom (1988) analyzed the use of political polling during congressional elections. The research team surveyed immediately after the 1982 congressional elections and discovered that 67 percent of respondents used polls and 33 percent did not. The average number of polls conducted per campaign was 2.5. Seventy-two percent of incumbents considered polling to be a major campaign research tool, while only 48 percent of nonincumbents considered it to be so. While incumbents and nonincumbents used political polling differently, the researchers concluded that "polls tend to be used, by the incumbent and winning campaigns, for fairly sophisticated determinations of 'elements of your image to stress,' 'attitudes of various groups,' and 'overall strategy'" (Weaver-Lariscy, Tinkham, & Nordstrom, 1988, p. 19). Nonincumbents who lose are more likely to use polls as a means of "surveillance, or monitoring 'who's ahead'" (Weaver-Lariscy et al., 1988, p. 22).

To reinforce the Weaver-Lariscy et al. findings, successful campaigns usually look to their polling to tell the campaign more than simply who seems to be ahead. Successful candidates use survey research to inform the campaign about matters of style and substance. The construction of polls that can validly elicit such information from the populace is much more difficult and requires more polling savvy than simply asking for whom the person on the other end of the telephone may vote, but the results are usually part of the tide that sweeps a candidate to victory.

Survey research may use either nonprobability samples or probability samples. A nonprobability sample, often called a convenience sample, is one in which the members of the parent population or universe, for example, all eligible voters in a city council election, did not have an equal chance of being selected. Examples of nonprobability polls would be the familiar television viewer call-in poll or the man-in-the street poll. The results of such polls have extremely limited use, because the manner in which the sample was selected prohibits using the laws of probability to analyze the data generated. Additionally, nonprobability samples can be very misleading about public opinion because there is no way to know whether the sample of people represents the population. Therefore, the gathered data do not lend themselves to scientific analysis; such polls do not aid in the scientific development of advertising strategies, and may mislead a campaign.

These types of samples remain popular because of convenience and economy despite their severe limitations. Some underfinanced candidates may indulge in nonprobability sampling as a means of cutting costs, but in this case, as with so many other things in life, one gets what one pays for. Because of the restricted utility of nonprobability samples, we don't recommend their use except in unusual cases.

On the other hand, probability samples do lend themselves to scientific analysis and are used to make informed judgments concerning advertising strategies and tactics. Probability samples are samples in which each member of the sample had an equal chance of being selected from the parent population. For this reason, the laws of probability can be applied, and meaningful analysis of the data can be conducted, within certain statistical constraints. Methods are available to generate various probability samples such as the random sample, stratified sample, cluster sample, or the multistage sample. For a review of these probability samples, see Babbie (1973), Sonquist and Dunkelberg (1977), or Weisberg and Bowen (1977).

There are two primary types of surveys: cross-sectional surveys, otherwise known as one-shot studies, and longitudinal surveys, which include trend, cohort, and panel studies (see Babbie, 1973). In the cross-sectional survey, "data are collected at one point in time from a sample selected to describe some larger population *at that time* [emphasis in the original]. Such a survey can be used not only for purposes of description but also for the determination of relationships between variables at the time of study" (Babbie, 1973, p. 62). Cross-sectional surveys are those studies with which the reader is most familiar. Many news organizations sponsor these types of polls in order to report what the citizenry is thinking at a particular period of time.

The critical element of a cross-sectional survey is that it tells only about what the people in the sample thought at the time the survey was taken. It is a snapshot of public opinion at that moment. A cross-sectional survey by itself can not tell how opinions may be changing.

It is possible to examine multiple cross-sectional surveys in an attempt to develop some understanding for how opinion may be moving. Attempts to understand opinion over a period of time by sampling at more than a single point in time constitutes longitudinal studies. Longitudinal studies "permit the analysis of data over time: either descriptive or explanatory. Data are collected at *different* [emphasis in the original] points in time, and the researcher is able to report changes in descriptions and explanations" (emphasis in the original, Babbie, 1973, p. 63). The longitudinal approach allows for the measurement of the change or stability of opinion on specified issues. By collecting information at more than one time in some type of controlled fashion, this approach provides a better understanding of what is happening in an electorate than the cross-sectional survey.

There are different types of longitudinal surveys. In a political trend study, the voting population is sampled and surveyed several times. The same set of questions is asked at different temporal points. However, different people participate in each survey; each sample is selected so as to represent the voting population. It is assumed that one random sample from a given population will respond in the same fashion as another random sample from the same population within known margins of error. Thus, asking the same set of questions to different random samples from the same population yields results similar to asking the same group of people the same set of questions at different points in time. One advantage of asking a different sample from the same population is the ease of collecting subsequent data; one need not track down the same individuals used in the last survey in order to complete the current round of questions. Another advantage is that the sample of respondents doesn't become sensitized to the questions being asked and begin to change their behaviors or responses.

In cohort analysis, a cohort "is any group of individuals who are linked in some way or who have experienced the same significant life event within a given period of time" (Wimmer & Dominick, 1991, p. 183). These significant events may be birth, matriculation, marriage, and so on during some specified period of time. Cohort analysis consists of sampling a cohort group at more than one point in time. As in trend studies, it is not necessary to interview the same people;

rather, the sample consists of members from the same cohort group at different times.

Normally cohort analysis compares results from more than one cohort against the response of another cohort group. By comparing cohort groups across time one can determine if differences are caused by being a member of a cohort or by changes that take place over time. For example, one cohort group might be people who served in World War II; a second cohort might be people who served during the Korean War. Samples from these cohort groups would be taken at different times and the results compared both within the cohort group and between the cohort groups.

Panel studies "involve the collection of data over time from the same sample of respondents. The sample for such a study is called the *panel*" (emphasis in the original, Babbie, 1973, p. 64). Unlike the previous two types of longitudinal approaches, the panel study does use the same group of people at multiple points in time. Trend and cohort studies allow the researcher to examine change over time; however, panel studies allow the researcher to tell exactly which people are changing their views. Political campaigns that employ panel designs usually use a continuous panel; that is, members of the panels are surveyed for their opinion at regular, set intervals. A second type of panel study is the interval panel, which differs from the continuous panel in that panel members are queried only when the researchers believe information is necessary.

Campaigns, whether using cross-sectional or longitudinal polling methods, should poll at specific points in the campaign. Three temporal stages of political polling we identified are: benchmark, intermediate, and summative. A benchmark poll is a precampaign poll that attempts to determine the base or benchmark attitudes of voters concerning various political issues, actors, and so forth (see Berkman & Kitch, 1986). Information from this poll will serve as the basis for the beginning campaign and will be used to compare the results with subsequent polls to see how the campaign is faring.

The intermediate poll is a follow-up poll that is used to investigate further the various findings of the original benchmark poll during a campaign. Such an analysis provides needed feedback as to how the political campaign is being received by the various target publics. Political strategies can be reevaluated and tactics reconsidered in light of the survey results. In well-financed campaigns, more than one intermediate poll is conducted.

Summative polls are polls that are used at the end of a political campaign. Most candidates regard summative polls as unnecessary luxuries. However, summative polls do provide important information. Political researchers are able to use statistical methods to analyze the results from all three polling periods. From this analysis, the researcher is able to judge what worked and didn't work with specific groups and convey this to the candidate.

The summative poll is particularly critical for incumbents in the U.S. House of Representatives, who are in effect continuously campaigning. Thus a victorious incumbent is able to identify those groups and organizations in his or her constituency that need extra attention during the next two years. Such polls may give early warning signals that may spell trouble in the next election. The national political party committees and the national news media are utilizing summative polls more and more in their analysis of political trends in America. Exit polling, which is frequently used by media organizations, is an example of summative polling.

One of the most important campaign research advances in recent years has been the tracking poll. The advent of the short-term tracking poll has revolutionized modern election campaigns, and in particular, political advertising tactics. The tracking poll is

a device that enables consultants to measure and describe the changes in voter sentiment about a campaign as often as every few hours. The quick response is possible because of the speed with which computers generate lists of randomly selected telephone numbers and process the data gleaned from phone polls. ("New Campaign Techniques," 1986, p. 30)

According to Congressional Quarterly's *Elections '86,* tracking polls have been utilized in presidential politics since the mid-1970s, but it was not until 1980 that the Republicans utilized the technique to identify vulnerable Republican senators who needed last-minute infusions of money to put them over the edge. By 1984, tracking polls were used in virtually all competitive senate elections (see "New Campaign Techniques," 1986).

Through the use of tracking polls, consultants and candidates are able to evaluate how various political advertising messages, both from their campaign and from their opponents, are being received. Because of the expense, tracking polls are primarily used in presidential, senatorial, and gubernatorial campaigns. Each night between 50 and 100 voters are contacted during the course of the campaign to detect early shifts in opinions. Questions concerning candidate evaluations, issues, and political advertising are administered. According to Berkman & Kitch (1986),

A system of "moving averages" is used. Five nights of consecutive interviews are considered to be the total sample. For example, five nights of 100 interviews means a sample of 500. The average shifts as the sixth night's results are added and the first night is dropped, and so on. (p. 150)

By having access to information that shows overnight changes in political opinions concerning candidates, advertising, and issues, the consultants can then create overnight changes in their political advertising tactics. Negative advertising can be pulled when it is wearing thin with the voters. And when opposition negative advertising is found to be damaging, a responsive ad can be created and disseminated within 24 hours (Squier, 1987). The key is to be adaptable to the changing opinions of the public.

This has created an instant-response capability that has been practically translated into instant response ads. Instant-response politics has brought great changes to the world of political advertising, and perhaps is one reason that negative political advertising, as we earlier noted, has come of age. Kern (1989) calls these instant response ads "poll-driven ads" (p. 28). One Democratic consultant, Gary Nordlinger, reminded his audience, "You have to remember that this was our response to his response to our response to his response to our original ad" ("New Campaign Techniques," 1986, p. 30). In effect, tracking polls and instant-response ads have created a situation where campaigns take on the "character of an electronic debate" ("Technology, Strategy," 1985, p. 2559).

Impact polling is not a distinct type of polling; rather, it is an approach to political polling that is particularly useful to the political advertising consultant. Harrison (1980) coined the term "impact polling" to refer to a polling approach that seeks to evaluate turnout of electorate, impact of issues, and degree of commitment to a candidate or cause (p. 9). Basically, impact polling attempts to evaluate the voters' knowledge base concerning political issues, candidates, and political parties. Voters are asked to identify major candidates, campaign themes, date of the election, their polling place, and other items. In addition, the survey instrument attempts to measure the intensity of feeling that voters hold toward specific political objects, such as how committed the voter is to Candidate X. In this way, the researcher is able to sort the attentive voter who has an informed opinion and who cares strongly about given issues from those who do not. By identifying those members of the attentive public who are most likely to make their beliefs known in society, researchers are able to advise candidates on highly sophisticated direct mail strategies that are likely to have a ripple effect through the community. Impact polling provides rich data for the political advertising strategist.

Impact polling by attempting to collect information that goes deeper than surface opinion attempts to approximate the "campaign like context" (Harrison, 1980, p. 11). In other words, impact polling gets beyond superficial responses to a closer look at the way people actually view political issues, candidates, and parties.   Impact polling could be accomplished through a variety of techniques: open-ended questions, probes, intensity scales, and various multiple indicator indices.

Laboratory Experiments

Survey research is primarily interested in describing what exists and inferentially how opinions may have been formed or influenced. Laboratory research is concerned with cause and effect.   In order to make statements about causality one must be able to demonstrate both the necessity and the sufficiency of a particular cause to create a specific effect. Only experimental designs are capable of exploring these cause-effect relationships by attempting to eliminate all other possible causes for any observed change. What makes statements about causality possible using experimental methods is that experiments almost always take place outside of the normal environment. Experiments are usually conducted in a place where the environment and other elements that might affect the experiment, that is, the observation of the cause-effect relationship, may be controlled.

A laboratory experiment utilizes "an experimental design executed in a non-naturalistic environment" where the participants are in effect members of a captive audience who are aware of the experimentation process (Haskins, 1968, pp. 4-5). Laboratory experiments are frequently used in advertising and marketing research and are very popular among academic investigators. "At base, experiments involve (1) taking action and (2) observing the consequences of that action" (Babbie, 1986, p. 181). Several different designs are used, each with its own costs and benefits (see Campbell & Stanley, 1963, for a thorough review). Laboratory experiments are hypothesis-driven in that they examine specific scientifically defined concepts in order to explain human behavior. Thus laboratory experiments should be thought of as offering primarily explanation, not description. The laboratory experiment usually contains both obtrusive exposure to the advertising message and obtrusive evaluative measures. In some situations, laboratory experiments may involve hidden cameras, physiological measurement devices, or masked evaluative measures, but these testing procedures are becoming less frequent, as people engaged in academic research must meet a stringent set of ethical criteria when dealing with human participants. Although an important academic research situation, the laboratory experiment is not used very often in political campaigns. However, knowledgeable consultants do pay attention and often incorporate knowledge that is derived from academic laboratory research into their repertoire of campaign techniques.

Physiological Response Measures

As mentioned above, some experimental work involves the use of physiological measures, but these measurement techniques may be applied to research beyond the experimental method. The problem with most methods for collecting data, whether the method selected is survey or experimental, is that the participant may lie or be unable to correctly express his or her response. As the name implies, physiological measures are measurements taken from the human body directly. One of the perceived advantages to physiological measures is that the researcher is not asking for any expressed response; rather, the researcher is measuring the actual physiological changes directly.

Two general areas of the nervous system, the central nervous system and the autonomic system, serve as primary areas for measurement. Fletcher (1985) describes three common physiological measures for the central nervous system: eye movement, alpha wave, and electromyogram. Eye movement studies utilize a device that continuously measures where the eye is looking. These are interpreted as indicating the area where the observer has an interest. Alpha wave studies use an electroencephalograph in order to record the alpha rhythms of the brain. Electromyography measures whether the muscles of the person tighten. Minor tightening and loosening of the muscles is usually a sign of tension or relaxation.

Fletcher (1985) details six physiological measures from the autonomic system: pupil response, heart rate, respiration, blood pressure, skin conductance, and electrical potential. All of these measures are thought to be the body's response to attention or change in emotion. When one is paying attention, for example, the pupils dilate, heart rate increases, respiration goes up, blood pressure rises, and skin resistance is lowered, while electrical potential of the skin increases.

All of these physiological measures have been used in academic research, and some have been used in advertising research. Pupil response research has been used in the evaluation of products and product advertising by manufacturers and advertisers for several years (Halpern, 1967; Krugman, 1964). Alpha brain waves measured by an electroencephalograph (EEG) have been used in advertising and media studies (Alwitt, 1985; Davidson, Schwartz, Saron, Bennet, & Goleman, 1979; Krugman, 1971). Examples of heart rate being used in communication research have been conducted by Lang (1990, 1991). But as we earlier noted, these types of measurements are not frequently used in political communication research.

Focus Groups

Focus groups are routinely used in traditional marketing and advertising product research, and they have also been found to have utility for testing various political advertising messages. The use of focus groups provides information to marketing and advertising specialists not readily accessible in survey research or experimental laboratory research methods. Krueger (1988) has defined a focus group as "a carefully planned discussion designed to obtain perceptions on a defined area of interest in a permissive, nonthreatening environment" (p. 18).

To achieve this carefully planned discussion requires the consultant or researcher to assemble between 7 and 12 people, with 8 to 10 the most popular number. These people are usually selected because they have some characteristic in common; for instance, all group members might be registered voters, or Democrats who voted for Ronald Reagan. Selecting participants for a common characteristic creates a homogeneous group, which fosters the "permissive, nonthreatening environment" needed for a focus group (Kern & Just, 1992). If the purpose of the focus group is to evaluate the possible effects or meanings of political media, the group members will be shown the specific artifact that is the focus of the discussion.

Following the exposure, group members are seated about a table where the discussion moderator—a consultant or member of the research firm who is organizing the focus group—will lead the group members through a set of questions that are organized into a script. These questions normally are developed by the consultant/researcher in consultation with the campaign. During the discussion, the moderator takes care that all members of the group have a chance to reply and interact with the other participants. This discussion is recorded either on audio or video tape so that a transcript and a subsequent detailed analysis may be made of the comments from the group members. Typically, a member of the sponsoring organization will also attend the session. In the case of a political campaign, this will usually be ranking members of the campaign organization but not the candidate.

It is the transcript of the focus group that serves as the source of the actual data from a focus group. The transcript provides a sense of both rational and emotional views held by the group members. The discussion of the group, as represented by the transcript, can detail what members of the group thought about not only minor points, such as the types of clothes being worn by people appearing in the spot, but also major points, such as how the group feels about the campaign, the issues, and so forth. It is standard practice to have more than a single group meet to discuss any topic. This redundancy serves to provide a bit more representativeness to the responses and to broaden the range of response.

Despite the use of additional groups, the focus group method is a qualitative method for gathering information. There is no attempt to claim that the findings that have come from the focus group are statistically similar to the population from which the group was drawn. Despite this limitation, focus groups provide a richness of information that is usually not available through quantitative research methods. Jamieson (1992) has made extensive use of focus groups in her descriptive and historical analysis of American political advertising.

Sometimes, campaign consultants pretest their political ads by showing them to focus group members before the ads are aired; the members are then asked to discuss the ads. Focus groups may be used to test concepts even before ads are created to determine whether such ads will strike a resonant chord. From the analysis of the transcript of the session, campaign consultants determine how various political advertising messages are perceived or may potentially be perceived by various types of individuals and how this perception evolves through the natural process of social interaction. It is important to note that to effectively evaluate possible political advertising within a campaign context, participants must be chosen from the actual electorate. For example, we know of campaign horror stories where national consultants used focus group participants from Washington, D.C., to approximate the voters of the deep South. And that "approximation" resulted in turning a lead into a loss.

The Bush campaign used focus groups in order to isolate effective campaign issues for its race against Dukakis. *Time* magazine reports,

The moderator began asking rhetorical questions. "What if I told you that Dukakis vetoed a bill requiring schoolchildren to say the Pledge of Allegiance? Or that he was against the death penalty? Or that he gave weekend furloughs to first-degree murderers?" "He's a liberal!" exclaimed one man at the table. "If those are really his positions," a woman added, "I'd have a hard time supporting him." ("Nine Key Moments," 1988, p. 49)

Such focus groups authenticated potent issues upon which the Bush campaign could be built.

According to Krueger (1988), focus groups allow individuals to evaluate a political advertising message "in part by interaction with other people" (p. 23). Because we know that we do not form opinions in isolation, researchers use focus groups to glimpse the complex process of social interaction that is involved in opinion formation. Newspapers have begun to look upon the focus group as another source of news about the campaign in much the same fashion as they view political polling (Traugott, 1992b).

However, focus groups are not a magical research method; the method has problems associated with it as well. Interpretation of self-reports remains a problem. For example, as one Republican consultant has stated: "Voters will tell you in focus groups that they don't like negative ads, but they retain the information so much better than the positive ones" (Roger Stone, quoted in "Negative Advertising," 1986, p. 104).

Q-Methodology

Q-methodology was first suggested by Stephenson (1953) and further developed for political applications by Brown (1980). Wattier (1982, 1986) has recommended the use of Q-sorts for both the development of campaign themes and the development of a voter targeting plan. Q-methodology is particularly attractive to low-financed campaigns, because it is relatively inexpensive compared to the more traditional survey research methods (Wattier, 1982, 1986). The technique requires the services of a Q-method consultant and a few representative but willing participants.

Q-methodology is an intensive method that creates conditions under which a few individuals are introduced to decisional situations approximating the individuals' internal dialog.   This method produces rich campaign information (Brown, 1980; Wattier, 1982). "The focus in Q is on what kinds or types of images people have, while in a poll, the focus is on who has which image and how many people have which image" (Wattier, 1982, p. 31).

The typical technique used in Q-methodology is to supply a small, selected group of people with a set of cards The cards constitute the Q sample. Typically about 100 cards compose the Q sample. Each card has a statement printed on it. A set of cards are supposed to represent the universe of ideas or concepts to be tested. People (called the P set) are then asked to sort the Q sample by placing the cards into piles. These piles are to represent cards that contained statements that the person feels are similar or related. The sorted cards are then statistically analyzed using a procedure called factor analysis (Brown, 1980). The resultant numbers allow the researcher to discover which ideas are perceived as being closely related and also the strength of the importance of those concepts.

Wattier (1986) writes of Q-method and politics, "In short, by asking a relatively small sample of persons, selected theoretically, relatively many questions—defined subjectively, inductively, and operantly—the strategist lets his subjects determine which messages to emphasize" (Wattier, 1986, p. 20).

Field Experiments

According to Haskins (1968), the field experiment "combines the advantages of field surveys and laboratory experiments and minimizes most of their disadvantages" (p. 39). The field experiment is used to expose subjects to various political advertising messages under naturalistic conditions. Optimally, participants should not feel as if they are part of a research study. Exposure to the messages and to the measurement should be as unobtrusive as possible within the confines of appropriate ethical use of human participants.

Field experiments are frequently an unrealistic alternative to lab experiments because of the often prohibitively high costs of conducting field research. For a discussion concerning both the advantages and the problems associated with field experiments in testing political advertising, see Tarrance (1982). However, modern electronic media technology may make the field experiment an attractive alternative in coming years.

Content Analysis

Content analysis is an important technique for analyzing messages. It is a technique that is equally appropriate as a tool of the campaign and for academic study. While the procedures by which the two groups may conduct content analysis may vary, the primary goal of systematically understanding content of messages is the same.

Content analysis is used in a variety of ways by today's sophisticated political campaigns. All news copy, whether broadcast or print, is carefully analyzed for material pertaining to the campaign, important events, and other occurrences that might affect the community.

Content analysis is also an important form of opponent analysis. An opponent's speeches, press releases, news interviews, position papers, and advertising messages should be carefully analyzed for important political themes. Frequently, valuable insights into the opponent's strategy will be gleaned from this approach. Keep in mind that these forms have the opponent on the record; and they may well make important contributions to the candidate's advertising themes. Content analysis can frequently bring a politician's own words back to haunt him or her.

In addition, campaign workers should content analyze the mail that the campaign receives much as they would the letters to the editor in local newspapers. With campaigns that monitor a call-in telephone line, a content analysis of all phone calls is conducted. If the time and resources are not available to content analyze the entire universe of political news, advertising copy, mail, and other political communications, then appropriate probability sampling techniques should be employed (Berelson, 1971; Holsti, 1969; Janowitz, 1976). This allows for a greater confidence that the findings actually reflect the universe of material studied.

Yet another important function for trained content analysts is the careful examination of all the campaign's own political communications. Content analysts ask the following evaluative questions:

Does it follow a consistent pattern?
Does the material say what the campaign intended?
Are the proper persuasive tactics used?
Is the material correctly targeted?
Are there any potential repercussions from what was said?

All political communications are usually previewed and cleared by the consultant, the campaign manager, and the candidate before dissemination.

There are two primary forms of content analysis: the hard and soft approaches (Frank, 1973). The hard approach may be viewed as defining and counting "discrete and concrete quantifiable bits of data" (Frank, 1973, p. 23) found in political communications. The soft approach allows the researcher "to evaluate the entire Gestalt package" of the political communication message (Frank, 1973, p. 23). The hard and soft approaches have both strengths and weaknesses. The hard approach reduces possible subjective coding error created by possible biases, but it results in a loss of information. The soft form, a more holistic approach, introduces a great deal of potential subjective error; however, it is quite possible that more of the coded information will be retained in its natural context. According to Frank (1973), the optimal technique is "the construction of a research design that utilizes both the hard and soft approaches to content analysis" (p. 25).

The content analysis of political messages is frequently engaged in by academic researchers. The academic researcher's goal is different from that of the campaign researcher. The academic is attempting to understand the messages being examined in terms of patterns and trends, without regard to who may win or lose an election. The campaign researcher, on the other hand, enters into content analysis specifically to provide information that may be used by the campaign for partisan purposes.

Academic content analysis may use relatively unsophisticated measures of content, for example, number of column inches or the number of times a name appears in print. However, more sophisticated content analysis procedures have also been developed. These procedures are both hard and soft. Increasing the explanative power of hard content analysis are such techniques as content analysis of verbatim messages (CAVE), which "allows blind, reliable ratings of archival material for explanatory style" (Zullow, Oettingen, Peterson, & Seligman, 1988, p. 673) and the Categorical Data Package (CATPAC), which "identi-fies [1] tallies of frequently occurring words, [2] conceptual clusters in the raw text of all spots, and [3] measures of association based on word co-occurrence" (Payne, Marlier, & Baukus, 1989, p. 368). An example of a research design incorporating both a hard approach and a complex soft content analysis approach that provides sophisticated levels of understanding is reconstructive content analysis (Johnson, 1984).

APPLICATIONS

All political advertising research must share the same goal; that is examining the effectiveness of various political communication messages within the context of an entire campaign. A single political television spot, a single press release, or a single media event simply is insufficient to describe the dynamics of the campaign and its surround-ing communication. All campaign messages, whether or not they are seen by their creators to be interrelated, are perceived by the potential voter as part of a single campaign, and thus interrelated. The interre-lated nature of these messages is most clear when viewed within the context of the synergism that is generated by the campaign in toto. There is a synergistic effect, meaning that the totality of the political campaign is greater than the sum of its parts.

In earlier work, we discussed this as the synergism problem (Johnson-Cartee & Copeland, 1991a, 1997; see also Jamieson, 1992). We noted that this problem is particularly apparent in the study of nega-tive political advertising. Most research findings tell us that people self-report that they do not like negative ads. Yet there is evidence to indicate that negative ads are more effective in garnering votes for a particular candidate than positive ads. Because the political commu-nication messages of a given campaign are interrelated, it is difficult to isolate the effectiveness of a single communication tool, such as a political ad, particularly when that tool is in reality should be the culmination of a carefully crafted persuasive message strategy propa-gated through the media over the course of a campaign.

Gronbeck (1992) recognizes the need for analyzing presidential campaign ads not as separate advertisements but interrelated much as

thrust-perry-riposte in fencing. Gronbeck turns to narrative performance theory when he discusses the enonce and the enunciation of the
narrative structures of negative political advertisements. While the
enonce is what is said, the enunciation is the actual performance of
that text within the unfolding pageant of the election. The enunciation becomes bardic, since it proclaims either the blackguardism of the
opposition or the heroism of the sponsoring candidate. The content of
the message itself, the enonce, merely speaks about past events. The
presentation of a message speaks not only about what is in the message
but about what type of person would deliver such a message. Gronbeck
seems to be making the point that one wouldn't simply find the use of
four-letter explicatives in a Sunday school class inappropriate, but one
would, in addition, make judgments about the person who used the explicatives.

   Thus it is with campaigns. If the goal is to understand the fluid
dynamics of the campaign and the resulting electoral outcome,
examining a single message from a campaign or even the complete set
of messages is insufficient. It is necessary to understand the presenta-
tional context for those messages. One must look at actions and the inferences that people may make about those actions to understand the
synergism that occurs in the contemporary media campaign.

Chapter 7

Political Advertising

In recent years, political advertising has become almost synonymous with political campaigning, because the news media have virtually ignored grassroots volunteer political organizations and instead concentrated its focus on political ads and the consultants that made them. This chapter is a brief examination of modern political advertising. It provides a review of the research literature relevant to understanding when, how, and under what conditions political advertising is effective. And it provides a classification scheme for all political advertising with explanations as to why different types of political advertising are used, along with examples of each. For an indepth examination of contemporary political advertising research and practice, see our *Negative Political Advertising* (1991a) and *Manipulation of the American Voter* (1997) or work by Biocca (1991); Diamond & Bates (1988); Jamieson (1984, 1992); Kern (1989); or Pfau & Kenski (1990).

THE RESEARCH DEMONSTRATING POLITICAL ADVERTISING EFFECTS

In 1972, McCombs and Shaw argued that a lack of research on the impact of political advertising on cognitive and information effects hampered a true understanding of the effects of the mass media. Studies conducted since this observation have generally supported the thesis that political advertising is related to cognitive and information outcomes. Hofstetter, Zukin, and Buss (1978); Kaid (1976); and Patterson and McClure (1976b) have all found that political advertising is related to knowledge about campaigns and beliefs held about the candidates. In a 1979 Harvard University Institute of Politics Report, it was observed that

the most competitive elections where the voters have the most information about candidates, are those in which the most money is spent. Election contests in [which] spending is comparatively high are also those in [which] voter participation tends to be highest. (reported in McGuiness, 1986, p. 38)

During the past 15 years, political advertising research has been recognized as an important component of the political process, and as such, worthy of academic inquiry. Political advertising research has taken a variety of paths since that time.

Kaid (1981) has divided effects into three types: cognitive, affective and behavioral; what people know, how people feel about what they know, and how people act based on what they know and feel. One of the problems with such a distinction is that these divisions are hard to maintain except as a heuristic device. For example, affective evaluations of a candidate are a cognitive function but are only definable through observation of some type of behavior. However, this tripartite division does reflect the perspective generally taken in attitude research (e.g., Rosenberg & Hovland, 1960) and provides bridges to that area of knowledge.

Cognitive Effects

Studies that discuss the cognitive effects of political advertising usually treat issues of increased knowledge about politics and political races. Atkin and his colleagues (Atkin & Heald, 1976; Atkin, Bowen, Nayman, & Sheinkopf, 1973) have demonstrated in a congressional campaign that exposure to political advertising leads to more knowledge about the campaign. The 1972 presidential election served to demonstrate through a number of studies that there exists a positive relationship between attention and exposure to political advertising and information about the presidential election (Hofstetter & Buss, 1980; Hofstetter, Zukin, & Buss, 1978; Mendelsohn & O'Keefe, 1976).

Evidence indicates that above a certain plateau, information gain by individuals from televised political advertising does not increase. Patterson and McClure (1976a) observed that viewers who watched moderate levels of political advertising demonstrated the same level of information gain as did heavy viewers. Other studies have indicated that a similar relationship exists for exposure and knowledge at lower-level races such as congressional (Atkin & Heald, 1976; Atkin et al., 1973), state house (Kaid, 1976), and mayoral (Mulder, 1979) elections.

One of the powers of the media is control over what issues seem important at a given time, generally called agenda setting. Cohen (1963) notes that the media may not be powerful enough to tell people how to think, but they can affect what people think about. This means that the media is primarily responsible for those issues that will be salient at any given time. This ability to control the important issues becomes particularly important in political campaigns (cf., Bowers, 1973; Shaw & Bowers, 1973), although Littlejohn (1989) suggests that the campaign may be too late, as "some researchers have come to believe that the issues reported during a candidate's term in office may have more effect on the election than the campaign itself" (p. 272). Bowers (1973) found that print political advertisements help set the boundaries for what issues are important in a campaign (cf., Shaw & Bowers, 1973; Patterson & McClure, 1976b).

Affective Effects

Cognition is a generic term that embraces knowledge and ratiocination. Affect is a generic term that embraces moods, feeling, and emotions or, to be a bit more technical, "'affect' refers to a subjective state which involves arousal of the autonomic nervous system or the interruption of attention" (Conover & Feldman, 1986, p. 51).

Affects are treated separately from cognitions, although both are manifestations of the brain. The research focus has traditionally been on the cognitive aspects of human behavior. As Gregg (1984) chides, "Despite the attempts of various 'rationalists' schools to transcend or downgrade, and thus deflect our attention from, such 'psychological' factors, emotions have always played a central role in human behavior" (p. 48). The increased interest in emotions, in part, derives from a theoretical perspective that provides the theory for emotions to be conceived of as a fundamentally different mental system, with cognitive and affective evaluations being independent (Zajonc, 1980).

Kaid (1981) defines affective effects as generally taking the form of evaluating the candidate in terms of attractiveness, credibility, and status. The second approach to affective effects looks more specifically to the inner feelings of the potential voter. Abelson, Kinder, Peters, and Fiske (1982) found that two distinct affective dimensions— negative affect and positive affect—were present when using their list of affects for 1980 presidential candidates. Their findings also indicated that negative and positive emotions about a candidate tend to be independent of one another; that is, that one can simultaneously have both negative and positive affects toward a politician.

The emotional response of the electorate toward a candidate is heavily influenced by communication. A candidate through the proper use of political advertising may build positive affective responses in the audience. Baskin (1975) supported this conclusion when he discovered that a candidate's image is primarily a function of his or her political advertising. This positive feeling towards an individual does not necessarily affect feelings towards other aspects of the person's candidacy. Atkin and Heald (1976) note that this increase in favorable regard toward a candidate by a member of the electorate is "a positive affective orientation toward the candidate as a person, independent of party affiliation or issue positions" (219). Meadow and Sigelman (1982) reported that issue-oriented political ads increased the candidate's perceived leadership and warmth. However, the relationship is curvilinear; that is, a moderate amount of repetition is better than a small or large amount of (Becker and Doolittle, 1975). These findings of repetition and familiarity had been predicted by Zajonc's (1968) mere exposure theory, which suggests that exposure will lead to a greater positive affect (discussed in Chapter 5 and also Chaffee, 1967a, 1967b; Ray, 1973; Zajonc & Rajecki, 1969). Wanat (1974) and Garramone and Smith (1984) demonstrate the mere exposure effect by showing that positive evaluation of a candidate increases with exposure to the candidate's advertising

Donohue has explored how the credibility of a source affects the way in which people selectively perceive information. In a study using radio messages from Kennedy, Humphrey, Lindsay, and Nixon presidential campaigns, Meyer and Donohue (1973) discovered that highly credible sources are often misapprehended as supporting the listener's position. Donohue (1973) found that this misperception is not as strong for television as for radio.

Andreoli and Worchel (1978) reported that candidates and current politicians are not as convincing in expressing opinions on television as newscasters and retired politicians. Though no explanation is offered by Andreoli and Worchel, we suggest that there is a difference between retired and existing officeholders. A retired politician has a sympathetic component usually not shared with an incumbent. This sympathy perhaps grows out of the myth of the elder statesman. In addition, the candidate in the experimental situation was a fictional candidate created for the experiment. There is a likelihood that an unknown candidate would be perceived more suspiciously than a retired politician when the audience has no other information upon which to base its decisions.

Behavioral Effects

Political advertising has been assumed to have an impact on an individual's voting decisions. However, the conditions under which this is true remain undefined. When asked, most people say that political advertising does not shape their voting behavior (Atkin, Bowen, Nayman, & Sheinkopf, 1973; Mendelsohn & O'Keefe, 1976). If such a view were true, it would be expected that no relationship between political advertising expenditures and election outcomes would exist. Rather than no relationship, there seems a preponderance of evidence demonstrating a positive relationship between moneys spent and voter turnout and election outcome (Dawson & Zinser, 1971; Grush, McKeough, & Ahlering, 1978; Jacobson, 1975; McCleneghan, 1980; Palda, 1975).

The influence of political advertising is also demonstrated in ticket splitting. Ticket splitting, voting for members of different parties in the same election, has been shown to increase with an increase in political advertising (DeVries & Tarrance, 1972; Hofstetter & Buss, 1980; Joslyn, 1981). The 1996 election results of reelection of President Clinton and return of a Republican majority to the Congress is an example of ticket splitting.

Other research has found that the media—specifically political advertising—result "in considerable voter impact" (Kaid, 1981, p. 251). Palda (1975), for example, found in Canada that political advertising was the second most important variable affecting voter behavior. Indeed, in Joslyn's (1981) analysis, exposure to political commercials was the third most important criterion on voter defections. The evidence does support the proposition that political advertising does promote some forms of behavioral change.

POLITICAL ADVERTISING EFFECTIVENESS

Effectiveness is an evaluation concept (Nothstine & Copeland, 1983). In other words, how well does political advertising work? Research has demonstrated that the effectiveness of political advertising will be strongest in low-level and local races such as primary elections, nonpartisan races, and races for state positions and campaigns for the House of Representatives (Kitchens & Stiteler, 1979; Rothschild, 1975; Wanat, 1974).

Rothschild (1975) tested the effectiveness of political advertising for high- and low-involvement races in an experimental setting and discovered that political advertising did have a greater impact for the low-involvement races. Swinyard and Coney (1978) conducted a field experiment for high- and low-involvement races and came to the same conclusions. The evidence is convincing that political advertising is much more powerful in low-involvement races. Similar findings have been reported by a number of researchers (Grush, McKeough, & Ahlering, 1978; Hofstetter & Buss, 1980; Hofstetter, Zukin, & Buss,

1978; McClure & Patterson, 1974). Swinyard and Coney (1978) suggest that power of political advertising to influence low-involvement races exists because "voters in high-level races question, defend against, and otherwise counter-argue against promotions [and thus] are able to protect themselves from much promotional influence" (p. 47).

The study of the political advertising effects has stimulated some (e.g., Atkin & Heald, 1976) to create typologies of the purposes for which political advertising may effectively be used. Devlin (1986) provided 10 potential goals for political advertising. Devlin's enumeration describes the utility and power of political ads.

Devlin's Typology of Advertising Goals

Devlin recognized that political advertising develops name recognition for a candidate. This recognition is particularly important for challengers, but is also important for incumbents. Political advertising puts the names of the candidates before the voters. It reaches noninvolved and late deciding voters. Political advertising for noninvolved voters may stimulate their interest or simply keep those people informed about the race. For late deciders, political advertising often is helpful in making a decision (Mulder, 1979), and television is a popular source of information for this group (Strand, Dozier, Hofstetter, & Ledingham, 1983). Independents are examples of late deciders who frequently utilize political advertising messages in order to make their decisions close to election day.

Political advertising acts as a reinforcing agent for those who have selected a candidate to support. Sheinkopf, Atkin, and Bowen (1972, 1973) found that this reinforcement extends to campaign workers for a candidate. Those who are already committed to a particular candidate will often seek information to reinforce their preexisting preference. In addition, political advertising often provides reasons to vote against the opposition candidate. In recent years, voters were more likely to cast their ballots against someone rather than for someone. Thus it has become increasingly important to provide prospective voters with reasons for not voting for the opposition. Political advertising also creates the issue agenda for the campaign. Political advertising defines or creates the issues and gives them their public character. Political advertising gives the candidate some control over what the issues will be in the election. Thus advertising helps to structure the debate in the campaign.

Political advertising may be used to redefine the perceptions of a candidate or party. The "New Nixon" in the 1968 presidential campaign was a classic example of redefinition of a candidate. This restructuring is an attempt to change voter perception. Political advertising may target specific groups of voters. The time-honored persuasion axiom of "specific messages for specific audiences for specific results" is utilized by political advertising consultants. Selecting the advertising medium is but one way to reach the selected demographic and psychographic target audiences. Political ads, though costing money, may be used to increase the financial base of the campaign. Whether through direct appeals for money in the advertising or through the visibility that advertising gives the candidates, money is easier to raise for candidates who advertise. Political advertising may be used tactically. As issues change in a campaign, political advertising is an effective instrument to counter the thrust and parry of the opponent. (See Witherspoon, 1984 for anecdotal evidence from several campaigns).

Finally, political advertising is used because it is expected behavior for a candidate. Television advertising is a campaign ritual, and therefore running a campaign without advertising violates the expectations of the voters. For any statewide or federal race, a candidate without television advertising will be perceived as the losing candidate.

Political advertising is an important part of the U.S. political process. These ads legitimize both the political institution and members of the political institution. The advertising demonstrates that this political system provides voters with choices, and the "voters' selection of one candidate over the other will make a difference" (Jamieson, 1984, 2nd par., pp. 452-453).

POLITICAL ADVERTISING: CONTENT AND STYLE

Political advertising is effective, strategic, and necessary. Previous discussions have treated political spots without a serious examination of the elemental content of those spots. The content and style of the ad help determine its impact.

Issues and Images

Traditionally, a political candidate's advertising has been viewed by researchers and political consultants as comprised of issues and images. In discussing political imagery, a number of conceptual problems exist in the literature, problems that we have discussed throughout this book. At this point, we will simply review what appears in the literature. For this reason, images and issues will be treated as separate and discrete constructs.

The image construct has been used in a variety of ways. For the most part, political advertising imagery has been used to denote both the graphic representation of a candidate and the attributes of a candidate's character, though the latter is the more common association (Shyles, 1986). We view issues as public concerns and policies or as "specific policy stands" (Shyles, 1986, p. 116). For the purposes of reviewing what is known about political advertising, we will use these two subdivisions—images and issues—for organizational purposes.

Issues

Studying the messages in political advertising has been the subject of much academic interest. Various approaches to understanding the messages in political advertising have been used. Interviews with people who have been behind the scenes are sometimes used to gain knowledge about how messages came to be crafted and used. These behind-the-scenes informants include major political advertising producers, media coordinators, and political ghostwriters (Benson, 1968, 1974; Berkovitz, 1985; Devlin, 1981). Benson (1981), Jamieson (1984), and Rudd (1986) have also used participant-observer methods to study how political commercials were created.

Political observers have long debated the merits of political advertising for the political system. However, research examining the issues presented in television political commercials generally indicates that issues are presented. Studies have indicated that a sizable number if not a majority, of political ads may be considered issue presentations (Bowers, 1972; Hofstetter & Zukin, 1979; Joslyn, 1980; McClure & Patterson, 1974; Winneg, 1986). Joslyn (1980) studied television political ads from a number of races and discovered that over half (57.7%) of the advertisements mentioned issues. The number of times that issues are mentioned in political ads may be more frequent than Joslyn reports. Hofstetter and Zukin (1979) reported that 85 percent of presidential candidates' advertisements in the Nixon and McGovern race contained some reference to issues, while McClure and Patterson (1974) reported 70 percent in the same election. Shyles (1983) reported 649 mentions of issues in the 140 spots he coded. Latimer's (1984) data show that Alabama candidates for the House of Representatives put more issue messages in their political advertising than do candidates for the U.S. Senate, who have more image messages. Elebash and Rosene (1982) found that in the 1978 Alabama gubernatorial race, 30-second televised political spots averaged 1.35 issues per spot while, 60-second spots averaged 2.11 issues. This favorably compares with the amount of issue discussion in print advertising (Bowers, 1972).

While the evidence is clear that there are issues presented in political advertising, the candidate's position on those issues may not always be presented in the ad. In his 1986 study, Joslyn found that only 5 percent of the political advertisements studied contained specific policy preferences, and in 1980, he noted that the stands candidates took on the issues presented were not always clear. Patterson and McClure (1976b) report that there was a superficial treatment of issues in the political advertising they studied. This lack of specificity is probably intentional and strategic on the part of the candidate. For example, Bennett (1977) argues that candidates should not be too specific, since what matters is the mentioning of the issues rather than the position taken. He also sees these issue posi-tions as image building.

As noted earlier, politicians may not clearly delineate their own position on campaign issues, there does seem to be sufficient evidence to suggest that candidates at least allude to issues in their television advertising. There does not appear to be a lack of issues in political advertising; rather, there seems to be a lack of specific details concerning the issues. Many political ads merely uphold consensual values rather than deal directly with issues (Bennett, 1977; Joslyn, 1986; Rudd, 1986).

Joslyn's (1980) study of political advertising also revealed that a specific, target demographic group was the third most mentioned area in political spots. He found that candidates try to identify specific target groups, and candidates then try to link the groups with their campaigns. Although the mention of the candi-date's political party is frequently used in political advertising, the rate of this mention was a distant fourth. The mentioning of party affiliation may be affected by a number of campaign factors, such as the level of party competition within the voting electorate.

Again we caution not to view issues and images as discrete constructs. These constructs are so deeply intertwined that they must be considered as a whole.

Image

Rubin (1967) quotes James Reston in 1958 bemoaning, "Instead of the old-fashioned emphasis on what a candidate thinks, or what he says, the emphasis now seems to be on how he looks, especially on television, and on what kind of personality he has" (p. 32). Some writers (for example, Devlin, 1973; Kelly, 1960; O'Keefe & Sheinkopf, 1974) have echoed these sentiments. Others, such as Fenno (1978) and Napolitan (1972), note that personal characteristics of a candidate are more important to a large number of voters than the candidate's stand on a specific issue. Ogden and Peterson (1968) write, "The presidential candidate must convince the American people that he can lead the nation. . . . His qualities as a person and as a leader are far more important on the whole than are the stands he takes on particular issues" (p. 16).

Academic research has also used these concepts to explore the impact of political advertising. For example, Patterson and McClure (1976b) contend that voters react to content rather than style when they evaluate political advertisements. Garramone (1983) received mixed results when trying to determine how individuals form image impressions about the candidate's attributes from political advertising. Mansfield and Hale (1986) found that viewers of political advertising didn't make clear distinctions between image and issue advertisements.

An exception to this has been the work of Rudd (1986), who notes that the issue content of political advertising also affects the candidate's image. He notes that issue-oriented campaigning also creates an image for the candidate.

The second most popular element in television spots relates to the candidate's image (Joslyn, 1980). Joslyn (1986) found that 57 percent of the political advertising that he coded contained material about the personal attributes of the candidate. He found that this was the most common type of advertising information. Shyles (1983) has categorized the most popular areas of image as: experience, competence, special qualities (those unique to the given race), honesty, leadership, and strength.

That voters are influenced by candidate image has been established by a number of studies. Two studies that looked at the influence of candidate image on evaluations of political spots are Cundy (1986) and Boyd (1978). Both found that images portraying stylistic elements impact on viewers. A telephone survey conducted during the 1972 presidential campaign concluded that commercials by candidates are primarily image building in effect (O'Keefe & Sheinkopf, 1974). Brownstein (1971), not surprisingly, found that a candidate's image influences how favorably that candidate is viewed. People who are image rather than issue oriented seem to interpret political spots differently (Garramone, 1986). People who are seeking to form an impression of a candidate's personality are more likely to base their impressions on the material in political advertising (Garramone, 1983).

Image-oriented political commercials were found to be best for content recall (Kaid & Sanders, 1978; Kaid, 1982), and specifically, image advertising increased name recall for the candidate. Image advertising may also affect behaviors. Latimer's (1984) data suggest that the image content of ads may have increased vote totals.

Woman Candidates

The success of Diane Feinstein, Patty Murray, Barbara Boxer, Carol Moseley Braun, and Barbara Mikulski in their 1992 senatorial campaigns emphasizes the increasing number of women who are running for and winning elected offices. But 1992 was an unusual year in that a number of factors, including legislative redistricting, worked to create a favorable climate for the election of women. Carroll (1994) identifies these favorable factors as: "the check-bouncing scandal, the Thomas-Hill hearings, a strong desire for change among voters, a shift away from a focus on foreign affairs to a focus on domestic problems, and record levels of contributions to women candidates" (p. 164). In 1992, 24 women were elected to the U.S. House of Representatives (Carroll, 1994, p. 161). Five women were elected to the U.S. Senate in 1992 (Carroll, 1994, p. 163).

While no one would argue that the number of women who are elected is close to representing their actual numbers in the population, at least they are no longer the "novelty act" that Pat Schroeder once lamented (reported in Griffiths, 1985). The old reasons summarized by Hedlund, Freeman, Hamm, and Stein (1979) on why women did not run (specifically, personality differences, situational factors, and sex role socialization) are crumbling. There appears to be a growing acceptance of women as elected officials among the electorate (Carroll, 1985; Darcy, Welch, & Clark, 1987; Ekstrand, 1978; Hedlund, Freeman, Hamm, & Stein, 1979).

Benze and Declerq (1985) enumerated the types of women they perceive will fare the best in a campaign: (1) women who appear strong but not too aggressive, (2) women who appear professional, and (3) women who are not too attractive. Concerning appearance, a similar standard for men candidates also applies to women candidates; that is, the woman candidate should be "not too plain, not too pretty, women must find the perfect in-between in constructing a public image" (Mandel, 1981, p. 38).

All candidates must be able to raise money for the campaign. This appears to be a more difficult task for a woman than a man. The average amount of money raised in the 1984 campaign showed that women raised less money than their male opposition (Burrell, 1987). However, that may be a function of males tending to be the incumbents. Those women running as challengers or in open races, on the average, raised more money than their male counterparts. This was illustrated again in 1992. All three of the nonincumbent women running for the U.S. Senate were able to raise more money for their campaigns than their male opponents. However, all three were running for open seats. The need for money specifically to buy media is acute in campaigns for women because, as Declerq, Benze, and Ritchie (1983) report, woman candidates rely more heavily on advertising, and particularly television advertising, than males.

The strategy used by a male candidate whose opponent is a woman may have to be different than the male candidate running against another male. Consultants in the past generally did not want to use negative political advertising against women. They feared a boomerang effect from the voters against such tactics. And in the past, consultants warned female candidates to exercise caution when they themselves used negative ads. Jamieson (1988) and Trent and Friedenberg (1983) caution women that they must be careful about attacking their opponents because, as Jamieson writes, the woman might be considered "unfeminine, shrill, and nagging" (p. 86). More current research indicates that tougher stands by women are becoming more acceptable to voters. Leeper's (1991) experimental results led him to conclude, "Female candidates need not worry about appearing too strident or uncharacteristically tough" (p. 256).

Spots for a woman candidate have been found to be very similar and in some cases identical with spots for men (Benze & Declerq, 1985), and when set in the same surroundings, males and females make equally favorable impressions (Kaid, Myers, Pipps, & Hunter, 1985). Benze and Declerq (1985) concluded from their content analysis that men usually stress their toughness, while women usually stress their compassion. Kahn (1993) found in an analysis of 1984 and 1986 U.S. Senate candidates that "men tend to concentrate on economic issues, while women are much more likely to discuss social issues such as education and health policy (p. 481). Johnston and White (1994) found that female candidates running for the U.S. Senate in 1986 tended to dramatize their competency and showcase their past accomplishments as public officials. They also found that the female candidates were issue oriented and were less likely to use negative ads.

However, Trent and Sabourin (1993), in their analysis of negative campaign commercials used by female and male candidates who ran for major political offices during the 1980s, documented the emergence of a female style and a male style in the use of negative ads. "Ads used by males contained harder attacks, more frequently pictured the opponent, showed the candidate in strictly business attire, and did not feature the candidate live" (Trent & Sabourin, 1993, pp. 35-36). They conclude that the male style can be characterized as being "opponent-centered" (p. 36). They also found that

ads used by female candidates contained more variety in types of negative ads, showed the candidate in professional clothing less often, did not picture the opponent, and less frequently showed the candidate in a close-up at the time of the attack. The female candidates were also more likely than males to use other people in the ad . . ., and to physically touch someone." (Trent & Sabourin, 1993, p. 36)

Trent and Sabourin (1993) characterize the female style as being "candidate-centered" (p. 36). They conclude that because females are generally underfunded and are more likely to be challengers, they have to utilize negative ads for a variety of purposes, and for this reason the ads, while attacking the opponent, still highlight the candidate. Interestingly, Dinzes, Cozzens, and Manross (1994) found that "respondents rated the candidate sponsors of negative political ads significantly more positively and were more likely to vote for the sponsor when the ads were directed against an opponent of the opposite sex" (p. 67).

Williams's (1994) analysis of 1992 Senate races found that female candidates "balanced compassion and competence by demonstrating a high level of . . . 'connected activity,' by recapping their personal histories of working *for* and *with* [emphasis in the original] other people in their life struggles" (p. 211). The unique set of circumstances that led to the 1992 election climate allowed female candidates to go beyond the simple blurring of traditional male and female candidate roles to establishing a new dynamic in female candidate advertising. "Female candidates could stress their competence, for example, but do so in a uniquely woman-centered fashion—they could stress a different sort of competence" (Williams, 1994, p. 211). Advertising for female candidates was less likely to use female announcers and more likely to depict women in nontraditional roles.

Whether female candidates will continue this new advertising dynamic and whether the voters continue to accept it is not certain; however, it does appear that female candidates are no longer penalized for pursuing traditionally "masculine" strategies. Research shows "an aggressive stance by a female candidate—one where she uses attacks on her opponent—is more desirable than a nonaggressive, passive stance" (Wadsworth et al., 1987, p. 91). For example, Procter, Aden, and Japp (1988) attribute Kay Orr's success in the 1986 gubernatorial race in Nebraska against Helen Boosalis to Orr's strategy of combining female compassion traits with male aggression traits in her political advertising. In addition, a female candidate exhibiting a career orientation was evaluated higher than one who exhibits a family orientation. Clearly these findings are contrary to traditional beliefs about female candidates, and may be an artifact of using college students as the sample in many studies. However, it is time to reevaluate the early research and thinking about female candidates' campaigns. It is quite possible that with the rapid societal changes expe-

rienced in the late seventies and eighties and the increasing number of
female candidates, society's expectations concerning appropriate female candidate behavior has changed as well.

POLITICAL ADVERTISING STRATEGIES

Political consultants have a repertoire of political advertising
strategies that they draw upon during political campaigns. There are
four genre of political advertising:

1. Positive ads designed to position the candidate on the political spectrum, state
   his or her perspectives on issues and increase the candidate's perceived ideal
   personal leadership qualities
2. Negative ads designed to question the opponent's fitness for office
3. Reactive response ads that answer the opposition's negative ads
4. Proactive inoculation ads that are used to undermine, deflect, and reduce the
   power of anticipated negative attacks (Johnson-Cartee & Copeland, 1991a)

The majority of political advertising falls within the first two categories, because political consultants primarily want to provide reasons
for voters to vote for their candidate and against the opposition. Since
the 1980s, the dominant form of political advertising has been negative; however, roughly 30 percent of political advertising remains positive. Both reactive response ads and proactive inoculation ads are
used to combat candidate liabilities.

Positive Ads

Although positive political advertising is still widely used, it is
not used as a primary means of persuading voters. In today's political
culture, positive ads do not carry the persuasive power that they once
had in the 1960s, when people were primarily aligned behind the two
political parties. As political parties have become less important and
electoral contests have become more competitive, many electoral
outcomes ultimately turn on the independent vote, and for this reason,
political consultants have relied on negative advertising to persuade
voters. However, positive ads continue to be used for six primary reasons:

1. Improve candidate's name recognition
2. Develop or improve candidate's association with positive leadership characteristics
3. Demonstrate homophily with the voters
4. Develop the heroic image of the candidate
5. Develop or improve candidate's association with issues having a positive
   evaluation by the voters

6. Link candidate with positive figures or groups (Johnson-Cartee & Copeland, 1997)

In our earlier writings we identified three types of positive political spots: Identification spots, Mythical Character spots, and Political Issue spots (Johnson-Cartee & Copeland, 1997).

Identification Spots

Ads that develop name recognition for a candidate or attempt to associate the candidate's name with particular issues or societal values are called identification spots. These positive political ads often take the approach of presenting a brief biography of the candidate that highlights the candidate's life with an emphasis on how his or her life experiences have affected what the candidate believes. Biographical spots are particularly effective if the candidate's biography highlights traditional American myths such as success through hard work. Generally identification spots are used by either challengers who wish to improve their low name recognition or by incumbents in low-visibility campaigns who wish to remind the voter of the candidate's incumbency status.

In 1994, Ryan deGraffenried ran for lieutenant governor in the Democratic primary in Alabama. This was deGraffenried's first attempt at a statewide race. While he was well known in his area where he had served as a state senator, he needed to increase his name recognition throughout the rest of the state. His campaign used a series of ads that highlighted his name in a humorous fashion while still linking the candidate with critical voter concerns.

The 1994 deGraffenried "Long Name" Ad

Video	Audio
White letters on black background: "deGraffenried";	Female Announcer [VO]: "How do you say this man's name?"
a white-haired man appears to the side, dressed in a blue work shirt.	White-haired man, grinning SOT]: ["deGraffenried?"
Super: "Hold it" in green on white with black speckled background; white-haired man still grinning. Super: "You know his record" in blue on white and black speckled background.	Female Announcer [VO]: "Hold it. Now that you know his record, you ought to know his name."

Super: "That's it. Good job!"	White-haired man, grinning [SOT]: "deGraffenried. That's right."
deGraffenried pointing to a large board with economic figures, new employment, investments, etc.	Female Announcer [VO]: "Who's the candidate who is nationally recognized for creating jobs in Alabama?"
Black-haired man in front of statistics on board; Super: "Right."	Black-haired man [SOT]: "Ryan deGraffenried."
Man in cowboy hat outside of Anders hardware.	Man with Cowboy hat [SOT]: "He's done more than all of his opponents put together."
White letters on black: "deGraffenried." deGraffenried at desk working Super: "The Experience to be Lt. Governor."	Female Announcer [VO]: "Who's the candidate with the experience to be Lieutenant Governor?"
Brown-haired man talking with "deGraffenried" written in blue in syllables to his right.	Brown-haired man [SOT]: "deGraffenried."
Elderly black man talking.	Elderly black man [SOT]: "He's the honest man.
White-haired woman talking in front of a chalkboard. Someone is writing "deGraffenried" on the board behind her while she speaks.	White-haired woman [SOT]: "He's the man spearheading education reform."
Super: "Ryan deGraffenried Democrat for Lt. Governor."	Female Announcer [VO]: "Ryan deGraffenried."
deGraffenried talking to camera, holds his arms apart.	deGraffenried laughing [SOT]: "Just remember; it's the big guy with the long name."
White-haired man in blue shirt.	White-haired man [SOT]: "deGraffenried! Right?"

Mythical Character Spots

Ads that utilize American cultural myths to strike responsive chords within the voters stored political memories are called mythical character spots. Such an approach uses the resonance strategy by attempting to evoke what is latent within the individual. Mythical character spots often include the American Dream political myth, which is closely linked with materialism. The candidate born to lowly beginnings but who worked hard and ultimately achieved great accomplishments is presented as an American hero. Warner (1976) observed, "The myth of ultimate success and the creation of the symbolic role of the successful man who rises from lowly beginnings to greatness and final heights is a necessary part of the apparatus of our social and status system" (p. 207). In the 1992 U.S. Senate race in Colorado, Ben Nighthorse Campbell ran a positive ad that emphasized his Native American heritage and his poor background. Campbell is presented as a true American hero.

The 1992 Campbell "American Dream" Ad

Video	Audio
White letters on black: "Imagine this." Photo of Campbell as a little boy in a sailor suit. Black and white photo as a boy, smiling. Close-up of photo.	Announcer [VO]: "Imagine this: a young Native American, his mother a victim of tuberculosis, his father of chronic alcoholism. Early on the young boy learns first hand what happens when people are divided from one another. His sister and he are placed in separate orphanages. The odds are against them, but the odds themselves could not rob the young boy of his most valuable possessions: his dreams and his courage. At 17, he dons his country's uniform in the
Photo of Campbell in Korea. Photo of Campbell as athlete at Olympic games with a medal around his neck.	Korean War. In 1964, he again wears the uniform of his country. As a member of the United States Olympic team, his fellow athletes chose the young Native American to carry the flag in the closing ceremony. His name:
Super: "Ben Nighthorse Campbell" Campbell in cowboy attire saddles horse and rides.	Ben Nighthorse Campbell. Throughout his life he has known how important real jobs

	are. A lesson he learned early loading and hauling crates of tomatoes and pears from the fields to the markets. He taught high school during the day and rode in the back of an ambulance as a
Dusk scene. Ambulance workers. Super: "Pro-Choice"	young deputy at night. His strong pro-choice stand comes from seeing a young woman in that ambulance one night, the victim of a back alley abortion. And as a
Black and white photo of Campbell as young boy; Close-up of face, Super: "Pro-Health Care."	man who saw his own family broken by poverty and illness, Ben Nighthorse Campbell's commitment to affordable, quality health care for all Americans is
Campbell in Native American dress on horseback.	real. And as a chief of the Northern Cheyenne, his respect for the earth, the land, and the
Black and white photo of family.	water is also real. As a husband and father, as a lawmaker who
Black and white photo of Campbell talking with elderly. Color photos of Campbell with children, with young people.	has made a difference in people's lives. Ben Nighthorse Campbell knows you cannot lead unless you can heal. He has put the real lessons of an extraordinary life to work. To heal, to lead, and to bring us together. And while the politics of the past have sought to divide us. Ben Nighthorse Campbell has united us.
Black with white lettering: "Real life. Real work. Real leadership."	Real life. Real work. Real leadership.
Campbell on horse riding. Super: "Ben Nighthorse Campbell for U.S. Senate."	Ben Nighthorse Campbell for Colorado's U.S. senator. The time is now."

Political Issue Spots

Political issue spots are ads used by candidates to associate themselves with particular issues that are important to various groups in the candidate's coalition of potential voters. These ads are rarely specific in that they will say that the candidate supports, say, social security or education but typically will not offer potential solutions for funding either of these policy areas. In a 1990 North Carolina state senate race, Ted Kaplan ran a reelection campaign that featured his stands on the issues. The ad below illustrates the frequently used technique of highlighting an issue without providing a solution (Johnson-Cartee & Copeland, 1991a). This is an example of what Joslyn (1986) has termed bogus policy appeals.

The 1990 Kaplan "Issues" Ad

Video	Audio
Kaplan talking to camera Super: "Senator Ted Kaplan on Education . . ."	Kaplan SOT: "Money is not the answer. Parents and teachers have to become more and more involved in schools. And the
Kaplan talking to camera.	General Assembly has to see that they can do that. In the war to
Super: "Senator Ted Kaplan on Environment"	save our environment, the front line has got to be the reduction of waste that we produce. Our
Kaplan talking to camera. Super: "Senator Ted Kaplan on Crime & Drugs . . ."	problem is setting the examples for young people so enforcement of the law becomes secondary and respect for the law becomes
Still of Ted Kaplan. Super: "Ted Kaplan North Carolina Senate."	number one."

Negative Political Advertising

Negative political advertising is political advertising that implicitly or explicitly places the opposition in an inferior position. Such ads question the leadership ability of the opposition and in this way challenge the opposition's fitness for office. Because research reveals fitness for office is the critical voter test in deciding for whom to vote, negative political advertising has become a very powerful strategy in modern campaigns. However, in order for negative political advertising to work, it must be believable, be factually supported, and be considered fair. If voters perceive that a candidate is unfairly attacking or misrepresenting an issue while attacking the opposition, this can lead to backlash against the sponsoring candidate (see Johnson-Cartee & Copeland, 1991a). We (1991a) have identified three types of negative political advertising: the direct attack ad, the direct comparison ad, and the implied comparison ad (see also Gronbeck, 1985).

Direct Attack Ads

Direct attack ads only attack. They do not offer comparisons between candidates; rather, they focus on the weaknesses of the opposition. Such ads are very effective in reaching and converting the less-educated voter and serve as a powerful reinforcing device for those predisposed toward the sponsoring candidate (Johnson-Cartee & Copeland, 1991a; Weiss, 1966). Direct attack ads are often used during the last two weeks before election day when many less-educated, undecided voters are making their voting decisions.

A candidate's record is a popular subject for dirct attack ads. We (Copeland & Johnson-Cartee, 1990; Johnson & Copeland, 1987; Johnson-Cartee & Copeland, 1989b, 1991a) have shown the use of a candidate's record in attack ads to be one of the acceptable forms of negative political advertising. The 1992 Bush campaign used a direct attack spot that highlighted Clinton's record as governor of Arkansas.

The 1992 Bush "Clinton's Record" Ad

Video	Audio
An Arkansas sign on a steel bridge Photo of Bill Clinton as governor Super: Trailer parks More trailer parks Hosiery tax Beer tax Hotel with women taking photographs Clinton playing on TV with saxophone Bagging groceries Super: "Guess where he'll get the money?"	Fiddle music under. Announcer: "To pay for his increased spending in Arkansas, Bill Clinton raised taxes not just on the rich. He increased the sales tax by 33 percent. He imposed a mobile home tax. Increased the beer tax. He assessed a tourism tax. He added a cable TV tax. Supported a tax on groceries. And now if elected president, Bill Clinton has promised to increase government spending by 220 billion dollars. Guess where he'll get the money?"

The opponent who is attacked does not have to be specifically named. The ad may speak of "the other candidate" or of the sponsor's "opponent." Sometimes the opponent isn't a single individual but a collective. George Wallace was known for running against such collectives as the electric company and "pointy headed intellectuals." It is becoming more and more common for the collective that is attacked to be the legislative group for which the candidate is seeking office. In 1992 an incumbent congressman, Rick Santorum of the 18th

Congressional District in Pennsylvania, used a series of ads that attacked the Congress, portraying the legislative body as a bunch of unfeeling, insensitive, loudmouthed, gluttonous drunks.

The 1992 Santorum "Restaurant" Ad

Video	Audio
Large table of men and women in a nice restaurant. They're smoking, drinking liquor, and eating large quantities of food. They're laughing and hugging each other.	Piano music in background. Man [SOT]: "Hey! Waiter! Bring us a bottle of your very best champagne."
Waiter is seen.	Waiter [VO]: "Of course you know, sir, that it's very, very expensive."
	Man [SOT]: "Hey! Don't worry about it, if we don't have enough money, just give the bill to them."
He points to a table of children with no food or drinks. Close-ups of children's very sad expressions.	
Rick Santorum enters the room holding a child.	Santorum [SOT]: "I'm Rick Santorum. Believe it or not, that's exactly what the leaders in Congress are doing. They're wasting our tax dollars, running up the deficit, and then passing the bill on to your children and mine. That's simply not fair and costs Americans jobs. That's why I'll continue my fight to clean up Congress and its greedy spending practices."
Table of men and women partying. Man receives bill from the waiter.	Man [SOT]: "Hey! I'll just write a check." (Laughter)
Super: "Join the Fight!" "For our children's future, vote Santorum for Congress."	Announcer [VO]: "Join the fight! For our children's future. Vote Santorum for Congress."

In one 1992 congressional election, the incumbent ran a highly vituperative but very funny ad against his opponent Donna Peterson.

The ad was titled "The Great Pretender," and underneath the narrative the popular fifties and sixties tune "The Great Pretender" played.

The 1992 Wilson "The Great Pretender" Ad

Video	Audio
Super: "She's the great pretender." Photo of young beautiful redhead posed in a provocative pose (like a glamour shot).	Woman singing VO: "Yes, she's the great pretender." Song under. Announcer V0: "Donna Peterson, the great pretender who's running for Congress. Donna pretends she flew helicopters for the army. In fact, she never had a flying assignment and doesn't even have a pilot's license.
A little green helicopter flies across the screen from the left side It falls off the screen.	
A model of a house with a sign in the front yard reading "A-1 Enterprises." The sign floats by.	Donna pretends she was general manager of A-1 Enterprises, a company that doesn't exist.
Red convertible	Donna Peterson pretends she paid $42000 cash for a foreign-made sports car on a $13,000 a year salary.
Photo of real Donna Peterson, blond middle-aged woman	Hunh! You figure!"

Although direct attack ads have been shown to decrease both the candidate evaluation scores and the candidate preference scores of targeted candidates, the drop was not as great as that for a direct comparison spot (Johnson-Cartee & Copeland, 1991a).

Direct Comparison Ads

Direct comparison ads compare one candidate with another. Direct comparison ads work on the assumption that voters compare candidates when making voting decisions (Choi & Becker, 1987; Gronbeck, 1985). Most important, the direct comparison spot creates a greater decrease in the opponent's evaluation and voting preference scores than other types of negative ads (Johnson-Cartee & Copeland, 1991a). Additionally, these spots give the illusion of fairness presenting two sides though the sponsoring candidate always appears superior. Such two-sided arguments are far more effective than one-sided arguments in persuading the highly educated and in fighting future counterpropaganda (Weiss, 1966).

In 1986, Claude Harris, an Alabama circuit judge, ran in the Democratic Seventh Congressional District primary. Harris faced Billy Hill, a Shelby county district attorney, in the primary.

The 1986 Harris "Finances" Ad

Video	Audio
White type on black screen	Announcer [VO]: "Compare your congressional candidates.
Split screen with Hill on left. Harris on right. Type is under each respective photo. After each point made about Hill, his photo gets smaller. After Harris's points, his photo gets larger	The majority of Billy Hill's campaign contributions was $1,000 gifts and came from a small group of influential people. Claude Harris, the people's candidate, received contributions from more than 600 people, with the majority giving $100 or less. Billy Hill's campaign is more than $175,000 in debt. Seventy-five thousand to out-of-state consultants.
Full frame of Claude Harris.	Claude Harris's primary campaign has no debt. A lot of people gave what they could to Claude Harris, because they know he'll represent all the people . . . not a select few.
Two squares as if in voting machine, large Red X in one beside Claude Harris's logo	On June 24th, elect Claude Harris. He'll do the job he is elected to do."

Implied Comparison Ads

Implied comparison ads are often perceived by voters as being positive political spots. The implied comparison ad never refers to the opposition either euphemistically or specifically. "The implied comparison ads are not negative in and of themselves, but it is their public's interpretation of those ads that give them their negative character" (Johnson-Cartee & Copeland, 1991a). Unlike the direct attack or direct comparison ad, the implied comparison ad are deductive in that voters must (1) infer who the opposition is and (2) understand how that candidate is being criticized. Implied comparison ads can only be used in political contests where the voters have a significant degree of knowledge about the candidates, their positions, the issues, and so on. It is this store of information that is being tapped by the ad, and it is within the voter that the comparison is made. Typically, this means implied comparisons are more often used in high-visibility, high-involvement elections. Research shows indirect comparison ads create statistically significant decreases in the targeted candidate's evaluation scores and voting preference scores while elevating both of these for the sponsoring candidate (Johnson-Cartee & Copeland, 1991a). Generally, implied comparison ads are used in campaigns only after the voters have acquired the necessary knowledge about the candidates and issues to make the comparison. This often means these ads are used in the final weeks of a campaign.

In 1980, Robert Goodman, a political consultant, produced a spot for presidential candidate George Bush that indirectly compared his background with that of the Democratic incumbent, Jimmy Carter.

The 1980 Bush "President in Training" Ad

Video	Audio
Camera up on Bush in happy crowd.	Announcer [VO]: "This time, Americans have seen the opportunities of the 1980s—for the country and for the world. This time, there'll be no replays of the past. This time, there is George Bush.
Cut to audience, standing ovation; cut to Bush and wife Barbara shaking hands with supporters.	"George Bush has emerged from the field of presidential candidates because of what he is—a man who has proven that he can do the tough jobs and lead this country,
Cut to white letters against blue background: "GEORGE BUSH FOR PRESIDENT"	George Bush—a president we won't have to train. This time."

Source: Diamond & Bates, 1988, p. 267.

Proactive Inoculation Ads

Proactive inoculation ads are particularly important for candidates with liabilities in their backgrounds such as past voting decisions or past policy positions. Inoculation ads are defensive in nature in that by using them, candidates are able to deflect or neutralize subsequent attacks. By warning voters of potential negative attacks, the candidate has neutralized the effectiveness of those attacks. Such spots provide voters with the raw materials to use when counterarguing against the opposition's negative ads (Johnson-Cartee & Copeland, 1991a; 1997).

In 1990, U.S. Senator Jesse Helms of North Carolina faced Harvey Gantt, the mayor of Charlotte, in the general election. The national news media focused on Helms because he was either involved in or led a number of conservative crusades. Helms had gone on record as being opposed to such diverse groups as the National Endowment for the Arts, the pro-choice movement, and the entertainment industry. He had singled out birth control, affirmative action programs, and gays and lesbians as targets for his negative attacks. Much of the national news was critical of Helms's ideas and his conduct in the U.S. Senate, and the Helms campaign expected that some of this criticism would come back to haunt Helms in the Gantt campaign ads. The Helms campaign chose to prepare voters for this criticism by having then Governor Jim Martin present an inoculation ad for Senator Helms.

The 1990 Helms "Martin" Ad

Video	Audio
Scenes of the Tiananmen Square episode in Chinese history; Chinese tanks facing a lone male.	Governor Martin [VO]: "You remember the picture of this courageous martyr standing in the path of a Chinese tank just off Tiananmen Square, July 1989? It was not just one tank or even four as in some pictures."
Martin holding a blowup photograph of tanks. Super: Governor Jim Martin	Martin [SOT]: But a column of 19 tanks with another 50 waiting to get in line. America needs leaders with the courage to stand up for what's right regardless of what the liberal critics say. For 18 years, Senator Jesse Helms has stood up for us, for North Carolina, for America. On November 6th, he needs us to stand up for him."

In a 1986 Alabama gubernatorial campaign, the Democratic attorney general, Charlie Graddick, faced numerous political enemies in the Democratic primary. The Graddick campaign prepared itself for a tough fight and pursued the proactive strategy of warning Alabama voters that Graddick had political enemies because he was the people's champion. In this way, the Graddick campaign hoped to deflect any future negative ads.

The 1986 Graddick "In Charge" Ad

Video	Audio
Longshot of Graddick in a courtroom, speaking to a jury. Super: "Charlie Graddick." Slow zoom on Graddick. Super of a newspaper headline replaces other super: "Mobil to pay $2 million for illegal bay dumping."	[Drum rolls.] Announcer: "Attorney General Charlie Graddick. He's made some powerful enemies. [Drum rolls.] He got the largest fine in Alabama history imposed for water pollution.
New super: "Graddick says teacher test ruling his biggest victory."	[Drum rolls.] He blocked the politicians trying to certify incompetent school teachers.
Graddick points in courtroom. New super: "Graddick to appeal inmate release. Plans to sue governor too."	[Drum rolls.] When Fob James let convicted criminals go free, Charlie sued him and won. Yes, Charlie Graddick has made some enemies, that's why he's won so many friends.
Close-up of Graddick speaking. Picture is replaced by Super: "Graddick for Governor."	Charlie Graddick. When he's governor, you'll know who's in charge."

Responsive Ads

In some situations, candidates are not able to anticipate all of their liabilities, and a negative ad may catch them by surprise, or a public opinion poll may highlight a negative voter attitude that the campaign had previously not tapped. Under these conditions, the candidate must go into a defensive posture that attempts to rebuild a political argument that is in jeopardy (see McBurney & Mills, 1964). The campaign must decide how to react to the negative perceptions. In some cases, candidates may be well aware of their liabilities but will not want to draw attention to them for fear of creating a greater problem for themselves, and for this reason decide not to use proactive inoculation ads. The candidate will hope that the opposition may either be unaware of the liability or will choose not to use it during the campaign. But despite the candidate's hopes, the campaign should have previously prepared a reactive strategy to combat any known liabilities that voters have not been inoculated against. In this way, campaigns are able to react immediately with pretested advertising responses (Johnson-Cartee & Copeland, 1991a, 1997).

Response ads are not the most ideal means to deal with candidate negatives. Campaigns should never be surprised but, unfortunately, they sometimes are. In such situations, a response ad may be the only tools left to the consultant. It is always important to remember that an attacked candidate should not be put in the position of simply answering charges against his or her candidacy, for the public and the media should not get the impression that the opposition is controlling the public debate surrounding the election. Such a belief is a death knell for a political candidacy, for it means that the attacked candidate is no longer in charge of his or her own campaign, and the candidate has, in effect, turned over the campaign's script to the opposition, a terrible sign of weakness. For this reason, response strategies frequently include a number of tactics that emphasize attacks on the opposition to show that the candidate is still in charge and still fighting.

We have identified eight modes of response: (1) silence, (2) confession/redemption, (3) sanctimonious admission, (4) denial/campaign attack, (5) counterattack, (6) refutation, (7) obfuscation, and, (8) counterimaging (Johnson-Cartee & Copeland, 1991a, 1997; cf. Baukus, Payne, & Reisler, 1985).

Silence

Before 1980, consultants habitually told candidates to ignore negative attacks, because they believed that negative ads simply didn't work and the only damage that would be done would be to the sponsor of the ad by a voter backlash. But after a series of prominent U.S. senators fell to negative ads during the 1980 election, consultants began to reassess their traditional advice (Johnson-Cartee & Copeland, 1991a, 1997). Today it is recognized that silence is no longer a legitimate strategy in responding to negative advertising, for negative ads that go unanswered are then given credibility and believed by the voters. And perhaps most important, as Ed McCabe explained in his criticism of the 1988 Dukakis presidential campaign's ineptitude in dealing with negative attacks, "there's one thing the American people dislike more than someone who fights dirty. And that's someone who climbs into the ring and won't fight" (1988, p. 48).

Confession/Redemption

Candidates who publicly confess their mistakes to the voters and apologize are likely to be "forgiven" by the voters. This interesting phenomenon may be explained by the Judeo-Christian influence on our culture, in that this belief structure establishes a means by which individuals can redeem themselves before their God and their community (Johnson-Cartee & Copeland, 1991a, 1997). The confession/redemption tactic has been called an apologia or an apology strategy by other researchers (Berkman & Kitch, 1986; Sabato, 1981). In 1969 New York Mayor John Lindsay confessed that he had made numerous mistakes but was trying and doing his best, and after all, wasn't that all voters could ask?

The 1969 Lindsay "Mistakes" Ad

Video	Audio
Fade-in to extreme close-up of Lindsay.	(Birds are faintly audible in background throughout.)
Slow zoom out, revealing his casual dress. He is sitting on a porch.	Lindsay (SOF): "I guessed wrong on the weather before the city's biggest snowfall last winter, and that was a mistake. But I put 6,000 more cops on the street, and that was no mistake. The school strike went on too long, and we all made some mistakes. But I brought 225,000 new jobs to this town, and that was no mistake. And I fought for three years to put a fourth police platoon on the streets, and that was not a mistake. And I reduced the deadliest gas in the air by 50 percent, and I forced the landlords to roll back unfair rents, and we did not have a Detroit, or a Watts, or a Newark in this city, and those were no mistakes. The things that go wrong are what make this the second toughest job in America. But the things that go right are what make me want it."
Fade to black, then white Super:	

"Vote for Mayor Lindsay. It's the second toughest job in America."	

Source: Diamond & Bates, 1988, pp. 321-322.

Sanctimonious Admission

In some situations when candidates are attacked, they will turn the tables on their accusers by taking the attitude "Yes, I did that, and I'm damn glad I did it, and furthermore, if I had to do it all over again, I'd do exactly the same thing." In some situations, a candidate may decide to address a personal liability that his opposition is covertly exploiting in ads. Such tactics make the opposition look bad for even indirectly bringing such matters before the public (see Johnson-Cartee & Copeland, 1991a, 1997).

In 1988, Paul Simon entered the Democratic presidential primaries. Simon recognized that he did not have a very mediagenic appearance, and he knew that he certainly could not be considered charismatic. Both of these factors could prove to be serious liabilities for him in a race for the presidency. Newspapers in primary states featured cartoon caricature of Simon that ridiculed not only his looks but his personal mannerisms. And photos in opposition advertising made Simon appear even less attractive than he actually was. Although no opponent had openly attacked Simon on such superficial grounds, Simon knew that his image was a problem in the eyes of the voters. For this reason, Simon decided to make his "less than attractive" public image a virtue rather than a liability. He attempted to do this through a sanctimonious admission ad.

The 1988 Simon "Bow Tie" Ad

Video	Audio
Cartoon caricature from newspapers of Paul Simon with giant bow tie	Simon [VO]: "I was running for the Illinois House of Representatives, newspapers identified me as the candidate with the bow tie."
Simon talking to camera.	[Patriotic fife and drum music under.] Simon [SOT]: "And now it is more than a symbol for me. Because the public relations specialists tell me: get rid of the bow tie, get rid of the horn-rim glasses, change your views to accommodate public opinion polls.

	My bow tie is my declaration of independence. I'm going to be my own person, you have to take me for what I am."
Super: "Paid for by Paul Simon for President. "Photo of Paul Simon	

Denial/Campaign Attack

One means of addressing a negative attack is to create an ad that both denies the charges and tells voters that the opposition is telling lies about the candidate. This strategy is by far the most popular response to a negative ad. In some situations, the candidate may not want to go on record as denying the charges (usually because the candidate is guilty as charged), but the candidate will air an aid that implies a denial of the charges by accusing the opposition of mudslinging or unfair campaign practices (Johnson-Cartee & Copeland, 1991a; 1997).

In 1990, U.S. Senator Jesse Helms of North Carolina was attacked on his environmental record by his Democratic opponent, Harvey Gantt. Helms used the denial and attack response when he chose to deny the accusations and countercharge Gantt with dirty campaign tactics.

The 1990 Helms "Environment/Exempt" Ad

Video	Audio
Photo of Gantt with Super: "Can you believe Harvey Gantt's negative ads about our environment? "Photo of Gantt with Super: "Ducked Federal Clean Air Act." New Super: "Gantt's ads don't tell the truth." Photo of Helms with Super: "For Environment." Photo of soft ocean waves coming in at twilight. Super: Jesse Helms supported making Exxon and other oil companies pay to clean up oil spills . . . sponsored $5.7 billion to clean up toxic wastes." Photo of shoreline and seabirds. Scene of New River. Super: ". . . sponsored the law saving our New River, the oldest river in America, from being dammed by power	Announcer [VO]: "Can you believe Harvey Gantt's negative ads about our environment? When it was Mayor Gantt himself who asked to exempt his city from the Clean Air Act. Gantt's ads don't tell the truth. Jesse Helms supported making Exxon and other oil companies pay to clean up oil spills . . . sponsored 5.7 billion dollars to clean up toxic wastes . . . sponsored the law saving our New River, the oldest river in America, from being dammed by big power companies. That's the real Jesse Helms."

companies." Super: "That's the
<u>real</u> Jesse Helms."

Counterattack

When denial or refutation is not an option because the evidence for the factual basis of the attack is too well known or too well substantiated by sources other than the opponent, candidates often put into practice the trite advice, "A good offense makes the best defense." Rather than respond to the charge, the candidate will often go on the offensive, using a counterattack strategy. Consultants hope that voters will be distracted from the original negative attack by heightening the negativity of the campaign, In order to be successful, the counterattack must be far more powerful and devastating than the initial attack ad as it must draw attention away from the original charge (see Johnson-Cartee & Copeland, 1991a, 1997).

In the Wisconsin 1992 U.S. Senate campaign, Russ Feingold had attacked incumbent Bob Kasten's record using condemning newspaper headlines in his ads to back up his charges. Kasten chose to counter-attack.

The 1992 Kasten "Too Liberal" Ad

Video	Audio
Black lettering on white background: "A New Democratic Party?" Clinton and Gore in background of frame.	Announcer [VO]: "They say there's a new Democratic party? The party of Bill Clinton and Al Gore. (Cymbal crashes in background with each point made.) A party that favors a middle class tax cut, the death penalty, and reforming welfare. Russ Feingold opposes not only Bob Kasten on these issues but even his own party, Bill Clinton and Al Gore. When asked about Bill Clinton's tax proposals, Feingold said he thought Clinton could be convinced to raise taxes a little more. Now if Russ Feingold is out of step with his own party, isn't he out of step with Wisconsin?"
Super: "Middle-Class Tax Cut"; "Death Penalty"; "Welfare Reform."	
Feingold in background. Super: "Feingold opposes." Boxes with the words: "Welfare Reform, Death Penalty, Middle-Class Tax Cuts. "Super: "Feingold to Clinton: 'Raise taxes a little more.'"—*Milwaukee Sentinel*, 10/17/92; Feingold in background using saltshaker. Super: "Out of step with Wisconsin"	

Refutation

Refutation spots are by far the most effective and therefore the optimal mode for response ads (Garramone, 1985a; Johnson-Cartee & Copeland, 1991a, 1997; Salmore & Salmore, 1985). Refutation ads destroy the credibility of the negative attack by refuting the charges made by presenting convincing evidence to the contrary. Evidence presented as part of the refutation works as an inhibitor against future attacks from the opposition (McCroskey, 1970).

In 1994 the National Rifle Association targeted a number of incumbent senators who had voted for the assault rifle ban. U.S. Senator Bob Kerrey was one of the senators the NRA decided to target. An ad sponsored by the National Rifle Association's Political Victory Fund was run that featured a leading conservative spokesperson, Charlton Heston. In the ad, Heston condemned Kerrey for his vote in favor of the ban and urged voters not to vote for Kerrey's reelection. Kerrey, a Viet Nam War veteran who lost a leg in that military confrontation, produced a powerful spot refuting the NRA ad by appealing to the voters' reason and emotions.

The 1994 Kerrey "No AK47 Needed" Ad

Video	Audio
Bob Kerrey with other hunters, practicing skeet shooting. White print on blue background: "A message to Charlton Heston from Bob Kerrey."	Announcer [VO]: "This is a message to Charlton Heston from Senator Bob Kerrey."
Kerry talking.	Kerrey [SOT]: "I'm a hunter, and I believe in the constitutional right
·Kerrey opens breech on shotgun and closes it.	to bear arms. When it's time to hunt birds, you need a good gun like this Reuger Red Label.
Hands gun to someone off screen. Off-screen person hands him an AK47.	Twenty-five years ago in the war in Viet Nam, people hunted me. They needed a good weapon like this AK47. But you don't need one of these to hunt birds."

Obfuscation

Obfuscation ads use dramatic assertions and protestations that are disguised as evidence to refute negative attacks. The strategy is to confuse and distract the voter with hot language from the issue at hand. They may appear to be refutation spots, but on close examination, the candidate has not actually provided any evidence to refute the original charge, but it looks and sounds as if the candidate has.

In 1990, Senator Helms was attacked by Democratic challenger Gantt for Helms's involvement in a variety of highly controversial radical conservative issues and neglecting the interests of his home state, North Carolina. In addition, Gantt in his positive spots told North Carolina voters what he stood for and what he promised to do if elected. Helms chose to respond by obfuscating the issue at hand by introducing racial stereotypes and prejudices into the discussion.

Gantt is an African American. While the ad can be considered to be a direct comparison ad in that it draws a comparison, it can also be typed as an obfuscation spot. Helms discounts Gantt's promises to look out for North Carolina's interests, suggesting that Gantt is simply promising something for nothing. "The phrase 'Something for nothing' taps the racial stereotype that African-Americans expect something for nothing, that is, money for no work, and Helms's warning that there is 'no such thing as a free lunch' harks back to the individualist creed that diametrically opposes the community or social welfare creed that is stereotypically viewed as being supported by political liberals" (Johnson-Cartee & Copeland, 1997).

The 1990 Helms "Free Lunch" Ad

Video	Audio
Helms in an office. Super: "Senator Jesse Helms."	Helms [SOT]: "This is Jesse Helms, and I'll never try to get your vote by promising something for nothing. There's no such thing as a free lunch. Now, Harvey Gantt is a liberal. He's promised everything to everybody with you paying the bill. The question is, Who will cast your vote in the United States Senate, a liberal Harvey Gantt or a conservative Jesse Helms. I hope you'll help me Tuesday."

Counterimaging

In some situations, candidates may not want to deal with criticisms or negative public perceptions in a direct fashion because such a tactic may call more attention to the liability. Because negative perceptions should never go unanswered, the candidate may choose a subtle counterimaging ad that presents voters with a counterproposition to the the negative ad or to a widely held public belief about the candidate. Counterimaging ads are frequently mistaken for positive spots. Usually counterimaging ads are used in combination with other response ads and positive political spots that associates the candidate with desired leadership traits and favorable public issues (see Johnson-Cartee & Copeland, 1991a, 1997).

In 1992, the California state controller, Gray Davis, ran in the Democratic primary for the U.S. Senate. Davis's public image was the stereotype of the accountant, a numbers-and-balance-sheet type of individual who has little empathy or understanding for his fellow man. That is not the ideal image of a U.S. senator, who is expected to be a compassionate idea person, a statesman. Davis produced a counterimaging spot that on the one hand linked him with idolized Democratic leaders of the past and on the other demonstrated his compassion and statesmanlike rhetoric.

The 1992 Davis "Truth" Ad

Video	Audio
Film showing Los Angeles at night, sirens flashing; scenes of black men dragging a white man from truck. White girl being knocked down and hit in head with brick. Smoke over L.A., at night, burning. Oriental girl crying, sweeping up debris from riots. Rescue worker clearing debris. Martin Luther King, Jr., in upper left. John F. Kennedy in lower right, juxtaposed over people cleaning up.	Davis [VO]: "It's not white people's fault that there were riots in L.A.. It's not black people's fault that there were riots in L.A. A few thousand thugs—black, brown, white—terrorized all of us. It's time to stop categorizing people by race. Each of us, every race, must be held accountable for what we do. That's what I learned from Dr. King and President Kennedy. And that's why I am running for U. S. Senate."
Photo of Gray Davis Super: "State Controller Gray Davis, Democrat for U. S. Senate."	Announcer: "Truth, for a change. Gray Davis, Democrat for U.S. Senate."

Today, most political candidates will face negative political ads at some point in the campaign. As we have shown, the candidate and the candidate's campaign have a number of viable options available to deal with negative ads. Selecting the correct response is part of the art of media consulting. The decision for the response approach must be made keeping in mind the political context, the voters' view of the candidate and the candidate's opponent who issued the attack.

Chapter 8

Legal and Ethical Considerations

An individual's actions may be guided by legal, ethical, and moral constructs. By following the law of the land, individuals avoid going to jail or losing substantial economic assets. For the political communication consultant, this awareness of the legal boundaries has necessarily focused on libel and the "actual malice" standard for public officials. However, a political communication consultant may follow the letter of the law and still violate the ethical boundaries of modern American political culture. Ethics are the unwritten values, beliefs, and norms that bind members of a society together. Ethical considerations are germane to the society of professional advertising consultants and/or to the society at large. The freedom of political expression enjoyed in the United States necessitates a responsible holistic approach that examines both legal and ethical considerations within the political communication context. In addition, we will also review federal campaign finance law and its effect on political campaigns.

It has been noted more than once that there are more regulations concerning the marketing of soap or cornflakes than concerning the marketing of political candidates. "Because advertising is verifiable, the Court said there is less reason to tolerate false and misleading statements in commercial ads than in political debate where government attempts to prohibit falsehoods may stifle Democratic decision making" (Middleton & Chamberlin, 1988, p. 320; see also *Virginia State Board of Pharmacy v. Virginia Citizens Consumer Council*, 1976, at 771-772, n. 24.). The marketplace of ideas in many ways is wide open, while the marketplace of goods is severely controlled and regulated. And it is the First Amendment of the

Constitution that provides such a free marketplace of ideas with its protection.

Congress shall make no law respecting an establishment of religion, or prohibiting the free exercise thereof; or abridging the freedom of speech, or of the press; or the right of the people peaceably to assemble, and to petition the Government for a redress of grievances. (*Constitution of the United States, Amendment I*)

THE FIRST AMENDMENT AND POLITICAL ADVERTISING

Many legal scholars consider the First Amendment to be one of the most important tenets of the American system of government (see Meiklejohn, 1948, pp. 88-89; Middleton & Chamberlin, 1988). And for the most part, the American court system has encouraged political expression as part of our First Amendment rights (see *Federal Election Commission v. Central Long Island Tax Reform*, 1980 citing *Monitor Patriot Co. v. Roy*, 1971, and *Mills v. Alabama*, 1966). The courts have found, "There is a national commitment to principle that debate on public issues should be uninhibited, robust, and wide-open, and that it may well include vehement, caustic and sometimes unpleasantly sharp attacks on government and public officials" (U.S.C.A., Const. Amend. 1). "The constitutional protections for speech and press do not turn upon the truth, popularity, or social utility of the ideas and beliefs which are offered" (U.S.C.A., Const. Amend. 1). And "the constitutional protections for speech and press require a federal rule that prohibits a public official from recovering damages for a defamatory falsehood relating to his official conduct unless he proves that the statement was made with 'actual malice,' that is, with knowledge that it was false or with reckless disregard of whether it was false or not" (U.S.C.A. Const. Amends. 1, 14). The ability of public officials to sue and win damages in a libel case is drastically reduced by the "actual malice" standard.

In *New York Times Co. v. Sullivan*, the Supreme Court ruled that the constitutional guarantees of freedom of speech and of the press apply to political advertisements and reaffirmed that in order for public officials to recover damages for libelous statements made about their official conduct, they must prove "actual malice." The *Times* decision defined actual malice as "with knowledge that it was false or with reckless disregard of whether it was false or not" (*New York Times v. Sullivan*, 1964). Justice Brennan quoted an opinion written by Justice Burch of the supreme court of Kansas:

[I]t is of the utmost consequence that the people should discuss the character and qualifications of candidates for their suffrages. The importance to the state and to society of such discussions is so vast and the advantages derived are so great that they more than counterbalance the inconvenience of private persons whose conduct may be involved, and occasional injury to the reputations of individuals must yield to the public welfare, although at times such injury may be great. The public benefit from publicity is so great and the chance of injury is to private character so small that such discussion must be privileged. (*New York Times v. Sullivan,* 1964)

The *New York Times* decision reiterated the Supreme Court's ruling in the *Cantwell v. Connecticut* decision:

In the realm of religious faith, and in that of political belief, sharp differences arise. In both fields the tenets of one man may seem the rankest error to his neighbor. To persuade others to his own point of view, the pleader, as we know, at times, resorts to exaggeration, to vilification of men who have been, or are, prominent in church or state, and even to false statement. But the people of this nation have ordained in the light of history, that, in spite of the probability of excesses and abuses, these liberties are, in the long view, essential to enlightened opinion and right conduct on the part of the citizen of a democracy. '*Cantwell v. Connecticut,* 84 L. Ed. 1213, 1940, 84 S. Ct. 710 (1964).

It must be noted that while the *New York Times* decision's actual malice requirements only apply to defamatory comments concerning a public official's "official conduct," the Court "has interpreted official conduct broadly" (Middleton & Chamberlin, 1988, p. 107). In *Garrison v. Louisiana,* the district attorney of Orleans Parish, Louisiana, held a press conference in which he made disparaging comments about the parish's criminal district court judges. The district attorney attributed "a large backlog of pending criminal cases to the inefficiency, laziness, and excessive vacations of the judges." (1964, 13 L ed 2d 125, 85 S. Ct. 209). Although the lower courts had viewed these comments as pertaining to the judges' personal life, the Supreme Court disagreed. Justice Brennan wrote: "Anything which might touch on an official's fitness for office is relevant. Few personal attributes are more germane to fitness for office than dishonesty, malfeasance, or improper motivation, even though these characteristics may also affect the official's private character" (1964, 13 L ed 2d 125, 85 S. Ct. 209).

Political candidates for public office are considered public officials by the courts, which makes winning a libel suit by a candidate very difficult. The courts have held that public officials and, later, public figures—those who are "intimately involved in the resolution of important public questions or, by reason of their fame, shape events in areas of concern to society at large" (*Gertz v. Robert Welch, Inc.,* 1974)—invite attention and comment upon their public lives, and for this reason, the court has made it more difficult for a public official (or public figure) to prove libel. Thus *Gertz v. Welch* establishes two types of public figures: those who are public figures for all purposes and those who are public figures for a limited range of issues (limited-purpose public figures).

Judicial decisions suggest that it would be difficult for a candidate to win a libel suit against his or her opponent. Proving malice or reckless disregard is very difficult, and the courts, as we have seen, lean toward allowing a wide range of opinions in political settings.

Campaign Falsity Laws and Fair Campaign Practice Codes

As contemporary society has grappled with an increasingly negative political arena, a series of campaign falsity laws have been enacted in a number of states. These statutes—which are "usually enacted as part of a state's corrupt practices act—forbid the making, publishing or circulating of false statements about a candidate for public office" (Ryder, 1986, p. 73). And it is important to note that in *Friends of Phil Gramm v. Americans for Phil Gramm* (1984), the federal district court wrote,

The act nowhere specifically addresses the problem of fraud in political advertising. Congress obviously did not intend completely to preclude state regulation in the area, thus giving political organizations license to mislead. The only reasonable conclusion is that Congress intended to leave regulation of fraud in political advertising to the states. (p. 776)

From our own analysis of state election laws, as of August, 1995, 22 states had some type of campaign falsity laws (for earlier studies, see Albert, 1986; Caywood & Preston, 1989; Ryder, 1986; Winsbro, 1987). These laws range from a voluntary Fair Campaign Practice Code to mandatory libel and slander guidelines that may carry fines or imprisonment penalties. And in some instances, convicted candidates or officeholders may be removed from public office or removed from the party's nomination. Those states with some type of falsity laws or a Fair Campaign Practice Code are Alaska, California, Colorado, Florida, Hawaii, Illinois, Louisiana, Massachusetts, Minnesota, Mississippi, Montana, Nebraska, New York, North Carolina, North Dakota, Oregon, Tennessee, Texas, Utah, Washington, West Virginia, and Wisconsin.

The states of Montana, Illinois, California, New York, and Montana have adopted a Code of Fair Campaign Practices. These codes are restatements of the Fair Campaign Practices Commission's "Code of Fair Campaign Practices" (see Archibald, 1971; Sabato, 1981). No two codes are exactly alike; and the administration and enforcement of these codes varies as well. The Illinois Code of Fair Campaign Practices is provided as illustration (see Figure 8.1). In all four cases, the subscription to the code is voluntary, which precludes enforcement or punishment for lack of compliance. The Illinois Code stipulates the following:

Figure 8.1
The Illinois Code of Fair Campaign Practices

There are basic principles of decency, honesty, and fair play which every candidate for public office in the State of Illinois has a moral obligation to observe and uphold, in order that, after vigorously contested but fairly conducted campaigns, our citizens may exercise their constitutional right to a free and untrammeled choice and the will of the people may be fully and clearly expressed on the issues.

THEREFORE:

(1) I will conduct my campaign openly and publicly, and limit attacks on my opponent to legitimate challenges to his record.

(2) I will not use or permit the use of character defamation, whispering campaigns, libel, slander, or scurrilous attacks on any candidate or his personal or family life.

(3) I will not use or permit any appeal to negative prejudice based on race, sex, sexual orientation, religion or national origin.

(4) I will not use campaign material of any sort which misrepresents, distorts, or otherwise falsifies the facts, nor will I use malicious or unfounded accusations which aim at creating or exploiting doubts, without justification, as to the personal integrity or patriotism of my opposition.

(5) I will not undertake or condone any dishonest or unethical practice which tends to corrupt or undermine our American system of free elections or which hampers or prevents the full and free expression of the will of the voters.

(6) I will defend and uphold the right of every qualified American voter to full and equal participation in the electoral process.

(7) I will immediately and publicly repudiate methods and tactics that may come from others that I have pledged not to use or condone. I shall take firm action against any subordinate who violates any provision of this Code or the laws governing elections.

I, the undersigned, candidate for election to public office in the State of Illinois or chairman of a political committee in support of or opposition to a question of public policy, hereby voluntarily endorse, subscribe to, and solemnly pledge myself to conduct my campaign in accordance with the above principles and practices.

Date   Signature

Source: "Illinois Code of Fair Campaign Practices," 1990 (§ 3, eff. Sept. 8, 1989).

Any candidate or chairman of a political committee who subscribes to the Code of Fair Campaign Practices and fails to comply with any provision of such Code shall not be guilty of a criminal offense and nothing in this Act or any other law shall be construed to impose any criminal penalty for noncompliance with this Act. (1990, § 8, added by P.A. 86-1435, § 2, eff. Sept. 21, 1990)

In California, candidates are issued and are encouraged to sign a code form of the Code of Fair Campaign Practices when they declare their candidacy for public office. Completed forms are retained in the county clerk's office where the candidate resides and are available for public review until 30 days after the election. A California attorney general's opinion advises, "a state law or county ordinance requiring ballots to indicate whether candidates for elective county office have signed or refused to sign the Code of Fair Campaign Practices would violate guarantee of freedom of speech" (69 Op. Atty. Gen. 278, 1986). And on a similar matter, the California attorney general presented an opinion that stated,

A state law or county ordinance providing for a citizens advisory committee appointed by the board of supervisors which would hold hearings on complaints of unethical campaign practices and would publicize its findings prior to the election would violate guarantee of freedom of speech. (69 Op. Atty. Gen. 278, 1986)

Clearly the Fair Campaign Code in California has no teeth.

The New York Code was amended by the legislature to delete the passage that had candidates and campaign committee chairpersons pledge not to allow "attacks based on racial, religious or ethnic background and deliberate misrepresentations of a candidate's qualifications, position on a political issue, party affiliation or party endorsement" (L. 1978, c. 8, § 3, eff. Mar. 7, 1978). That amendment destroyed any ethical authority that the code may have had. The Montana "Fair Campaign Practice Code" exists without discussion of enforcement mechanisms. California and Montana statutes have certain falsity provisions in addition to the Code. Colorado's campaign falsity statute provides a brief example of the type of statutes that exist in 20 states (in that they deal in some manner with the issue of falsity):

§ 1-13-109. **False statements relating to candidates or questions submitted to electors—penalty.**

(1) No person shall knowingly make, publish, or circulate or cause to be made, published, or circulated in any letter, circular, advertisement, or poster or in any other writing any false statement designed to affect the vote on any issue submitted to the electors at any election or relating to any candidate for election to public office.
(2) Any person who knowingly violates any provision of this section commits a class 2 misdemeanor and, upon conviction thereof, shall be punished as provided in section 18-1-106, C.R.S. 1973.

Mississippi and Montana have more narrowly drawn their prohibitions against false political advertisements. Mississippi's statute declares that it is unlawful for a candidate to make any charge "reflecting upon the honesty, integrity, or moral character of any candidate, so far as his/her private life is concerned, unless the charge be in fact true and capable of proof" (Mississippi Corrupt Practices Law of 1935, § 23-3-33). Montana's statute makes it unlawful for a candidate to "publish any false statement or charge reflecting on any candidate's character or morality or knowingly misrepresent the voting record or position on public issues of any candidate" (*Montana Code Ann.* § 13-35-234, 1989).

Some states, such as Massachusetts, Minnesota, Mississippi, and Oregon, also make it illegal for candidates to make misrepresentations about themselves. Such misrepresentations might include who sponsored a political ad (Texas), the incorrect reporting of an endorsement in an ad or other publicity material (Texas, Washington, Utah), or misrepresentation of incumbency status by either using the title or requesting reelection for a post not previously held (Oregon, Texas).

Unlike the Fair Campaign Practice Codes, falsity laws potentially carry criminal penalties. Seven states provide guidelines for fines (West Virginia, less than $10,000; Florida, less than $5,000; Hawaii, greater than $100 and less than $1,000; Louisiana, less than $500; Massachusetts, less than $1,000; New York, less than $1,000; and Tennessee, less than $50) and five of those states provide additional specific imprisonment guidelines within the falsity law itself (West Virginia, less than 1 year; Hawaii, less than 2 years; Louisiana, less than 6 months; Massachusetts, less than 6 months; and Tennessee, less than 30 days). Hawaii, Oregon, Wisconsin, and Mississippi require that convicted candidates be removed from public office.

At least in some states, these codes have been upheld and enforced. In *Skibinski v. Tadych* (1966), the Wisconsin court held, "The making or publishing of false statements concerning a candidate must be deliberate, willful and substantial in order to constitute the basis of an ouster from office" (1966). In 1968 in *Cook v. Corbett*, the Oregon Supreme Court set aside Corbett's nomination because the court judged that the candidate had made misleading statements about herself during the campaign. Cook was declared the nominee, because he had finished the race in the number two spot (see Winsbro, 1987; *Cook v. Corbett*, 446 P. 2d 179, 1968). However, it is interesting to note that Oregon's falsity law isn't as tough as it seems, for the Oregon legislature that passed the law saw fit to exclude themselves from any removal-from-office penalty. The law reads,

260.532.(7). If a judgment is rendered in an action under this section against a defendant who has been nominated to public office or elected to a public office other than state Senator or state Representative, the defendant shall be deprived of the nomination or election and the nomination or office shall be declared vacant. (*State Political Action Legislation and Regulations*, 1984, pp. 483-484)

Hawaii's falsity law is very, very specific. It deals with only the publication of "a false statement of the withdrawal of any candidate at the election" (*Hawaii Code*, § 19-3 Election frauds. (6)). Yet the punishment is severe:

Every person found guilty of an election fraud shall be fined not less than $100 nor more than $1,000, or imprisoned at hard labor not more than two years, or both. Besides the punishment, the person shall be disqualified from voting and from being elected to, holding or occupying any office, elective or appointive. If the person so convicted holds office, either elective or appointive, at the time of the conviction, the office shall at once and without mention in the sentence or other proceeding be vacated by the conviction. (§ 19-4 Penalties)

Since 1900, however, there have been only two such instances where the state courts have set aside the results of an election because of violations of campaign falsity laws (Winsbro, 1987).

And in some instances, the campaign falsity laws may discourage voters and political candidates from bringing charges against a candidate for possible violations of the law because the law sets penalties for those making accusations, if the person charged is found innocent. In Florida, the Code begins with the following passage:

104.271 False or malicious charges against, or false statements about, opposing candidates; penalty.
(1) Any candidate who, in a primary election or other election, willfully charges an opposing candidate participating in such election with a violation of any provision of this code, which charge is known by the candidate making such charge to be false or malicious, is guilty of a felony of the third degree, punishable, as provided in § 775.082 or § 775.083; in addition, after his conviction he shall be disqualified to hold office.

In Mississippi if the alleged offender is acquitted, then the individual(s) bringing the charge shall be required to pay for all court proceedings (Mississippi Corrupt Practices Law of 1935, § 23-3-33).

While on the surface these campaign falsity laws may appear to rectify certain political grievances that may occur during the course of a campaign, the vast majority of these statutes are not worth much more than the paper they are written on. In *Vanasco v. Schwartz* (1975), the court warned that any "state regulation of campaign speech must conform to the 'actual malice' standard applicable to public fig-

ures set forth in *New York Times Co. v. Sullivan*" (Bott, 1990, p. 336).
Two states, Florida and Washington, have the "actual malice" provision, and four states—Montana, North Carolina, Ohio, and Oregon—
have chosen to use the legal definition of actual malice in their
statutes.

Courts in many states have effectively voided these acts by ruling
that they violate constitutional guarantees. In Louisiana, the falsity
law that prohibited anonymous publication of "scurrilous, false, or
irresponsible adverse comments" about candidates was found by the
courts to be in violation of the federal and state constitutional
guarantees of free speech (*State v. Burgess*, Sup. 1989). In that same
opinion, the court found as well that the law's prohibition against
falsely stating and circulating false information that a candidate was
endorsed or was supported by a particular group was also in violation
of the constitutional guarantees of free speech (*State v. Burgess*, Sup.
1989). And in Louisiana, in *Guste v. Connick*, the court held that although a political advertisement contained false comments regarding
an incumbent's official conduct and were also presented, in a deceptive
manner, there was not sufficient grounds to grant an injunction to stop
the broadcast of the ad. Further, such an injunction, if enacted, would
violate the opponent's rights of freedom of speech under the
Constitution (Sup. 1987). In Minnesota, the court held that false representation as to where a candidate obtained negative information concerning his opponent for a political ad did not violate the campaign
falsity law (*Grotjohn v. McCollar*, 1971). And "false and illogical inferences" and misleading campaign charges were found not to violate
the Minnesota falsity law (*Kennedy v. Voss*, 1981; *Bundlie v.
Christensen*, 1979).

While some state courts have found these acts to be unconstitutional, other state courts have allowed the application of the *New
York Times v. Sullivan's* "actual malice" standard, thus avoiding a
constitutional challenge (see Ryder, 1986; Malchow, 1981). Small
fines and short jail sentences have been added as criminal penalties to
the existing civil libel remedies. Because the "actual malice" standard is a difficult standard of proof to meet, few cases have been prosecuted under these statutes, and fewer defendants have been convicted.
A New York statute was held to be unconstitutional by a federal district court in New York in 1975 (*Vanasco v. Schwartz*). And the state
of Michigan repealed such a statute in 1975. Campaign falsity laws
are little more than a symbolic attempts to encourage fair campaigning.

One federal district court decision stands out as an anomaly. In
Tomei v. Finley (1981), Judge Milton Shadur stopped a local
Democratic party organization in Lyons Township, Illinois, from iden-

tifying itself as the "Representation for Every Person Party" and running ads that closed with "Vote REP April 7" (Albert, 1986). Shadur found the Democrats use of "REP" to be "deliberately false expression to the voters of the idea that the defendants are Republicans" (*Tomei v. Finley*, 1981). Therefore, he reasoned that their use of the acronym "REP" did not deserve First Amendment protection. Judge Shadur quoted the *Garrison v. Louisiana* decision in justification of his own ruling.

The use of the known lie as a tool is at once at odds with the premises of democratic government. . . . Hence, the knowingly false statement and the false statement made with reckless disregard of the truth do not enjoy constitutional protection. (*Garrison v. Louisiana, 1964,* at 75)

Shadur's use of "reckless disregard" or the actual malice standard is likely why the ruling has stood. However, in addition to the application of the actual malice standard, Shadur's decision made extensive use of false commercial advertising decisions which heretofore had not been used in political advertising decisions (see Albert, 1986). Because of the use of commercial advertising decisions, the *Tomei v. Finley* ruling stands alone among political advertising rulings. It is likely that if Shadur had used only the commercial speech arguments, the ruling would have been struck down by a higher court.

Because of our First Amendment protection, U.S. courts may find that a given ad is within the legal boundaries of political discussion, but the ad may still violate the ethical constructs of the political advertising profession and/or society at large. Such violations of accepted ethical constructs impact negatively on the quality of political debate.

POLITICAL ADVERTISING ETHICS

As we have discussed in Chapter 3, inherent in the social contract theory is the assumption of the rational actor, or the "rational human." The concept of the rational human describes an individual who not only is knowledgeable about politics but has an interest in it. Such individuals seeks information concerning the political issues of his or her day, they discuss and debate points of view with their friends, family, and business associates, and this discourse is characterized by thoughtful, informed reason and analysis. Ultimately, society arrives at a decision that is based, then, on reason.

Philosophically, the ultimate decision based on reason would reflect the public interest or shared values of society (Cooper, 1991). However, decisions that are based on the public interest can be made

only when the individuals involved have access to reliable information and have a process and environment established for open
discussion and debate.

Introductory courses in political science introduce students to the
social contract theory and its attendant concept's of the reasoned
human and the public interest. And while so doing, the instructors
warn that the social contract theory is an ideal of democratic government—one in fact that political scientists know we fall far short of as
a society. Many scholars blame our falling short of the ideal on the
use of television in American society (Cooper, 1991; Denton, 1991). As
mentioned in Chapters 1 and 2, Americans receive the majority of their
political information from television. And as Patterson (1980) and
others have indicated, voters receive the majority of their political
campaign information from political commercials, not political news.
Because this is true, an analysis of the ethical considerations in the
composition of political advertising is very important to the American
polity. Kaid (1991) warns that many political observers believe that
"political advertising is inherently unable to meet the tests of communication necessary to create good decision making" (p. 146).

Situational Ethics

In American society, there is no set of agreed-upon guidelines as to
how politicians should behave or act at all times. Rather, our society
has adopted an ethical view known as situational ethics. In short, the
behavior that our society will tolerate on the part of our political
leaders is related to the situation in which the behavior is performed
(Gronbeck, 1991). The situational ethics approach is not an ethical
philosophy that allows our political leaders "to get by with anything
and everything." Rather, we expect communication and other behaviors appropriate to the candidate's role in a given situation. These
behaviors are dictated by societal expectations or rules. Thus, voters
have "come to expect exaggeration in political campaigning but more
straightforward analyses of domestic and foreign problems in state-of-
the-union addresses." (Gronbeck, 1991, p. 60)

Judging the ethical posture of candidates situation by situation, thus, is terribly
complicated; situational ethics by its very nature is comparative rather than ab-
solutist, and demands of its adherents a willingness to make multiple readings
over time and a power to factor in many candidate performances before drawing
moral conclusions about the person. (Gronbeck, 1991, p. 61)

Gronbeck (1991) draws from Aristotle for an analysis of voters'
perceptions of ethical decision making in campaigns. From the *Poetics*,
Gronbeck uses Aristotle's three primary elements of drama: "action or

plot (mythos), character (ethos), and thought (dianoia)" (p. 52) to construct an analysis of the "ethical pivots around which assessments of campaign morality are made" (p. 52). For Gronbeck, voters make decisions based upon their ethical judgments of candidates, which are based on perceptions of public acts, most noticeably, talk. These ethical judgments are based on three things:

1. Candidates' actions and the *motives* they offer in justification of those actions.
2. Candidates' *character* (to Aristotle, the degree to which they exhibit good sense, goodwill, and acceptable morals in their talk).
3. Candidates' discussions of issues and the extent to which they illustrate their *competence* [emphasis in original] as governors. (Gronbeck, 1991, p. 52)

We believe ethical decisions are those decisions used to improve the public discussion of political issues by calling attention to, defining, clarifying, criticizing, and debating the issues of the day. For the most part, American political advertising is an ethical campaign practice. But in a small percentage of cases, deliberate misrepresentations, half-truths, lies, distortions, or innuendoes are used to smear a candidate's political record or personal qualifications for office (which includes the candidate's personal life). This type of deceptive campaign practice we have called dirty politics (Johnson-Cartee & Copeland, 1991a, 1991b).

In addition to dirty political ads we have also identified two other forms of political ads the use of which we judge to have an overall negative effect on the body politic. Ads that ignite social hatred among voters are examples of what we have termed hatred politics (Johnson-Cartee & Copeland, 1991b). Ads that offend the sensibilities of voters we have called bad taste ads (Johnson-Cartee & Copeland, 1991b)

Ultimate Accountability

Denton (1991) reminds the political observer that both political candidates and political consultants are intimately involved in the decision-making process of the campaign. But who is ultimately responsible for political advertising? It is our position that the ultimate responsibility must rest with the candidate. For it is the candidate who both approves of and pays for the political ad. Yet political candidates often try to escape their responsibility.

Career politicians, incumbents and challengers alike, try to place the blame for questionable ads on the backs of political consultants. In this way, candidates obfuscate who in fact is in charge. All too often, journalists and political leaders portray political consultants as political Svengalis who transform malleable candidates into fire-breathing dragons of unethical polispots.

In reality, political consultants and political candidates have a symbiotic relationship. They are mutually dependent on each other. One cannot exist, in this modern campaign age, without the other. But, it is an uneasy relationship in that the candidate is always the one who holds the purse strings and thus the one who should ultimately makes the decisions. The political consultant is an employee of the political candidate, and as such falls prey to the whims and prejudices of the candidate. Granted, the political consultant has an unusual advantage in that the consultant is a specialist in persuasive communication. Because of this, political consultants may have an advantage in any campaign discussion for two reasons: (1) they are able to articulate their rationale in a persuasive manner, and (2) they are able to remind their employer that they were hired in the first place to be expert political communicators.

The point that must be stressed here is that the political consultant wields power only with the awareness and approval of the candidate. All candidates know that after the election they must live with the legacy of their campaign behavior. In other words, a candidate cannot afford to be disgraced by dirty lies, hatred politics, or bad taste ads. If these tactics are used and later exposed by either the media or an opponent, the candidate may not be able to afford the loss of credibility. After the election, it will be the candidate who must explain his or her unethical behavior. And it will be the candidate that history remembers as a dirty trickster. Consultants also carry their own baggage with them. Consultants are fond of saying that they are only as good as their last race, meaning only as good as their last win. But that saying is a double-edged sword, in that consultants have their own ethical credibility problems as well. A consultant who sells his or her soul in order to win is forever tainted, and only those candidates willing to sell their own souls will darken their doors. The result is a permanent position on the fringes of acceptable political society.

Unfortunately, negative political advertising has been inaccurately portrayed and perceived as being the only unethical form of political campaigning (Felknor, 1992; Johnson-Cartee & Copeland, 1991a, 1991b). For this reason, negative political ads have received far more attention than other forms of political advertising when dealing with the question of ethics. Journalists analyze negative polispots as part of their metacampaign analysis. Yet they rarely, if at all, bother to examine a positive political commercial. Political ads, whether they are positive or negative, may be true or false, ethical or unethical, and as such, they should be judged on the basis of the quality of the argument, not upon the mode of argumentation.

A 1990 Alabama attorney general race provides numerous examples of positive ads that crossed ethical boundaries. Democratic candidate Jimmy Evans told voters in a positive spot that as Montgomery County district attorney, he had been a champion for child support collections. But in reality, Evans had one of the worst records in the state, ranking 62 out of 67 child support collection officials. In a series of political spots, Evans told Alabama voters that he had personally prosecuted more than 17,000 cases in his years as Montgomery county district Attorney. In reality, Evans had personally prosecuted only about 200, and one fourth of those had been overturned by the Alabama Supreme Court because of "prosecutorial errors" in the courtroom, that is, Evans's mistakes. This case illustrates that all forms of political advertising—positive, negative, inoculation, or response ads—should be examined.

Dirty lies are deliberate lies or half-truths propagated about a candidate's political record or personal qualifications in order to destroy his or her candidacy. Most frequently, dirty lies appear during the last days of the campaign, when the likelihood of discovery and exposure is drastically reduced because of time constraints (see Jamieson & Campbell, 1983). Many of these so-called dirty tricks have been associated with independent political action committees such as the Christian Voice Moral Government Fund, the National Conservative Political Action Committee, and other organizations (Johnson-Cartee & Copeland, 1991a; Kaid, 1991). However, examples of candidate-sponsored dirty lies during any recent campaign season are all too abundant.

Society determines for itself what is true and what is false. These determinations may vary over time, as societal ethics are constantly evolving. An examination of the significance of truth and relevance for political debate in the United States and a discussion of the various manifestations of dirty lies and hatred politics will be presented.

"Truth becomes important to us, one must assume, in part because certitude is comforting in a world of flux, in part because truths are measuring rods against which we can assess the motives, character, and competence of others" (Gronbeck, 1991, p. 59). Andreñ (1980) argues that truthful advertising is a rarity, and therefore ads should be judged on a continuum of truth or falsity. He maintains that the truthfulness of an ad should be judged on the basis of whether it is objective and informative. "Communication designed to influence the behavior of an audience is objective and informative to the extent that it corresponds to the facts, is relevant, comprehensive, adequately supported, intelligible, and propositional" (Andreñ, 1980, p. 75). Similarly, Felknor (1992) suggests that the key to an ethical analysis of political advertising rests in the "dual issue of truth and relevance" (p. 30).

In a 1990 congressional race in Alabama, the Republican challenger promised to reduce property taxes and to increase taxes on "trees." A central issue in this local race dealt with the equity of extremely low property taxes for unimproved land and timberland. Billboards and other printed advertisements promised action on these two property tax issues. Yet the ad was not relevant. The Congress of the United States does not have anything to do with property taxes; therefore, the argument was specious. In addition to being irrelevant, the ads were misleading, in that they suggested to the unwary voter that the candidate if elected to Congress would have domain over this issue.

In the 1990 North Carolina and Minnesota Senate races, candidate-sponsored ads reported that their opposition supported abortions in the last month of pregnancy at taxpayers' expense. In both situations, these charges were outright lies. In 1988, the "Illinois Republican Party mailed leaflets charging that murderers, rapists, drug pushers and child molesters vote for Dukakis" (Martz, Warner, Fineman, Clift, & Starr, 1988, p. 16).

As modern digital technology has become more advanced, the possibility for visual lies has increased (see Kaid, 1991). Kaid (1991) has identified the principal areas of concern with the use of television technology: "(1) editing techniques, (2) special effects, (3) visual imagery/dramatizations, (4) computerized alteration techniques, and (5) subliminal techniques" (p. 153). We have already begun to see abuses of these modern technologies.

In the 1992 presidential campaign, the Bush team ran an ad that featured Bill Clinton on the cover of *Time* magazine with the cover headline: "Why Voters Don't Trust Clinton." The cover was a complete fabrication. In the 1990 Alabama gubernatorial campaign, Republican incumbent Guy Hunt used a series of negative spots that charged that Democratic challenger Paul Hubbert, president of the Alabama Education Association, had stopped the governor's education bill in the legislature. The ads used a newspaper story and headline that supported the charge. The problem was that on close inspection, the newspaper copy concerned postal workers and the story's headline had been computer generated. The ad was a total fabrication. When Hunt was asked by a Birmingham television reporter why this had occurred, he responded by saying that "everybody does it." The Hunt campaign pulled the ads. In the 1990 Texas gubernatorial race, Democratic candidate Ann Richards used "doctored" newspaper headlines in order to portray her Republican opponent Clayton Williams as a financial deadbeat. But Clayton Williams wasn't clean in the dirty politics arena, either. According to *The People for the American Way*, Williams produced a spot that presented a totally "inaccurate depiction of Treasurer Richards' role in the savings and loan crisis" (1990, p. 8).

The source of political advertising is a particularly critical bit of information for voters to know, for voters often make their assessment of the truth or veracity of the ad based upon the source of the ad. For this reason, the Federal Election Commission as well as various state election laws have required political commercials to display the sponsorship of the ad. Yet political candidates and their consultants often work to weaken the impact of that notification either by imbedding the disclaimer within the ad or by using innocuous names to neutralize their own political affiliations.

Highly vituperative ads often have the sponsorship appearing in the opening seconds of the ad; in this way, consultants hope that the viewer might forget or not even notice the source of the scurrilous attack by the end of the ad. The source of the ad often does not seem important to the viewer until the end of an ad. Viewers are more likely to make note of the source of the negative attack when the sponsorship message is at the end of the ad. When the source is at the beginning, viewers have not had the opportunity to discover the negativity of the ad at the time they see the source. Therefore they do not attempt to remember the source in order to place blame on it. Are these sleights of hand, legal? Yes. Are they ethical? That is not as clear.

Political consultants have found clever ways of obfuscating the sponsor disclosure requirements for political advertising. Perhaps the most popular disclosure is "Paid for by the Friends of John Doe," although some consultants have done as Tony Schwartz has suggested and ended with an even more informal disclosure: "And that's exactly why this message was brought to you by a lot of people who want Bob Jones in the Senate" (Schwartz, 1976, p. 349). Such folksy tags have been called "no-tag tags" (Jamieson & Campbell, 1983). The use of these no-tag tags increases the likelihood that political advertisements will be mistaken for other programming such as news (see Jamieson & Campbell, 1983).

Often political ads will simply obfuscate the political realities of the time. During the 1992 election cycle, the Republican National Committee ran a series of spots attacking the Democratic-controlled Congress. The spots told a story of a Congress totally dominated by one party. The spots ignored the bipartisan nature of the American legislative process, which can only be characterized by individualism, negotiation, and incrementalism, and instead presented

the American Congress as a functioning legislature in the British par-
liamentary mode, which can only be characterized by its strict adher-
ence to party discipline. These ads attempted to oversimplify the
democratic process, and by so doing, mislead the voters.

Frequently an incumbent's voting/attendance records are unfairly
manipulated to form damning attacks by the challenger. Many people
do not understand or they may not even be aware of how a bill becomes
a law, and for this reason, political action committees and some
candidates have often slanted the facts for their own political gain.
Ads that attack a politician's voting record may be very misleading in
that, frequently, unrelated riders are attached to popular bills so that
they can sneak into law through the back door. A congressman or
senator may feel forced to vote against a bill that he or she might
ordinarily support because of the unsatisfactory rider.

In other situations, the original bill may be so important to the
individual congressional representative or senator's constituency that
he or she feels forced to support the bill even though the member of
Congress may disagree with the rider. Frequently, these riders are not
minor pieces of legislation, but rather are significant in not only scope
but also cost and effect. In other situations, congressional representatives and senators may vote for a rather general funding bill that gives
moneys to various agencies for distribution. Frequently decisions about
how the money is actually spent are decided on the state or local
level. A number of misleading ads have been used to suggest that a
member of Congress voted Nay or Yea on a very specific controversial
program, when in fact the political leader may have voted for a very
general bill that is later translated into specific policy by others much
farther down the ladder of command. The representative or senator is
then blamed for how the money was distributed when election time
rolls around. As George Will has so aptly put it, "They use something
technically true . . . in a fundamentally dishonest way" (1989, p. 92).

In a 1990 Michigan Senate race, Republican U.S. Representative
Bill Schuette produced a spot titled "Levin of Arabia" attacking
Democratic Senator Carl Levin. Because Levin had voted against
several Pentagon recommendations, Schuette showed pictures of our
troops in the Persian Gulf and told Michigan voters: "If Levin had his
way, he wouldn't have a ship to stand on . . . and neither would our
troops" (Garfield, 1990, p. 28). Garfield (1990) concluded that
Schuette did everything but call Levin a traitor (p. 28).

Felknor (1992) wrote that "Concerns over loyalty and patriotism
have bubbled through the American polity at irregular intervals and
levels of intensity since colonial days. . . . But stewing about what
loyalty and patriotism may demand of a free people has never en-
tirely subsided" (p. 125). This bubbling concern over patriotism raised

its head during the 1988 presidential campaign when Bush attacked
Dukakis over his stand on the so-called flag and pledge of allegiance
controversy. And during the 1992 campaign, Bush attacked Clinton for
avoiding the draft and for protesting against the Viet Nam War on
foreign soil. Patriotism, like beauty, is in the eye of the beholder.
Many Viet Nam War protesters thought that they were exercising
their freedom of political speech in protesting what they perceived to
be an unjust war. Many of these young men and women viewed their actions as being patriotic.

Hatred politics is a form of the Us versus the Different political
strategy (Johnson-Cartee & Copeland, 1991a, 1997). Such ads employ
a strategy of fear. Candidates and their consultants discover what
people fear the most, and then they focus on those themes, riding a
wave of discontent. Alabama's George Wallace's long career as an
Alabama legislator, judge, governor, and presidential candidate was
sprinkled with negative political advertising that can only be
characterized as hatred politics. Wallace channeled people's fears,
whether they were fears concerning blacks, economic displacement,
competition, or loss of social status (see Carlson, 1981; Hogan, 1984;
Orum, 1972), into support for Wallace, the leader. Wallace crusaded
against the so-called enemies of the people such as African-
Americans, tax-exempt foundations, public utilities, state universities,
pointy-headed intellectuals, know-nothing federal judges, and a host
of others. Wallace offered no solutions. What he did offer the people
was a belief in George Wallace. Wallace's type of protest politics
thrives on "turmoil, excitement, discord. He is interested in exploiting
issues, not solving problems" ("Poisoned Cup," 1972, p. 36).

Republican Senator Jesse Helms of North Carolina provides
another example of hatred politics. In Helms's early years, we find
the same antiblack rhetoric now forever associated with George
Wallace, but recently Helms has expanded his campaigns' most hated
list to include those who support birth control, sex education, rock music, and abortion as well as feminists, teachers, homosexuals, and
artists. In 1990, Helms reintroduced race into his campaign against
black challenger Harvey Gantt. Helms exploited white voters' fears
concerning economic displacement by blacks and the effects of affirmative action on white blue-collar workers. In addition, Helms used implied negative arguments that contained highly emotion-laden negative stereotypes of African American behavior in society.

Hatred politics introduces a divisive element in any campaign.
Its tactics are troubling in that they promote alienation and they
capitalize on the troubling divisions in American society. With the
introduction of destructive, centrifugal forces into the political arena,
society often fails to move forward in harmony but instead scatters in

disharmony. Hatred politics obfuscates the very real issues facing American voters and their political leaders. We believe that America should be an egalitarian society—a society where all individuals are equal with respect to social, political, and economic rights without regard to race, ethnicity, religion, gender, and sexual preference. We believe that to suggest otherwise is to violate the very principles on which the United States was founded.

Some ads are simply in bad taste. Ads that are in poor taste anger the viewer, yet the anger is not directed toward the desired target but rather the sponsor. One consultant said that "bad taste" ads leave the audience with a sense of revulsion. Democratic pollster Mark Mellman suggests that bad taste spots are like bad situation comedies, "they don't last very long" (Hagstrom & Guskind, 1986, p. 2621).

We (Johnson and Copeland, 1987; see also Johnson-Cartee & Copeland, 1989b) found that many voters believe that attacks against a candidate's personal life are "out of bounds" (see also Roddy & Garramone, 1988; Shapiro & Rieger, 1989). In 1990, Republican Senator Rudy Boshwitz of Minnesota ran a bad taste ad against his underfunded Democratic challenger Paul Wellstone. Both Wellstone and Boshwitz are Jewish. In a direct mail campaign, Boshwitz criticized Wellstone for raising his children as "non-Jews" and suggested that Wellstone had neglected his Jewish roots. Minnesota voters rejected their incumbent senator in favor of Wellstone.

In addition, some analysts suggest that not all attacks on a candidate's record are accepted by the voter. In a 1986 Missouri Senate race, Democratic candidate Harriet F. Woods aired a "crying farmer" spot against her opponent former governor Christopher S. ("Kit") Bond. The spot, which was produced by Democratic consultant Robert Squier, showed a farmer sobbing "as he recounted losing his family farm and an announcer linked Bond to the company that foreclosed on the farm" (Hagstrom & Guskind, 1986, p. 2624). "'Almost as sad as a family leaving its farm,' says the announcer in Bond's response, over a split-screen image of Bond and the sobbing farmer, 'is a politician using their pain for political advantage'" (Hagstrom & Guskind, 1986, p. 2624). The news media heavily criticized the original spot, calling it "sleazy and shallow" and in "poor taste" (Hagstrom & Guskind, 1986, p. 2624). Bad taste ads don't make good sense. They are one type of negative spot that is almost sure to boomerang.

Summary

Dirty political ads, hatred ads, and bad taste ads harm the election process by eroding voter confidence in political advertising. If a campaign is filled with ads that are lies or are built on gross distortions of the truth, the electorate will come to discount political advertising. The loss of effectiveness of political advertising would mean the lack of ability to define issues, character, or style by a candidate's campaign.

Luckily, unethical ads are rare, for a number of reasons. First and foremost is the central role of the news media and its position as the self-appointed arbiter of the political system (see Diamond & Bates, 1988; Hagstrom & Guskind, 1986). Political consultant Bradley S. O'Leary explains that "the press regulates political broadcasts every day. If we say anything that's untrue, it's on the evening news the next day. And don't forget our candidates are also punished by the voters if we say or do something wrong" (quoted in Tucker & Heller, 1987, p. 46). Similarly, Democratic media consultant David Sawyer maintains that "the marketplace works. You try to put an unsubstantiated ad on TV and in 48 hours the press will be all over your case" (quoted in Taylor, 1986, p. A7). However, some research has indicated that media criticism of political advertising may actually create an undesirable effect as less-educated voters and female viewers may interpret the criticism as being in support of the targeted ad, and when this occurs, the influence of the ad goes up (Cappella & Jamieson, 1994; Jamieson, 1992; Pfau & Louden, 1994). And perhaps most important, research has shown that for well-educated viewers, media criticism may have the desired effect in terms of "punishing" the sponsor of the questionable ad; however, such criticism of the sponsor has not been shown to salvage the damaged reputation of the candidate who was attacked (Cappella & Jamieson, 1994).

Secondly, an unethical ad may give the attacked candidate an opportunity to counterattack the character and integrity of the attacking candidate. Dirty political ads leave the sponsor, whether it is a PAC or a candidate, vulnerable to counterattack (see Heller, 1987). No one likes a liar. The credibility of the sponsoring candidate is thrown into limbo, and everything said by the candidate is then called into question. Hatred political spots and bad taste ads alienate large segments of the population. In such a situation, the sponsor may be counterattacked by ads that call into question his or her judgment or moral authority.

PROPOSED REMEDIES FOR UNETHICAL POLITICAL ADVERTISING

Because dirty politics does exist in America—albeit constituting a small percentage of political advertising—journalists, political leaders, and other social commentators have suggested a variety of political advertising reforms. While reforms are often discussed, actual changes are much less common.

Review Committees

The Fair Campaign Practices Committee's mission was to condemn "the use of campaign material of any sort which represents, distorts, or otherwise falsifies the facts regarding any candidate" (Tucker & Heller, 1987, p. 45). The FCPC was formed in 1954 by a group of citizens concerned about both the potential and actual abuses of political advertising. Clearly the committee's focus was on "dirty politics." According to Tucker and Heller (1987), the FCPC

initially accomplished a great deal. The group acted as a clearinghouse of complaints, an investigator of wrongdoing, and an arbiter of fairness. It followed up alleged deviations from the code with an in-house investigation, discussions, and recommendations. (p. 45)

If the FCPC discovered unethical advertising, they would ask the offending party to either change the spot or retract it. And if the campaign refused, the FCPC would threaten to expose them in the news media (see Tucker & Heller, 1987).

The FCPC lasted twenty years. Felknor (1992) attributes its demise to its weak financial situation and to "almost unceasing harassment by the Internal Revenue Commission (later Service)" (p. 232). Felknor (1992) suggests that conservative House and Senate members "sicced the IRS" on the FCPC (p. 232). While in operation, the Fair Campaign Practices Committee averaged 65-67 complaints each year (Archibald, 1971; Tucker & Heller, 1987).

Spero (1980) has called for the formation of a "political fact bank" that would monitor all political campaign communication. The political fact bank would judge all political campaign communications by a "code of political campaign ethics and citizen action" that would be modeled after the standards used to measure false and deceptive product advertising. The political fact bank would identify violations of the code and would then produce and air counteradvertising that would expose the "untruths" to the voters. Felknor (1992) has warned that any such resurrection of the FCPC must have adequate funding, bipartisan support, and tax-exempt status.

Similarly, Garfield (1990) suggested that the Advertising Council take an active role in policing negative spots by what he called counteradvertising. This counteradvertising would be in the form of a "Just say no to sleaze" public service announcement campaign during election cycles (p. 29). In addition, Garfield recommended that all political ads contain a standard disclaimer: "WARNING: POLIT-ICAL ADVERTISING CAN LEGALLY DISTORT THE TRUTH" (1990, p. 29).

Congressional Legislation

Caywood and Preston (1989) warned that American political advertising is in jeopardy. They wrote, "'Jeopardy' as used here means a threat to the protected status of political advertising, which would mean increased regulation of this ever more controversial type of marketing communication" (p. 204). According to Caywood and Preston (1989), judicial rulings have relied on a laissez-faire theory when interpreting the First Amendment. Laissez-faire is a "broad and permissive theoretical framework designed primarily to protect the speaker by leaving the sender alone" (Caywood & Preston, 1989, p. 218). This concept allows government to take a nonactive role in eval-uating free speech. However, recently legal scholars have articulated a new interpretation of the First Amendment, which they have called affirmative theory. In his call for an affirmative theory of First Amendment interpretation, Emerson (1981) argues that the government should actively work to protect the listener. "The concept of right-to-know, listener's rights and balanced presentations are part of the af-firmative theory formula to give more power to the receiver of mes-sages including political advertising" (Caywood & Preston, 1989, p. 219; see Clinger, 1987, for discussion of affirmative theory).

The affirmative theory is clearly reflected in bills introduced in the U.S. Senate during the past ten years that would have regulated political advertising. However, none of these bills has been passed into law.

Professional Code of Ethics

Codes of ethics and behaviors have been created generally for protection: protection from the inside and outside (see Black & Barney, 1985-1986). People usually think of codes as primarily being for the use of the membership, a method for the organization to establish and enforce professional rules of conduct. These codes serve to guide neo-phytes as to what is acceptable practice (see Black & Barney, 1985-1986). Codes depict a professional as "bound by certain ethical princi-ples *and* [emphasis in the original] as incorporating those principles into his or her very character" (Lebacqz, 1985, pp. 63-91).

In many ways, codes of ethics are more important to an organi-zation for the protection they provide from outside critics. Codes serve as a shield against angry clients, audiences, and government. When someone objects to the behavior within the group, the group can claim such behavior as being aberrant because the individual failed to follow the code of ethics. Thus, codes serve to buffer the group from criticism targeted at a single member. Codes also provide evidence of self-regulation and self-control. Such codes serve as prima facie evidence that there is an internal mechanism available to control the behavior of members. With internal codes in place, there will be fewer calls for external controls to be imposed.

The writers of codes of behaviors generally take one of two approaches: delineating the minimal standards of conduct to comply with legal obligations or attempting to lift the profession by setting out behaviors that the ideal member would display (Elliott-Boyle, 1995-1986). These two different approaches to ethical codes suggest two separate approaches to their use for political consulting.

The minimalist code of ethics generally concerns itself with what is legal. Such a code serves as a reminder that there are laws that must be obeyed and as a warning that some actions may be criminal or actionable in civil courts (Elliott-Boyle, 1985-1986). What serves as its inspiration is not a sense of core values but an awareness of legal necessity. Following such minimalist rules is legally important but is not worthy of note. The behaviors are typical.

A minimalist code that stresses only the legal demarcations does not better the field. It also fails to inspire people to produce better work. Clearly an ad may be legal but still not ethical. Such a minimalist code does nothing to stop or inhibit the use of unethical ads. Deceptive political advertising, speaks to the worst in campaign tactics.

The establishment of a code of ethics that creates ideals to which practitioners should aspire moves the discussion away from one of jurisprudence to one of moral philosophy. It asks us to determine what set of core values we as an organized profession hold in common. Core beliefs serve as the force that holds organizations together. The assumption is that people want to meet the ideals of their normative reference group. The use of the ideal for the code of ethics provides a set of general guidelines that may be applied to test for consistency between actions and beliefs. It provides a ruler that may be applied across circumstances and time.

It should not be the intent of a code of ethics to create a situation where people may moralize; rather, the code provides guidance and consistency. As Black and Barney (1985-1986) note, there is a difference between moral philosophy and moralizing. Moralizing is usually a means of providing dogmatic decisions delivered from a self-perceived superior position. The most difficult part of establishing a code that expresses the ideals of the practice is attempting to exactly isolate core beliefs. In any organization, there are differing ideological views. However, a core of beliefs should stretch across the differences among ideologies.

In September of 1975, the American Association of Political Consultants (AAPC) adopted a code of ethics (see Figure 8.2). Sabato (1981) provides an excellent discussion of the AAPC and the ethics code. According to Sabato (1981), many of the clauses of the code were taken from the "Code of Fair Campaign Practices (drawn up by the Fair Campaign Practices Commission) and the 'Code of Ethics for Political Campaign Advertising' of the American Association of Advertising Agencies" (p. 304).

Figure 8.2
Code of Professional Ethics

As a member of the American Association of Political Consultants, I believe there are certain standards of practice which I must maintain. I, therefore, pledge to adhere to the following Code of Ethics:

I shall not indulge in any activity which would corrupt or degrade the practice of political campaigning.

I shall treat my colleagues and my clients with respect and never intentionally injure their professional or personal reputation.

I shall respect the confidence of my client and not reveal confidential or private information obtained during our professional relationship.

I will use no appeal to voters which is based on racism or discrimination and will condemn those who use such practices. In turn, I will work for equal voting rights and privileges for all citizens.

I will refrain from false and misleading attacks on an opponent or member of his family and shall do everything in my power to prevent others from using such tactics.

I will document accurately and fully any criticism for an opponent of his record.

I shall be honest in my relationship with the press and candidly answer questions when I have the authority to do so.

I shall not support any individual or organization which resorts to practices forbidden in this code.

_____   _____
Signature   Date
Code of Professional Ethics of the AAPC.

Source: Obtained from the American Association of Political Consultants, December 1989.

Today, new applicants for membership in the AAPC are required to sign the eight-point "Code of Professional Ethics." As practicing professionals, consultants are encouraged to have their clients read and sign the code as well. While members are required to sign the code, there is no enforcement mechanism for a member who should run afoul of one of the provisions of the code. An ethics committee does hear complaints against members, but it has no punitive powers.

While some would have the AAPC serve as the political advertising equivalent of the chief product advertising regulator, the Federal Trade Commission, the AAPC does not see its role in this light (Sabato, 1981). Although the AAPC has no enforcement procedures or punitive measures for violations of the code, the code still serves an important purpose.

The existence of the code presumes that as a group the AAPC has decided that political consultants should be guided by an ethical code that discourages political consultants from believing that the ends justify the means. The existence of the code suggests that there are limitations as to what a consultant should do for his or her candidate and against the opponents. The words of Tommy Ross, a pioneer in public relations, seem well suited for inclusion here: "Unless you are willing to resign an account or a job over a matter of principle, it is no use to call yourself a member of the world's newest profession--for you are already a member of the world's oldest" (quoted in Wilcox, Ault, & Agee, 1986, p. 119).

Journalists

David Broder (1990) has called upon American journalists to stem the tide of unethical advertising by working to police the political arena. According to Broder, journalists must exercise a "preemption strategy" that would successfully take the definition of the campaign agenda away from the candidates and their campaigns by offering through their news copy the voters' agenda. Journalists would determine what the voters cared about through the use of public opinion polls and discussions with voters. Candidates who attempted to turn the public debate to their own agenda would be called back to the voters' agenda through persistent questioning on the part of reporters. In addition, Broder suggests that reporters should remind voters of how their emotions have been manipulated in the past. And he suggests that old unethical ads should be shown again before the campaign season starts so that voters will be inoculated against such manipulations. Further, reporters should interrogate candidates about their ads. Broder wrote, "The press should establish, at the outset of the campaigns, one simple ground rule: The candidates will be available to answer questions about every ad, every piece of direct mail, that goes out of their headquarters, at the time it goes on the air or into the mail" (1990, p. B1).

In addition, Broder suggests that reporters should investigate the claims and evidence presented in the ad. They should require documentation from candidates as to the veracity of the ad, and they should maintain contacts with the opposition to receive any rebuttal information available. By carefully analyzing the ads and by reporting to the voters when they find ads that are unethical, reporters will improve the quality of political debate. Reports that discuss unethical ads should clearly highlight problem areas, provide evidence as to unethical nature of the ad, and report such information in plain language so that the voters understand the severity of the offense. And Broder does not stop with the reporters' role in this policing operation. He maintains that "columnists, commentators and editorial writers have the license—and the obligation—to apply verbal heat to those who sabotage the election process by their paid-media demagoguery. And the evidence suggests that such denunciations can have an effect" (1990, p. B1). He argues, as does Jamieson (1992), that news stories that merely focus on the "negativity" or "manipulative" nature of ads do little to hurt those who engage in unethical practices. Similarly, West (1992) writes,

Currently, reporters fall far short of the advertising coverage needed to uphold democratic elections. They devote extensive attention to candidate ads, but not necessarily in a way that furthers the substantive knowledge of citizens. They are more likely, for example, to use ads to discuss the horserace than the policy views of the candidates. (p. 76)

Broadcast news stories that replay deceptive ads accompanied by inadequate critical commentary merely serve to reinforce the ad's messages. To be effective, Broder (1990) argues, news stories must expose and denounce unethical ads. Similarly, West (1992) calls on the news media to develop a "truth in political advertising code which would feature a prominent oversight role for the media" (p. 76). Such a code, West argues, would "allow journalists to exercise their historic function of safeguarding the integrity of the elections process" (1992, p. 76). Broder ends his five-point agenda by arguing that reporters "need to become partisan—not on behalf of a candidate or party—but on behalf of the process" (1990, p. B1).

THE BROADCAST MEDIA

Although the American news media are said to be protected by the First Amendment, newspapers and other print publications enjoy a wider degree of freedom than do the broadcast news media. While the print media have no legal obligations to accept political advertising or to present political news in a fair or impartial way, the broadcast media do have certain legal obligations that must be met (see Middleton & Chamberlin, 1988; *Miami Herald Publishing Co. v. Tornillo*, 1974).

Historically, the public airwaves were considered to be a scarce public resource and because a radio station's signal could cross state lines, radio was placed under federal control because it was considered interstate commerce. Federal control of broadcasting was codified with the Radio Act of 1927. Stations were initially licensed to specific operators (Middleton & Chamberlin, 1988). In order to obtain a license, broadcasters had to agree to operate in the "public's interest, convenience, and necessity," and the Federal Radio Commission (FRC) was created to ensure that the broadcasters lived up to their license obligations (Radio Act of 1927). This tripartite standard of operating in the "public's interest, convenience, and necessity" has served as the yardstick by which regulating bodies have measured license applications and applications for license renewal since that time. This tripartite standard served as a "bootstrap" by which the FRC and later the Federal Communications Commission (FCC) were able to promulgate rules that would be deemed unconstitutional for the print medium.

Broadcast Political Commercials

Early in this century, broadcast political advertising was recognized as an important element of a democratic society. The Federal Radio Act of 1927 (Section 18) forbade the censorship of political broadcasts, and this commitment to freedom of speech was continued under the Section 315 of the Communications Act of 1934 and its subsequent renewals.

Access and Equal Opportunities

Although Section 315 does not require that stations provide time for political candidates, Section 312(a)(7) requires that broadcasters provide reasonable access for federal candidates 45 days before a primary election and 60 days before a general election. While stations are not obligated to sell a candidate a specific time during the day, they are required to provide advertising time during prime time and key viewing hours (see Middleton & Chamberlin, 1988). Although Section 312(a)(7) does not provide the same protection or benefits for state and local candidates, the FCC has ruled that its public interest standard requires broadcasters to devote substantial time to state and local political campaigns. However, the public interest standard and the requirement for substantial time have in no way been quantified, and no requirement exists that broadcast licensees must provide time and opportunity for every candidate (Middleton & Chamberlin, 1988, p. 555; see Law of Political Broadcasting and Cablecasting, 1978)

However, Section 315 requires broadcasters to provide equal opportunities for all candidates in the same political race. If a station airs an ad from one political candidate, other candidates for the same office must be given equal opportunities to purchase time, whether the race is federal, state, or local. "Equal opportunities" has sometimes been called "equal time," but the requirement for equal opportunities goes beyond just equal time. "It means the right to obtain time in a period likely to attract approximately the same audience as the period in which the opposing candidate appeared" (Law of Political Broadcasting and Cablecasting, 1978) for the same amount of money, that is, at the same rate. Section 315 forbids "any discrimination between candidates in rates or in any other way" (1978, 2219).

The equal opportunities provision applies only to uses of broadcast stations. A use is any broadcast that contains the candidate's voice or picture. A use may occur even if the candidate is not talking about his candidacy. During Ronald Reagan's 1980 and 1984 campaigns, television stations did not show any motion pictures in which Reagan appeared, as such a showing would constitute a use under FCC regulations, and the station would be required to provide equal opportunities to other candidates running for the same office. If a supporter of a candidate appears in the ad but the voice or picture of the candidate is not aired, then it is not considered a use. Newscasts and other news programs are exempted from the use rule, and therefore they are exempt from the equal opportunities provision.

However, broadcast stations are not under any legal obligations to notify candidates that their opposition has used the airwaves. Candidates and their campaign organizations must monitor the airwaves themselves; however, that information is not difficult to obtain, in that the broadcast station's political file is required to be open for public inspection. After discovering a use, a campaign must act to request equal opportunities within seven days of the opposition's use of the station, or the candidate will lose his or her right for equal opportunities (*Law of Political Broadcasting and Cablecasting*, 1978).

Legally Qualified Candidate

Candidates must be deemed legally qualified before they are provided equal opportunities. Legally qualified candidates are those individuals who meet the legal qualifications for office and who have publicly announced their candidacies. In addition, the candidate must have either qualified for a place on the ballot or have mounted a visible write-in campaign (*Law of Political Broadcasting and Cablecasting*, 1978).

No Censorship

Section 315 forbids broadcast stations from censoring any political messages broadcast by legally qualified candidates. This applies only to political programs or announcements (political advertising spots) that are aired because the candidate has purchased time from the station for their dissemination. Again, for the no-censorship rule to apply, the program or announcement must be considered a use. In other words, "if a candidate makes any appearance in which he is identified or identifiable by voice or picture, even if it is only to identify sponsorship of the spot, the whole announcement will be considered a use" (*Law of Political Broadcasting and Cablecasting*, 1984 , p. 20), and the spot cannot be censored.

The broadcast station

cannot refuse to carry his broadcast even if it contains libelous material or is vulgar or in "bad taste." It cannot require the candidate to appear either live or on tape, or even ask to preview his script or pre-audition his tape or film, except to learn (1) whether it contains the required sponsorship identification (if it is paid for), (2) whether it is the agreed-upon length for the period reserved for it, or (3) whether the candidate himself will appear on the program so that it becomes a "use" and is subject to equal opportunities, the political time rate, etc. (*Law of Political Broadcasting and Cablecasting*, 1978, 2220)

Libel and Potential Station Liability

Required to air political ads without controlling the content put stations at risk of being sued for libel. The Supreme Court ruled that because broadcast stations are not allowed to censor political advertising by a candidate, stations must be given absolute pro-tection from libel suits as the result of the dissemination of those messages (*Farmers Educational and Cooperative Union v. WDAY, Inc.*, 1959). However, if the political advertising is sponsored by someone other than a legally qualified candidate and therefore is not con-sidered a use, then "the non-censorship provision does not apply and the station is not protected against libel suits by the Supreme Court decision" (*Law of Political Broadcasting and Cablecasting*, 1984, p. 2220). A station can refuse to air any nonuse announcements or programs that the station believes contains libelous or false statements. Consequently, broadcast stations in recent years have refused to air political ads from political action committees that the stations have considered to be libelous or false, because of the jeopardy of being sued.

While broadcasters have absolute protection from possible libel suits as the result of the airing of political messages from legally qualified candidates, sponsors of political advertising may be held accountable for their political messages. Advertising sponsors may be sued under existing libel laws or prosecuted under existing campaign falsity or obscenity laws.

Broadcast Rates

Section 315 also controls the amount of money a broadcast licensee may charge a candidate for advertising time during certain periods. "The equal-opportunities provision requires that 45 days before a primary election and 60 days before a general election, broadcasters charge political candidates no more than the station's lowest advertising rates" (Middleton & Chamberlin, 1988, p. 551). The Lowest Unit Rate (LUR) for a particular length of spot and broadcast time is determined by discovering the LUR given to any sponsor for a given length of spot and broadcast time. Outside of the 45- and 60-day windows, the FCC has forbidden licensees to charge legally qualified candidates more than they would the commercial advertiser.

The LUR only applies to the purchase of air time. The spots must be legal uses in order for the LUR to apply. Spots from independent political action committees do not qualify for LUR. The costs of producing the ads such as studio time, film or video editing are not covered by this rule.

CAMPAIGN FINANCE LAW

Alexander and Bauer (1991) estimated that $2.7 billion was spent by and for political campaigns during the national, state, and local 1988 elections. Modern campaigns are big money media affairs. Spending by House incumbents increased 46 percent from 1990 to 1992. The average House campaign expenditure was $571,089. In 1992, the incumbent Senate campaign spent $4,149,198 (Morris & Gamache, 1994). "The average House incumbent's investment in broadcast advertising nearly doubled, from $76,109 in 1990 to $141,791 in 1992" (Morris & Gamache, 1994, p. 5). The average broadcast expenditure for incumbent Senators increased by 7 percent, from 33 percent of total campaign expenditures in 1990 to 40 percent of total campaign expenditures in 1992. In 1992, U.S. Senate campaigns spent $219,073,459. In 1992, U.S. House of Representative campaigns spent $323,175,852 (Morris & Gamache, 1994).

Raising political funds is also an expensive enterprise. In 1990 Jesse Helms paid $4.6 million to direct-mail consultants in order to finance his heavy campaign expenditures. In 1992 congressional races, nearly $85 million was spent on fund-raising activities, direct-mail funding requests, and telemarketing (Morris & Gamache, 1994). How and in what ways candidates raise money is a serious concern for professional consultants. Federal election laws will be reviewed with an emphasis on their potential impact on political communication expenditures.

The Federal Elections Commission (FEC) is mandated by Congress to serve as the watchdog over federal election campaign expenditures. In the 1970s, in an effort to deal with rising political campaign costs as well as ethical and legal problems associated with political campaign practices, the Congress of the United States passed two major campaign finance reform packages: the Revenue Act of 1971 and the Federal Election Campaign Act of 1971 (FECA).

The Revenue Act of 1971

The Revenue Act of 1971 established a mechanism where taxpayers could voluntarily contribute one dollar to a general presidential campaign fund each year during income tax time. Such voluntary contributions would go into a pool that would later help fund eligible presidential and vice presidential campaigns. In 1974, Congress extended the Revenue Act to include public funding for presidential primary elections and national nominating conventions. Eligibility standards and expenditure restrictions are as follows:

Candidates who raised $5,000 [total] in individual contributions of $250 or less in 20 different states were eligible for federal matching funds. Candidates may receive individual contributions of up to $1,000, but only $250 applies toward the $5,000 total. Each candidate may spend up to $10 million, with an inflation adjustment, in primaries. No more than $200,000 (plus an inflation adjustment) may be spent in a single state. ("Campaign Finance Debate," 1988, p. 122)

However, these spending limitations apply only to candidates who take the federal matching funds. John Connally in 1980 and Steve Forbes in 1996 have been the only major-party presidential candidates who refused to apply for public financing in order to avoid the primary expenditure limitations ("Campaign Finance Debate," 1988).

The Federal Election Campaign Act of 1971

The Federal Election Campaign Act of 1971 required that federal candidates (those seeking presidential or congressional offices) fully disclose both their campaign contributions and their campaign expenditures. The FECA also set ceilings on media expenditures for federal candidates (see "Controls on Political Spending," 1986); however, a 1974 amendment to FECA repealed the media spending ceilings for the House and the Senate. The 1974 amendment established the FEC, which was to serve as a watchdog over federal elections, ensuring candidate compliance with campaign finance regulations (see "Controls on Political Spending," 1986; The Campaign Finance Debate, 1988). In addition, the 1974 amendment set limits on how much individuals and political committees could contribute to federal candidates. Those contribution limits were changed in 1976 and 1979.

Contributions and Expenditures

In 1988, 10.2 percent of all Americans, or 18.6 million individuals, contributed to a candidate, political action committee, or political party (Sorauf, 1992). By FEC regulation, political contributions are "anything of value given to influence a Federal election. 100. 7 (a)(1)" (*Campaign Guide for Political Party Committees*, 1985, p. 4). Contributions include such things as gifts of money, in-kind contributions (services or goods that are received as either gifts or at a discounted rate), unpaid personal loans, unpaid endorsements and loan guarantees, proceeds from sales (e.g., money paid to attend a fund-raising dinner or to buy a campaign T-shirt), or extensions of credit beyond customary business practices (*Campaign Guide for Political Party Committees*, 1985).

The 1974 amendments to FECA put the following limitations on contributions:

- Individuals could contribute a maximum of $1,000 per candidate per election. In this and all other limits the primary and general elections came to count separately; thus the limit was in effect $2,000 per candidate in a two-year election cycle.
- Individuals were also limited to a calendar-year total of $25,000 in all contributions, with sublimits for the year of $20,000 to national party committees and $5,000 to a PAC or any other party committee.
- Political action committees (PACs) and party committees were limited to contributions of $5,000 per candidate per election (or $10,000 in the cycle).
- Party committees, too, could contribute no more than $5,000 per election to a candidate. The major party senatorial campaign committees, however, were permitted to contribute $17,500 to each of their party's senatorial candidates. (Sorauf, 1992)

Campaign expenditures are regulated, because they are purchases or payments used to influence a federal election or because they are a political contribution to a political committee, and subject to the Revenue Act's contribution limits. Expenditure examples include monetary contributions, in-kind contributions, or loans made to other committees (see *Campaign Guide for Political Party Committees*, 1985).

Political Committees

There are three types of political committees: political party committees, candidate committees, and political action committees. A political party committee is any "political committee which represents a political party and is part of the official party structure at the national, state or local level. 100.5(e)(4)" (*Campaign Guide for Political Party Committees*, 1985, p. 62). A candidate committee is "any political committee, including a principal campaign committee, authorized in writing by the candidate to receive contributions and make expenditures on his/her behalf. 100.5(f)(1)" (*Campaign Guide for Political Party Committees*, 1985, p. 61). The FEC refers to candidate committees as authorized committees. A political action committee (PAC) is a political committee that is "neither a party committee nor an authorized committee of a candidate. PACs sponsored by a corporation or labor organization are called separate segregated funds; PACs without a corporate or labor sponsor are called nonconnected PACs" (*Campaign Guide for Congressional Candidates and Committees*, 1988, p. 61). All political committees are either single-candidate or multicandidate committees and either authorized or unauthorized. Single-candidate commit-tees make "contributions or expenditures on behalf of only one candidate" (*Campaign Guide for Political Party Committees*, 1985, p. 63). An authorized committee is a committee sanction in writing by the candidate to act on the candidate's behalf. An unauthorized committee is not sanctioned by the candidate but makes contributions or expenditures on the candidate's behalf. The FEC defines a multicandidate committee as a political committee "with more than 50 contributors that has been registered for at least 6 months and, with the exception of State party committees, has made contributions to 5 or more candidates for Federal office" (110.1 (a) 110.2 (a)(1). (*Campaign Guide for Political Party Committees*, 1985, p. 62). If a PAC fails to qualify as a multicandidate committee, then it is "subject to the same contribution limits as an individual" (Sorauf, 1992, p. 247).

Campaign Disclosure Requirements

Political campaigns must keep careful and accurate contributor and expenditure records (Alexander, 1983). Today, accountants and lawyers who specialize in FEC guidelines have become integral parts of the campaign process. Ironically, the very act that was supposed to curb some of the financial excesses associated with mass media campaigns has helped usher in the New Politics era, which is characterized by media professionals and technocrats (see Alexander, 1983).

FECA's disclosure provisions provide that all contributors to a political campaign who give more than $50 must be listed by the political campaign in terms of name, address, occupation, date, and amount of expenditure and that this information be filed with the FEC. Only minor political parties that have demonstrated that their contributors may face harassment by the government or other political actors are exempt from these contribution disclosure requirements (see *Brown v. Socialist Workers '74 Campaign Committee,* 1982; *Federal Election Commission v. Hall-Tyner Election Campaign Committee,* 1982). All campaign expenditures greater than $200 must also be filed with the FEC.

There are three primary political advertising sponsors in American politics: candidates and their campaign committees, political parties, and political action committees. The sponsors of all political advertising that "expressly advocates the election or defeat of a clearly identified candidate, or that solicits any contribution, through any broadcasting station, newspaper, magazine, outdoor advertising facility, poster, yard sign, direct mailing, or any other form of general public political advertising" (11 C.F.R. sec. 110.11(a)(1) (1986)) must be fully disclosed. The sponsor must be clearly identified in a conspicuous place telling "who paid for the ad and whether it is authorized by the candidate" (Middleton and Chamberlin, 1988, p. 280; see 11 C.F.R. sec. 110.11(a)(2)). Small campaign items such as buttons, lapel pins, or bumper stickers are excluded from this requirement because of their size (11 C.F.R. sec. 110.11(a)(2).

SPONSORS

The sponsorship of political ads may be broken into three groups, political parties, political action committees, and the candidate or the candidate's campaign committee. The laws and regulations that govern each group is different.

Political Party Committees

Epstein (1967) has defined a political party as "any group, however loosely organized, seeking to elect governmental office-holders under a given label" (p. 9). A state or local political party committee may contribute only $1,000 per federal candidate, per election, unless it qualifies as a multicandidate committee, in which case it can contribute up to $5,000 per federal candidate, per election (110.1(a) and 110.2(a)(1); see *Campaign Guide for Political Party Committees*, 1985, p. 6). It is important to note that because all local party committees are considered to be state committee affiliates, all contributions received by or made by these local committees count against the state committee's limitations (*Campaign Guide for Political Party Committees*, 1985, p. 6). If the state committee is a multicandidate committee, then the

State committee and all of its affiliated local committees may contribute a combined total of $5,000 to a Federal candidate, per election. 110.3(b)(2)(ii). Similarly, the State committee and its local affiliates share the same limit on contributions received: an annual limit of $5,000 for contributions from an individual, organization or non party political committee. AOs 1976-104, 1978-39, 1979-68 and 1979-77. (*Campaign Guide for Political Party Committees*, 1985, p. 6)

Each major political party in the United States has three main national committees. The Democrats have the Democratic National Committee (DNC), the Democratic Senatorial Campaign Committee (DSCC), and the Democratic Congressional Campaign Committee (DCCC). The Republicans have the Republican National Committee (RNC), the National Republican Senatorial Committee (NRSC), and the National Republican Congressional Committee (NRCC). The DNC and the RNC work with all federal races, the DSCC and the NRSC work solely with senatorial races, and the DCCC and the NRCC work solely with House of Representative races (see "Political Party Campaigning," 1986).

The national party committees (RNC, DNC, DSCC, NRSC, DCCC, and NRCC) may each receive $20,000 per year from individuals, $20,000 per year from political committees or groups, or $15,000 per year from a multicandidate committee. The national committees are restricted to a $5,000 contribution to each candidate per election within a 2-year campaign cycle. The political party's senate campaign committee and its national committee are restricted to a combined contribution of $17,500 to each Senate candidate per campaign period.

Besides direct financial contributions, the national party committees provide in-kind contributions to political campaigns. An in-kind contribution is "services, goods or property offered free or at less than the usual charge to a political committee. 100.7(a)(1)(iii)" (*Campaign Guide for Political Party Committees*, 1985, p. 62). In-kind contributions are itemized in terms of their cash value as if they were cash contributions, and they are also itemized as operating expenditures (*Campaign Guide for Political Party Committees*, 1985). In-kind contributions might include such campaign services as media production assistance, polling information, and other technical assistance. Candidate training schools are also available.

It is also important to note that federal candidates are supported by party committees through more than just direct or in-kind contributions. Coordinated expenditures and soft money are two very important resources in federal campaigns. Coordinated party expenditures, also known as joint expenditures, are expenditures made by a political party committee after consulting with a given candidate. A coordinated expenditure is not considered a contribution by the FEC in that the state and/or national party committee spends the money itself rather than channeling it to a particular candidate for his or her discretionary use. The state or national party committee may consult with the candidate concerning the way in which the money is spent, but it is the party that spends the money, not the candidate. The party committee may make coordinated party expenditures only during general election campaigns. One of the most common forms of coordinated party expenditures is party sponsored-political advertising.

However, there are limits on coordinated party expenditures based upon a rather complicated formula involving the state's voting age population, the consumer price index, and the cost-of-living adjustment figures (COLAs) (see *Campaign Guide for Political Party Committees*, 1985). In 1980, the national party committee could spend up to $34,720 on a House election and as much as $987,548 on a Senate race ("Political Party Campaigning," 1986). If a coordinated party expenditure, for example, a political ad, benefits more than one candidate, "the money spent must be allocated among the candidates supported. The value attributed to each candidate must be in proportion to the relative benefit each candidate receives. 104.10 and 106.1(a) and (b)" (*Campaign Guide for Political Party Committees*, 1985, p. 11).

Advertising produced by the national party committees that dramatizes a particular issue and uses a fictitious candidate as an illustration is called canned advertising. The ads are "edited in such a way as to insert cuts of any number of candidates for whom the featured issue might be deemed appropriate" (Nimmo, 1986, pp. 77-78). Campaign brochures are also frequently canned. But canned advertising is not a coordinated expenditure. Rather, canned advertising is a campaign contribution, because it sells a particular candidate. The party committees only help produce the ads or brochures. The candidate's campaign places the ad and pays for its dissemination.

Canned advertising, or "donut ads" (Nimmo, 1986), should not be confused with generic advertising. Generic advertising is political advertising that promotes the political party rather than specifically supporting any political candidates. Both positive and negative generic advertising have been produced. Generic advertising is very important to both the party and its candidates; because no political candidate is specifically mentioned in the advertisement, the cost of the ad does not have to be reported to the FEC as either a coordinated party expenditure or a contribution.

One of the more illusive components of modern political campaigns is soft money. It is the loophole within the regulations governing federal campaign financing, in that such contributions are not regulated by law. "The exemption was made to encourage 'party-building' activities which benefit the political parties in general, but not specific candidates" (Markerson & Goldstein, 1994, p. 16). However, according to Markerson and Goldstein (1994), the end result has been something quite different. They write,

In reality, though, the loophole has emerged as the parties' primary means of raising tens of millions of dollars from wealthy contributors during the fall presidential campaigns, when direct contributions to candidates are prohibited. [It is] also used to support congressional candidates in key battleground states during off-year elections. (Markerson & Goldstein, 1994, p. 16)

Under new rules that became effective on January 1, 1991, "soft money contributions to the national parties must now be reported to the Federal Election Commission" (Markerson & Goldstein, 1994, p. 16). Soft money has four main benefits for both contributors and recipients:

- Soft money is not subject to any contribution limits. . . .
- Soft money contributions can be made by anyone—including groups prohibited from making contributions to federal candidates or parties. . . .
- Soft money offers an extra means of political giving for individuals who've already given the maximum to candidates and federal parties. . . .
- Soft money offers a way for corporations, unions and wealthy contributors to directly support presidential candidates in the fall elections. (Markerson & Goldstein, 1994, p. 16)

Political Action Committees

Political action committees are voluntary associations of individuals that support candidates, particular ideologies, or political parties, or that have particular political agendas. PACs that are "sponsored by a corporation or labor organization are called separate segregated funds; PACs without a corporate or labor sponsor are called nonconnected PACs" (*Campaign Guide for Congressional Candidates and Committees*, 1988, p. 61). Popularly, the separate segregated funds are called sponsored PACs, and the nonconnected PACs are known as independent political action committees.

The Federal Election Campaign Act of 1971 prohibits corporations and unions from making direct contributions to a candidate or from making independent expenditures on behalf of a candidate. Corporations and unions are, however, allowed to contribute money to state parties because of a 1979 amendment to the FECA. In addition, corporations and unions can also use their own money for political referenda (Middleton & Chamberlin, 1988).

In addition to corporate and union restrictions on expenditures, these organizations may not publicly declare their support for political candidates, but they may make such statements to their internal publics: management, employees, families of employees, and shareholders (see Boyle, 1985; Middleton & Chamberlin, 1988). The courts have held that nonprofit corporations whose primary role is ideological may finance public endorsements of federal candidates (see Middleton & Chamberlin, 1988).

However, corporations and unions may sponsor political action committees, that is, the PACs known as separate segregated funds or sponsored PACs. A corporation or union may pay all costs associated with setting up a PAC, and corporate and union officers may control the decision-making processes and financial resources of the PAC. However, corporate and union PACs may solicit funding only from management, stockholders, and their families. They may not solicit funding from the general public. And the corporation and union may not encourage their employees to contribute to the PAC through internal company communication tools.

As mentioned earlier, PACs can also be what the FEC calls nonconnected, or independent, in that they are not affiliated with any corporation or union. These PACs are "established by independent groups, partnerships, or unincorporated associations such as the California Medical Association" (Middleton & Chamberlin, 1988, p. 275). Unlike sponsored PACs, independent PACs may solicit money from the general public. However, they may not receive more than $5,000 from their parent organization for administrative and fund-raising expenses (Middleton & Chamberlin, 1988, p. 275).

In 1974, there were only 608 PACs in the United States. But by July 1, 1991, there were 4,123. However, the rate of growth of PACs has substantially declined. "Since the mid-1980s the number of PACs choosing to disband has just about equaled the number of new ones" (Sorauf, 1992, p. 104). Elliott (1980) views PACs as "the political manifestation of social and behavioral changes taking place in

America" (p. 554), in that PACs have become the natural replacement for precinct or neighborhood politics associated with the Old Politics era. She suggests that during the New Politics era, we are "not influenced by neighborhood leaders, but rather by particular occupational or socio-economic group leaders" (Elliott, 1980, p. 541).

PACs provide the necessary seed money early in the campaign to reach the small giver through direct mail and other communication channels. When PACs have contributed to a campaign, individuals are much more likely to look favorably upon the candidacy, because it is deemed as credible for having received the contribution (Elliott, 1980).

Because PACs' primary consideration when giving money is electability, incumbents have the edge over challengers (Elliott, 1980; Goldenberg & Traugott, 1984). During the 1987-1988 election cycle, 75 percent of the $147.9 million donated by PACs went to incumbents (*FEC Reports on Financial Activity: 1987-1988*, 1989). In the 1987-1988 election campaign cycle, 75 percent of PAC contributions went to congressional incumbents, 12 percent went to congressional challengers; and 13 percent went to congressional candidates in open seats (*FEC Reports on Financial Activity: 1987-1988*, 1989).

On January 30, 1976, the U.S. Supreme Court in the *Buckley v. Valeo* decision distinguished between campaign contributions and independent expenditures. Campaign contributions are direct contributions to a candidate. An independent expenditure, on the other hand, is an expenditure made on behalf of a candidate (that is, expenditures that may be viewed as helping or supporting a particular candidate). An independent expenditure is made "without cooperation or consultation with any candidate, or any authorized committee or agent" of a political candidate (*Buckley v. Valeo*, 1976, 28n. 31).

The Supreme Court concluded that limits on campaign contributions cannot be construed as violations of freedom of speech, because such contributions are not direct specific statements of support; rather, they are indirect, general expressions. But according to the Court, limitations on independent expenditures would be violations of freedom of speech, because they are direct statements of support for a given candidate. Limitations on independent expenditures would serve to impede the competitive flow of ideas in the political marketplace, and therefore they were judged by the Court to be unconstitutional.

Since 1976 some PACs, particularly the independent, ideological PACs, have taken full advantage of the *Buckley v. Valeo* decision to finance political advertising efforts in various federal elections (Sabato, 1984). By and large, these independent expenditures have been against a candidate, that is, they have paid for negative political advertising (Bannon 1982, 1983; Erickson, 1982; Jamieson, 1984;

Kitchens & Powell, 1986; Railsback, 1983; Tarrance, 1982; "Campaign Finance Debate," 1988).

Candidates and Their Campaign Committees

A candidate's campaign committee is technically called an "authorized candidate committee" by the FEC. An authorized candidate committee may also be the "principal campaign committee," which coordinates and controls the candidate's campaign. Authorized committees may receive $1,000 from an individual or other political committee or group per election. In addition, the authorized committee may receive $5,000 from multicandidate committees per election. It is important to note that the party primary, caucus, or convention with authority to nominate; the general election; the runoff election; and the special election are each considered a separate election (see *Campaign Guide for Congressional Candidates and Committees*, 1988).

References

Abelson, R. P., Kinder, D. R., Peters, M. D., & Fiske, S. T. (1982). Affective and semantic components in political person perception. *Journal of Personality and Social Psychology, 42,* 619-630.

Abramson, P. R. (1983). *Political attitudes in America.* San Francisco: Freeman.

Abramson, P. R. (1987). *Change and continuity in the 1984 elections* (Rev. ed.). Washington, DC: Congressional Quarterly Press.

Agranoff, R. (1976). *The management of election campaigns.* Boston: Holbrook Press.

Ajzen, I., & Fishbein, M. (1975). *Belief, attitude, intention, and behavior.* Reading, MA: Addison-Wesley.

Albert, J. A. (1986). The remedies available to candidates who are defamed by television or radio commercials of opponents. *Vermont Law Review, 11,* 33-73.

Aldrich, J. H. (1980). *Before the convention: Strategies and choices in presidential nomination campaigns.* Chicago: University of Chicago Press.

Alexander, H. E. (1969). Communications and politics: The media and the message. *Law and Contemporary Problems, 34,* 255-277.

Alexander, H. E. (1983). The regulation and funding of presidential elections. *Journal of Law and Politics,* 43-63.

Alexander, H., & Bauer, M. (1991). *Financing the 1988 election.* Boulder, CO: Westview Press.

Allen, V. L. (1975). Social support for nonconformity. In L. Berkowitz (Ed.), *Advances in experimental social psychology, Vol. 8* (pp. 1-43). New York: Academic Press.

Allport, G. W. (1935). Attitudes. In C. Murchison (Ed.), *A handbook of social psychology* (pp. 798-844). Worcester, MA: Clark University Press.

Almond, A., & Coleman, J. (1960). A functional approach to comparative politics. In A. Almond & J. Coleman (Eds.), *The politics of developing areas* (pp. 532-576). Princeton, NJ: Princeton University Press.

Almond, G., & Verba, S. (1963). *The civic culture.* Princeton, NJ: Princeton University Press.

Alsop, R. (1987, January 29). More companies squeeze ads into bargain 15-second spots. *The Wall Street Journal,* 31.

Alwitt, L. F. (1985). EEG activity reflects the content of commercials. In L. F. Alwitt & A. A. Mitchell (Eds.), *Psychological process and advertising effects: Theory, research and applications* (pp. 201-220). Hillsdale, NJ: Lawrence Erlbaum.

America: A regional review. *Public Opinion,* (1988, January/February). *5,* 25-30.

Anders, C., & Marlowe, H. (1987). On-line opposition research. *Campaigns & Elections, 7,* 61-64.

Andersen, K. E. (1989). The politics of ethics and the ethics of politics. *American Behavioral Scientist, 32,* 479-492.

Anderson, L. F., Watts, M. W., & Wilcox, A. R. (1966). *Legislative roll-call analysis.* Evanston, IL: Northwestern University Press.

Anderson, L. R., & McGuire, W. J. (1965). Prior reassurance of group consensus as a factor in producing resistance to persuasion. *Sociometry, 28,* 44-56.

Anderson, N. H. (1965). Averaging vs. adding as a stimulus-combination rule in impression formation. *Journal of Experimental Psychology, 70,* 394-400.

Andreñ, G. (1980). The rhetoric of advertising. *Journal of Communication, 30,* 74-80.

Andreoli, V., & Worchel, S. (1978). Effects of media, communicator and message position on attitude change. *Public Opinion Quarterly, 42,* 59-70.

Archer, D., Kimes, D. D., & Barrios, M. (1978, September). Face-ism. *Psychology Today,* 65-66.

Archibald, S. J. (1971). The dynamics of clean campaigning. In S. J. Archibald (Ed.), *The pollution of politics* (pp. 8-21). Washington, DC: Public Affairs Press.

Arterton, F. C. (1978). The media politics of presidential campaigns: A study of the Carter nomination drive. In J. D. Barber (Ed.), *Race for the presidency* (pp. 25-54). Englewood Cliffs, NJ: Prentice-Hall.

Arterton, F. C. (1984). *Media politics: The news strategies of presidential campaigns.* Lexington, MA: Lexington.

Ashmore, R. D., & Del Boca, F. K. (1976). Psychological approaches to understanding intergroup conflicts. In P. A. Katz (Ed.), *Towards the elimination of racism* (pp. 73-123). Elmsford, NY: Pergamon.

Atkin, C. K. (1980). Political campaigns: Mass communication and persuasion. In M. E. Roloff & G. R. Miller (Eds.), *Persuasion: New directions in theory and research* (pp. 285-308). Beverly Hills: Sage.

Atkin, C. K., Bowen, L., Nayman, O. B., & Sheinkopf, K. G. (1973). Quality versus quantity in televised political ads. *Public Opinion Quarterly, 40,* 209-224.

Atkin, C. K., & Heald, G. (1976). Effects of political advertising. *Public Opinion Quarterly, 40,* 216-228.

Axelrod, R. (1967). The structure of public opinion on policy issues. *Public Opinion Quarterly, 31,* 51-60.

Babbie, E. (1986). *The practice of social research* (4th ed.). Belmont, CA: Wadsworth.

Babbie, E. R. (1973). *Survey research methods*. Belmont, CA: Wadsworth.

Bagozzi, R. P. (1978). The construct validity of the affective, behavioral and cognitive components of attitude by analysis of covariance structure. *Multivariate Behavior Research, 13*, 9-31.

Baldwin, J. (1897). *Social and ethical interpretation in mental development*. New York: Macmillan.

Ball-Rokeach, S. J., & DeFleur, M. L. (1976). A dependency model of mass media effects. *Communication Research, 3*, 3-21.

Ball-Rokeach, S. J., Grube, W., & Rokeach, M. (1981). *Roots: The next generation*: Who watched and with what effect? *Public Opinion Quarterly, 45*, 58-68.

Bannon, B. (1982). NCPAC's role in the 1980 Senate elections. *Campaigns & Elections, 3*, 43-46.

Bannon, B. (1983). NCPAC in the 80s: Action vs. reaction. *Campaigns & Elections, 3*, 36-43.

Barber, J. (1974). *Choosing the president*. Englewood Cliffs, NJ: Prentice-Hall.

Barber, J. (1978). *Race for the presidency*. Englewood Cliffs, NJ: Prentice-Hall.

Bartels, L. M. (1985). Expectations and preferences in presidential nominating campaigns. *American Political Science Review, 79*, 804-815.

Bartels, L. M. (1987). Candidate choice and the dynamics of the presidential nominating process. *American Journal of Political Science, 31*, 1-30.

Bartels, L. M. (1988). *Presidential primaries and the dynamics of public choice*. Princeton, NJ: Princeton University Press.

Baskin, O. W. (1975). The effects of televised political advertisements on voter perceptions about candidates (Doctoral dissertation, University of Texas-Austin, 1975). *Dissertation Abstracts International, 36*, 6355A.

Baukus, R. A., Payne, J. G., & Reisler, M. S. (1985). Negative polispots: Mediated arguments in the political arena. In J. R. Cox, M. O. Sillars, & G. B. Walker (Eds.), *Argument and social practice: Proceedings of the fourth SCA/AFA Conference on Argumentation* (pp. 236-252). Annandale, VA: Speech Communication Association.

Baus, H. M., & Ross, W. B. (1968). *Politics battle plan*. New York: Macmillan.

Bayer, M. J., & Rodota, J. (1985). Computerized opposition research: The instant parry. *Campaigns & Elections, 6*, 25-29.

Becker, L. B., & Doolittle, J. C. (1975). How repetition affects evaluations of information-seeking about candidates. *Journalism Quarterly, 52*, 611-617.

Beniger, J. R. (1987). Personalization of mass media and the growth of pseudo-community. *Communication Research, 14*, 352-370.

Bennett, E. (1955). Discussion, decision, commitment and consensus in group decision making. *Human Relations, 8*, 251-274.

Bennett, W. L. (1977). The ritualistic and pragmatic bases of political campaign discourse. *Quarterly Journal of Speech, 63*, 219-238.

Bennett, W. L. (1980). Myth, ritual, and political control. *Journal of Communication, 30*, 166-179.

Bennett, W. L. (1988). *News: The politics of illusion* (2nd. ed.). New York: Longman.

Bennett, W. L., & Edelman, M. (1985). Toward a new political narrative. *Journal of Communication, 35*, 156-171

Benson, T. W. (1968, November). Conversation with a ghost. *Today's Speech, 16*, 71-81.

Benson, T. W. (1974, Summer). Conversation with a ghost: A postscript. *Today's Speech, 22*, 13-15.

Benson, T. W. (1981). Another shooting in cowtown. *Quarterly Journal of Speech, 67*, 347-406.

Benze, J. G., & Declercq, E. R. (1985). Content of television political spot ads for female candidates. *Journalism Quarterly, 62*, 278-283, 288.

Berelson, B. (1948). Communications and public opinion. In W. Schramm (Ed.), *Communications in modern society* (pp. 167-185). Urbana, IL: University of Illinois Press.

Berelson, B. (1971). *Content analysis in communication research*. New York: Hafner.

Berger, C. R. (1980). Power and the family. In M. E. Roloff and G. E. Miller (Eds.), *Persuasion: New directions in theory and research* (pp. 197-224). Beverly Hills: Sage.

Berger, P. L., & Luckmann, T. (1966). *The social construction of reality: A treatise in the sociology of knowledge*. New York: Doubleday.

Berkman, R., & Kitch, L. W. (1986). *Politics in the media age*. New York: McGraw Hill.

Berkovitz, T. L. (1985). Political television advertising objectives: The viewpoint of political media consultants (Doctoral dissertation, Wayne State University, 1985). *Dissertation Abstracts International, 46*, 1117A.

Bernard, S. (1988, October). Report on *NBC Nightly News*.

Bernays, E. (1955). *The engineering of consent*. Norman, OK: University of Oklahoma Press.

Berrigan, J. (1982). The cost-effectiveness of grass-roots campaign activities. *Campaigns & Elections, 3*, 25-33.

Biocca, F. (Ed.). (1991). *Television and political advertising*, Vol. 1 & 2. Hillsdale, NJ: Lawrence Erlbaum .

Bishop, G. F., & Frankovic, K. A. (1981). Ideological consensus and constraint among party leaders and followers in the 1978 election. *Micropolitics, 1*, 87-111.

Bishop, G. F., Oldendick, R. W., Tuchfarber, A. J., & Bennett, S. E. (1980). Pseudo-opinions on public affairs. *Public Opinion Quarterly, 44*, 198-209.

Bitzer, L. (1981). Political rhetoric. In D. Nimmo and K. R. Sanders (Eds.), *Handbook of political communication* (pp. 225-248). Beverly Hills: Sage.

Black, J., & Barney, R. D. (1985-1986). The case against mass media codes of ethics. *Journal of Mass Media Ethics, 1*, 27-36.

Bloom, M. H. (1973). *Public relations and presidential campaigns: A crisis in democracy*. New York: Thomas Y. Crowell.

Blumenthal, S. (1980, March/April). The candidate makers. *Politics Today*, 27-30.

Blumler, J. G., & Katz, E. (eds.). (1974). *The uses of mass communication: Current perspectives on gratifications research*. Beverly Hills: Sage.

Blumler, J. G., & McQuail, D. (1969). *Television and politics: Its uses and influence*. Chicago: University of Chicago Press.

Blydenburgh, J. C. (1971). A controlled experiment to measure the effects of personal contact campaigning. *Midwest Journal of Political Science, 15,* 365-381.

Boddewyn, J. J., & Marton, K. (1978). Comparison advertising: A worldwide study. In S. E. Permut (Ed.), *Proceedings of the annual conference of the American Academy of Advertising 1978: Advances in advertising, research, and management* (pp. 150-154). New Haven, CT: Yale University Printing Service.

Boorstin, D. (1961). *The image: A guide to pseudo-events.* New York: Atheneum.

Boorstin, D. (1962). *The image: Or what happened to the American dream.* New York: Atheneum.

Bormann, E. G. (1972). Fantasy and rhetorical vision: The rhetorical criticism of social reality. *Quarterly Journal of Speech, 58,* 396-407.

Bostrom, N. (1970). Affective, cognitive, and behavioral dimensions of communicative attitudes. *Journal of Communication, 20,* 359-369.

Bott, A. J. (1990). *Handbook of United States election laws and practices: Political rights.* Westport, CT: Greenwood Press.

Boulding, K. (1959). *The image: Knowledge in life and society* (2nd pr.). Ann Arbor, MI: University of Michigan Press.

Bowers, T. A. (1972). Issue and personality information in newspaper political advertising. *Journalism Quarterly, 49,* 446-452.

Bowers, T. A. (1973). Newspaper political advertising and the agenda-setting function. *Journalism Quarterly, 50,* 552-556.

Bowes, J. E., & Strentz, H. (1978). Candidate images: Stereotyping and the 1976 debates. In B. D. Ruben (Ed.), *Communication Yearbook 2* (pp. 391-406). New Brunswick, NJ: Transaction.

Boyd, J. M. (1978). An experimental analysis of source credibility and message discrepancy under differential levels of ego involvement in political television commercials (Doctoral dissertation, University of Southern California, 1978). *Dissertation Abstracts International, 38,* 5774A.

Boyle, L. (1985). PACs and pluralism: The dynamics of interest-group politics. *Campaigns & Elections, 6,* 6-16.

Brace, K., & Jaede, M. (1984). Computer graphics: Campaign targeting and micromapping. *Campaigns & Elections, 5,* 62-72.

Brady, H. E., & Johnston, R. (1987). What's the primary message: Horse race or issue journalism. In G. R. Orren & N. W. Polsby (Eds.), *Media and momentum* (pp. 127-186). Chatham, NJ: Chatham House.

Brady, H. E., & Sniderman, P. M. (1985). Attitude attribution: A group basis for political reasoning. *American Political Science Review, 79,* 1061-1078.

Briscoe, M. E., Woodyard, H. D., Shaw, M. E. (1967). Personality impression change as a function of the favorableness of first impressions. *Journal of Personality, 35,* 343-357.

Broder, D. (1990, January 14). Five ways to put some sanity back in elections. *The Washington Post,* p. B1.

Brody, R., & Page, B. (1973). Indifference, alienation, and rational decisions: The effects of candidate evaluations on turnout and vote. *Public Choice, 15,* 1-17.

Brody, R., & Page, B. (1975). The impact of events on presidential popularity: The Johnson and Nixon administrations. In A. Wildavsky (Ed.), *Perspectives on the presidency* (pp. 126-148). Boston: Little, Brown.

Broh, C. A. (1980). Horse-race journalism: Reporting the polls in the 1976 presidential election. *Public Opinion Quarterly, 44,* 514-529.

Brown, S. R. (1980). *Political subjectivity.* New Haven, CT: Yale University Press.

Brown v. Socialist Workers '74 Campaign Committee, 459 U.S. 87 (1982).

Brownstein, C. N. (1971). Communication strategies and the election decision-making process: Some results from experimentation. *Experimental Studies of Politics, 1,* 37-50.

Brummett, B. (1980). Towards a theory of silence as a political strategy. *Quarterly Journal of Speech, 66,* 289-303.

Brummett, B. (1988). The homology hypothesis: Pornography on the VCR. *Critical Studies in Mass Communication, 5,* 202-216.

Buckley v. Valeo, 424 U.S. 1, 46 L. Ed. 2d. 65 9, 96 S. Ct. 612, 76-1 USTC P 9189 (1976).

Buckley, W. (1967). *Sociology and modern systems theory.* Englewood Cliffs, NJ: Prentice-Hall.

Bundlie v. Christensen, 276 N.W. 2d 69 (1979).

Burgoon, J. K., & Hale, J. L. (1984). The fundamental topoi of relational communication. *Communication Monographs, 51,* 193-214.

Burgoon, J. K., & Hale, J. L. (1987). Validation and measurement of the fundamental themes of relational communication. *Communication Monographs, 54,* 19-41.

Burgoon, J. K., Pfau, M., Parrott, R., Birk, T., Coker, R., & Burgoon, M. (1987). Relational communication, satisfaction, compliance-gaining strategies, and compliance in communication between physicians and patients. *Communication Monographs, 54,* 307-324.

Burrell, B. (1987, January/February). Not a Cinderella story. *Campaigns & Elections, 7,* 32-37.

Buss, T., & Hofstetter, C. R. (1976). An analysis of the logic of televised campaign advertisements: The 1972 presidential campaign. *Communication Research, 3,* 367-392.

The campaign finance debate. (1988). *Elections '88* (pp. 119-126). Washington, DC: Congressional Quarterly.

Campaign guide for congressional candidates and committees (1988, July). Washington, DC: Federal Election Commission.

Campaign guide for political party committees (1985, October). Washington, DC: Federal Election Commission.

Campbell, A. (1964). Voters and elections: Past and present. *Journal of Politics, 26,* 745-757.

Campbell, D. T., & Stanley, J. C. (1963). *Experimental and quasiexperimental designs for research.* Chicago: Rand McNally College Publishing.

Cantor, J. R., & Zillmann, D. (1973). Resentment toward victimized protagonists and severity of misfortunes they suffer as factors in humor appreciation. *Journal of Experimental Research in Personality, 6,* 321-329.

Cantwell v. Connecticut, 310 U.S. 296, 310, 60 S.Ct., 906 (1940).

Cappella, J. N., & Jamieson, K. H. (1994). Broadcast adwatch effects. *Communication Research, 21*, 342-365.

Carey, J. (1976). How media shape campaigns. *Journal of Communication, 26*, 50-57.

Carlson, J. (1981). *George C. Wallace and the politics of powerlessness.* New Brunswick, NJ: Transaction Books.

Carmichael, C. W., & Cronkhite, G. L. (1965). Frustration and language intensity. *Speech Monographs, 32*, 107-111.

Carmines, E. G., & Stimson, J. A. (1982). Racial issues and the structure of mass belief systems. *The Journal of Politics, 44*, 2-20.

Carroll, R. (1980). The 1948 Truman campaign: The threshold of the modern era. *Journal of Broadcasting, 24*, 173-188.

Carroll, S. (1985). *Women as candidates in American politics.* Bloomington, IN: Indiana University Press.

Carroll, S. J. (1994). *Women as candidates in American politics* (2nd. ed.). Bloomington, IN: Indiana University Press.

Caywood, C. L., & Preston, I. L. (1989). The continuing debate on political advertising: Toward a theory of political advertising as regulated speech. *Journal of Public Policy and Management, 8*, 204-226.

Chaffee, S. (1967a). Salience and homeostasis in the communication process. *Journalism Quarterly, 44*, 439-444.

Chaffee, S. (1967b). Salience and pertinence as a source of value change. *Journal of Communication, 17*, 25-38.

Chaiken, S. (1979). Communicator's physical attractiveness and persuasion. *Journal of Personality and Social Psychology, 37*, 1387-1397.

Choi, H. C., & Becker, S. L. (1987). Media use, issue/image discriminations, and voting. *Communication Research, 14*, 267-291.

Christenson, R. M., Engel, A. S., Jacobs, D. N., Rejai, M., & Waltzer, H. (1981). *Ideologies and modern politics.* New York: Harper & Row.

Clean Campaign Act of 1985, Senate Bill 1310, Sec. 2.

Clinger, J. H. (1987). The clean campaign act of 1985: A rational solution to negative campaign advertising which the one hundredth Congress should reconsider. *Journal of Law & Politics, 3*, 727-748.

Cohen, B. C. (1963). *The press, the public and foreign policy.* Princeton, NJ: Princeton University Press.

Colford, S. (1992a, January 27). Buchanan takes off the gloves in N.H. *Advertising Age*, 3.

Colford, S. (1992b, January 13). Bush may launch ads vs. Buchanan. *Advertising Age*, 1, 42.

Colford, S. (1992c, March 2). Campaign ads get down and dirty. *Advertising Age*, 32.

Colford, S. W. (1988, October 24). Duke-ing it out: Troubled campaign tries longer ads. *Advertising Age, 59*, 3, 89.

Colorado Election Law, 1-13-109.

Combs, J. (1979). Political advertising as a popular myth making form. *Journal of American Culture, 2*, 231-340.

Combs, J. E. (1980). *Dimensions of political drama.* Santa Monica: Goodyear.

Combs, J., & Nimmo, D. (1993). *The new propaganda: The dictatorship of palaver in contemporary politics*. White Plains, NY: Longman.

Communication Research, 6. (1979, January) [Entire issue].

Communications Act of 1934, 47 U.S.C.A.

Congressional Campaign Spending Limit and Election Reform Act of 1993, S. 3 (1993).

Conover, P. J., & Feldman, S. (1986). Emotional reactions to the economy: I'm mad as hell and I'm not going to take it any more. *American Journal of Political Science, 30*, 50–78.

Constitution of the United States, Amendment I, U.S.C.A.

Constitution of the United States, Amendment 14, U.S.C.A.

Consultants scorecard. (1986, November/December). *Campaigns & Elections, 33*-40.

Controls on political spending. (1986). *Elections '86* (pp. 37-46) Washington, DC: Congressional Quarterly.

Converse, P. (1962). Information flow and stability of partisan attitudes. *Public Opinion Quarterly, 26*, 578-599.

Converse, P. E. (1964). The nature of belief systems in mass publics. In D. Apter (Ed.), *Ideology and discontent*, pp. 206-261. New York: Free Press.

Converse, P. E. (1970). Attitudes and non-attitudes: continuation of a dialogue. In E. R. Tufte (Ed.), *The quantitative analysis of social problems* (pp. 168-189). Reading, MA: Addison-Wesley.

Cook v. Corbett, 251 Or. 263 (1968).

Cooley, C. (1902). *Human nature and the social order*. New York: Scribner's.

Cooley, C. (1909). *Social organization*. New York: Scribner's.

Coombs, S. L. (1981). Editorial endorsements and electoral outcomes. In M. B. MacKuen & S. L. Coombs (Eds.), *More than news* (pp. 145-230). Beverly Hills: Sage.

Cooper, E., & Jahoda, M. (1947). The evasion of propaganda: How prejudiced people respond to antiprejudice propaganda. *The Journal of Psychology, 23*, 15-25.

Cooper, M. (1991). Ethical dimensions of political advocacy from a postmodern perspective. In R. Denton (Ed.), *Ethical dimensions of political communication* (pp. 23-47). New York: Praeger.

Cooperative Union v. WDAY, Inc., 360 U.S. 525 (1959).

Copeland, G. A., & Johnson-Cartee, K. S. (1990). Southerners' acceptance of negative political advertising and political efficacy and activity levels. *Southeastern Political Review, 18*, 86-102.

Cover, A. D. (1977, August). One good term deserves another: The advantage of incumbency in congressional elections. *American Journal of Political Science*, 523-542.

Cox, D. F., & Bauer, R. A. (1964). Self-confidence and persuasibility in women. *Public Opinion Quarterly, 28*, 453-466.

Crespi, I. (1980). Polls as journalism, *Public Opinion Quarterly, 44*, 464.

Cronkhite, G. (1969). *Persuasion: Speech and behavioral change*. Indianapolis: Bobbs-Merrill.

Crotty, W., & Jacobson, G. (1980). *American parties in decline*. Boston: Little, Brown.

Cundy, D. T. (1986). Political commercials and candidate image: The effect can be substantial. In L. L. Kaid, D. Nimmo, & K. Sanders (Eds.), *New perspectives on political advertising* (pp. 210-234). Carbondale, IL: Southern Illinois University Press.

Cusumano, D., & Richey, M. (1970). Negative salience in impressions of character: Effects of extremeness of salient information. *Psychonomic Science, 20,* 81-83.

Cutlip, S. M., Center, A. H., & Broom, G. M. (1985). *Effective public relations* (6th ed.). Englewood Cliffs, NJ: Prentice-Hall.

Dahlgreen, P. (1981). TV news and the suppression of reflexivity. In E. Katz & T. Szecsko (Eds.), *Mass media and social change* (pp. 101-113). Beverly Hills: Sage.

Darcy, R., Welch, S., & Clark, J. (1987). *Women, electronics, and representation.* New York: Longmans.

Darnton, R. (1975). Writing news and telling stories. *Daedalus, 104,* 175-194.

Davidson, R. J., Schwartz, G. E, Saron, C., Bennet, J., & Goleman, D. J. (1979). Frontal versus parietal EEG symmetry during positive and negative affect. *Psychophysiology, 16,* 202-203.

Dawes, R. M., & Smith T. L. (1985). Attitude and opinion measurement. In G. Lindzey and E. Aronson (Eds.), *The handbook of social psychology,* Vol. 2 (3rd ed., pp. 509-566). New York: Random House.

Dawson, P. A., & Zinser, J. E. (1971). Broadcast expenditures and electoral outcomes in the 1970 congressional elections. *Public Opinion Quarterly, 35,* 398-402.

Deaux, K. (1972). To err is human: But sex makes a difference. *Representative Research in Social Psychology, 3,* 20-28.

Declercq, E. R., Benze, J., & Ritchie, E. (1983, September). *Macha women and macho men.* Paper presented at the annual meeting of the American Political Science Association, Chicago.

Declercq, E., Hurley, T. L., and Luttbeg, N. R. (1975). Voting in American presidential elections, 1956-1972. *American Political Quarterly, 3,* 222-246.

Delbecq, A. L., Van de Van, A. H., & Gustafson, A. H. (1975). *Group techniques for program planning.* New York: Scott Foresman.

Denton, R., Jr. (1982). *The symbolic dimensions of the American presidency: Description and analysis.* Prospect Heights, IL: Waveland Press.

Denton, R. E., Jr. (1991). Primetime politics: The ethics of teledemocracy. In R. Denton (Ed.), *Ethical dimensions of political communication* (pp. 91-114). New York: Praeger.

Devlin, L. P. (1973). Contrasts in presidential campaign commercials of 1972. *Journal of Broadcasting, 35,* 17-26.

Devlin, L. P. (1981). Reagan's and Carter's ad men review the 1980 television campaigns. *Communication Quarterly, 30,* 3-12.

Devlin, L. P. (1986). An analysis of presidential television commercials, 1952-1984. In L. L. Kaid, D. Nimmo, & K. R. Sanders (Eds.), *New perspectives on political advertising* (pp. 21-54). Carbondale, IL: Southern Illinois University Press.

Devlin, L. P. (1989). Contrasts in presidential campaign commercials of 1988. *American Behavioral Scientist, 32,* 389-414.

DeVries, W. (1971). Taking the voter's pulse. In R. Hiebert, R. Jones, E. Lotito, & J. Lorenz (Eds.), *The political image merchants: Strategies in the NEW POLITICS* (pp. 62-81). Washington, DC: Acropolis Books.

DeVries, W., & Tarrance, V. (1972). *The ticket splitters.* Grand Rapids, MI: Eerdmans.

Dewey, J. (1925). *Experience and nature.* Chicago: Open Court.

Dexter, L. A. (1954). The use of public opinion polls by political party organizations. *Public Opinion Quarterly, 18,* 53-61.

Diamond, E., & Bates, S. (1988). *The spot: The rise of political advertising on television* (Rev. ed.). Cambridge, MA: MIT Press.

Diamond, E., & Marin, A. (1989). Spots. *American Behavioral Scientist, 32,* 382-388.

Dinzes, D., Cozzens, M. D., & Manross, G. G. (1994, June). The role of gender in "attack ads": Revisiting negative political advertising. *Communication Research Reports, 11*(1), 67-75.

Dion, K. K., & Stein, S. (1978). Physical attractiveness and interpersonal influence. *Journal of Experimental and Social Psychology, 14,* 97-108.

Dionne, E. J. (1980, May 4). Experts find polls influence activists *New York Times,* p. 26.

Dolbeare, K. M. (1981). *American political thought.* Belmont, CA: Wadsworth.

Donohue, T. R. (1973). Impact of viewer predispositions on political TV commercials. *Journal of Broadcasting, 18,* 3-15.

Dunn, A. W. (1986). *Public relations: A contemporary approach.* Homewood, IL: Irwin.

Dunn, S. W., & Barban, A. M. (1986). *Advertising: Its role in modern marketing* (6th ed.). New York: The Dryden Press.

Dybvig, H. E. (1970). *An analysis of political communication through television produced by the Robert Goodman Agency, Inc.* Unpublished doctoral dissertation, Southern Illinois University.

Eagley, A. H. (1978). Sex differences in influenceability. *Psychological Bulletin, 85,* 86-116.

Eagley, A. H., & Carli, L. L. (1981). Sex of researchers and sex-typed communications as determinants of sex differences in influenceability: A meta-analysis of social influence studies. *Psychological Bulletin, 90,* 1-20.

Edell, J. A., & Keller, K. L. (1989). The information processing of coordinated media campaigns. *Journal of Marketing Research, 26,* 149-163.

Edelman, M. (1964). *The symbolic uses of politics.* Urbana, IL: University of Illinois Press.

Edsall, T. B., & Edsall, M. D. (1991, May). Race. *The Atlantic Monthly,* 53-86.

Ekstrand, L. (1978, May). *An experiment to determine the effect of candidate's sex on voter choice.* Paper presented to the annual meeting of the Midwest Political Science Association, Chicago.

Eldersveld, S. J. (1956). Experimental propaganda techniques and voting behavior. *American Political Science Review, 50,* 154-165.

Elebash, C., & Rosene, J. (1982). Issues in political advertising in a Deep South gubernatorial race. *Journalism Quarterly, 59,* 420-423.

Elliott, L. A. (1980). Political action-committees—precincts of the '80s. *Arizona Law Review, 22,* 539-554.

Elliott-Boyle, D. (1985-1986). A conceptual analysis of the purpose of ethics codes. *Journal of Mass Media Ethics, 1,* 22-26.

Emerson, T. L. (1981). The affirmative side of the first amendment. *Georgia Law Review, 15,* 795-849.

Entman, R. (1981). The imperial media. In A. Meltzer (Ed.), *Politics and the oval office* (pp. 79-102). San Francisco: Institute for Contemporary Studies.

Entman, R. (1989). How the media affect what people think: An information processing approach. *Journal of Politics, 51,* 347-370.

Epstein, L. (1967). *Political parties in Western democracies.* New York: Praeger.

Erickson, J. (1982). The Democrats: Rebuilding with support groups. *Campaigns & Elections, 3,* 4-14.

Erikson, R. S. (1976). The influence of newspaper endorsements in presidential elections: The case of 1964. *American Journal of Political Science, 20,* 207-233.

Erikson, R. S., Luttbeg, N. R., & Tedin, K. L. (1991). *American public opinion* (4th ed.). New York: Macmillan.

Eron, L. D., Huesmann, L. R., Brice, P., Fischer, P., & Mermelstein, R. (1983). Age trends in the development of aggression, sex typing, and related television habits. *Developmental Psychology, 19,* 71-77.

Faber, R. J., & Storey, M. C. (1984). Recall of information from political advertising. *Journal of Advertising, 13,* 39-44.

Farmers Educational and Cooperative Union v. WDAY, Inc., 360 U.S. 525 (1959).

FEC reports on financial activity: 1987-1988. Final report: U.S. Senate and House campaigns. (1989, September). Washington, DC: Federal Election Commission.

Federal Election Commission v. Central Long Island Tax Reform, 616 F. 2d 45 (1980).

Federal Election Commission v. Hall-Tyner Election Campaign Committee, 678, F/ 2d 416 (2d. Cir. 1982).

Feldman, S. (1966). Motivational aspects of attitudinal elements and their place in cognitive interaction. In S. Feldman (Ed.), *Cognitive consistency: Motivational antecedents and behavioral consequences* (pp. 75-108). New York: Academic Press.

Felknor, B. (1992). *Political mischief: Smear, sabotage, and reform in U.S. elections.* Westport, CT: Praeger.

Fenno, R. F., Jr. (1978). *Homestyle: House members in their districts.* Boston: Little, Brown.

Festinger, L. (1957). *A theory of cognitive dissonance.* Stanford, CA: Stanford University Press.

Fiorina, M. (1977). *Congress: Keystone of the Washington establishment.* New Haven, CT: Yale University Press.

Fiorina, M. P., & Shepsle, K. A. (1990). A positive theory of negative voting. In J. A. Ferejohn & J. H. Kuklinski (Eds.), *Information and democratic processes* (pp. 220-239). Urbana, IL: University of Illinois Press.

Fishel, M. (1983). Electoral targeting, part I: For the do-it-yourself campaign. *Campaigns & Elections, 4,* 11-19.

Fishel, M. (1985a). Group process techniques and campaign planning, part I: Four Basic Sessions. *Campaigns & Elections, 6* (2), 17-22.

Fishel, M. (1985b). Group process techniques and campaign planning, part II: A case study. *Campaigns & Elections, 6* (3), 12-18.

Fisher, H. N. D. (1976). How the "I dare you!" candidate won. In R. Agranoff (Ed.), *The new style in election campaigns* (pp. 79-86). Boston: Holbrook Press.

Fisher, W. (1984). Narration as a human communication paradigm: The case of public moral argument. *Communication Monographs, 51,* 1-22.

Flanigan, W. H. (1972). *Political behavior of the American electorate* (2nd ed.). Boston: Allyn and Bacon.

Fletcher, A. D., & Bowers, T. A. (1988). *Fundamentals of advertising research* (3rd ed.). Belmont, CA: Wadsworth.

Fletcher, J. E. (1985). Physiological responses to the media. In J. R. Dominick & J. E. Fletcher (Eds.), *Broadcasting research methods* (pp. 87-106). Boston: Allyn and Bacon.

Florida Code (1990), 104.271.

Frank, R. (1973). *Message dimensions of television news.* Lexington, MA: Lexington Books.

Freedman, J. L., & Steinbruner, J. D. (1964). Perceived choice and resistance to persuasion. *Journal of Abnormal and Social Psychology, 68,* 678-681.

Frey, D. (1982). Different levels of cognitive dissonance, information seeking and information avoidance. *Journal of Personality and Social Psychology, 43,* 1175-1183.

Friends of Phil Gramm v. Americans for Phil Gramm, 587 F. Supp. 769 (1984).

Furbay, A. (1965). The influence of scattered versus compact seating on audience response. *Speech Monographs, 32,* 144-148.

Gans, H. (1979). *Deciding what's news.* New York: Vintage Books.

Garfield, B. (1990, November 5). Let voters take warning: Political advertising in this country is a travesty. *Advertising Age,* 28-29.

Garramone, G. (1985a). Effects of negative political advertising: The roles of sponsor and rebuttal. *Journal of Broadcasting and Electronic Media, 29,* 147-159.

Garramone, G. M. (1983). Issue versus image orientation and effects of political advertising. *Communication Research, 10,* 59-76.

Garramone, G. M. (1984). Voter responses to negative political ads. *Journalism Quarterly, 61,* 250-249.

Garramone, G. M. (1985b). Motivation and political information processing: Extending the gratifications approach. In S. Kraus & R. M. Perloff (Eds.), *Mass media and political thought: An information processing approach* (pp. 201-219). Beverly Hills: Sage.

Garramone, G. M. (1986). Candidate image formation: The role of information processing. In L. L. Kaid, D. Nimmo, & K. R. Sanders (Eds.), *New perspectives on political advertising* (pp. 235-247). Carbondale, IL: Southern Illinois University Press.

Garramone, G. M., Atkin, C. K., Pinkleton, B. E., & Cole, R. T. (1990). Effects of negative political advertising on the political process. *Journal of Broadcasting & Electronic Media, 34,* 299-311.

Garramone, G. M., & Smith, S. J. (1984). Reactions to political advertising: The roles of sponsor and rebuttal. *Journalism Quarterly, 61*, 771-775.

Garrison v. Louisiana, 379 U.S. 64 (1964).

Gergen, K. J. (1985). The social constructionist movement in modern psychology. *American Psychologist, 40*, 266-275.

Gersh, D. (1992, November 21). Voters feel better about the press, themselves. *Editor & Publisher, 125* (47), 13, 49.

Gertz v. Robert Welch, Inc., 94 S. Ct. 2997 (1974).

Getter, R. W., & Titus, J. E. (1984). Voter registration tapes: Mining for new votes, new voters & new money. *Campaigns & Elections, 4* (4), 4.

Gilligan, J. (Ed.). (1988). *Elections '88*. Washington, DC: Congressional Quarterly.

Glass, D. P. (1985). Evaluating presidential candidates: Who focuses on their personal attributes? *Public Opinion Quarterly, 49*, 517-534.

Glenn, N. D. (1972). The distribution of political knowledge in the United States. In D. Nimmo & C. Bonjean (Eds.), *Political attitudes and public attitudes.* (pp. 273-283). New York: McKay.

Glenn, N. D. (1973). Class and party support in the United States: Recent and emerging trends. *Public Opinion Quarterly, 37*, 1-20.

Goffman, E. (1959). *Presentation of self in everyday life.* New York: Doubleday.

Goldenberg, E. N., & Traugott, M. W. (1984). *Campaigning for Congress.* Washington, DC: Congressional Quarterly.

Goldenberg, E. N., & Traugott, M. W. (1987). Mass media in U.S. congressional elections. *Legislative Studies Quarterly, 12*, 317-339.

Golding, P. (1981). The missing dimensions—news media and the management of social change. In E. Katz & T. Szecsko (Eds.), *Mass media and social change* (pp. 63-81). Beverly Hills: Sage.

Goldman, P., & Matthews, T. (1989). *The quest for the presidency: The 1988 campaign.* New York: Simon & Schuster.

Gollin, A. E. (1980). Exploring the liaison between polling and the press. *Public Opinion Quarterly, 44*, 449.

Graber, D. A. (1976). *Verbal behavior and politics.* Urbana, IL: University of Illinois Press.

Graber, D. A. (1980). *Mass media and American politics.* Washington, DC: Congressional Quarterly Press.

Graber, D. A. (1989). *Mass media and American politics* (3rd. ed.). Washington, DC: Congressional Quarterly.

Grass, R. C., & Wallace, H. W. (1969). Satiation effects of TV commercials. *Journal of Advertising Research, 9*, 3-9.

Gray-Little, B. (1973). The salience of negative information in impression formation among two Danish samples. *Journal of Cross-Cultural Psychology, 4*, 193-206.

Greenberg, B. S. (1965). Voting intentions, election expectations and exposure to campaign information. *Journal of Communication, 15*, 149-160.

Gregg, R. B. (1984) *Symbolic inducement and knowing: A study in the foundations of rhetoric.* Columbia, SC: University of South Carolina Press.

Griffiths, M. (1985, November). "Make no heroines" may be newspapers' attitude. *Press Women*, 7-9.

Gronbeck, B. (1985, November). *The rhetoric of negative political advertising: Thoughts on the senatorial race ads in 1984.* Paper presented at the annual meeting of the Speech Communication Association Convention, Denver.

Gronbeck, B. (1992). Negative narratives in 1988 presidential campaign ads. *Quarterly Journal of Speech, 78,* 333-346.

Gronbeck, B. E. (1978). The functions of presidential campaigning. *Communication Monographs, 45,* 268-280.

Gronbeck, B. E. (1991). Ethical pivots and moral vantages in American presidential campaign dramas. In R. Denton (Ed.), *Ethical dimensions of political communication* (pp. 50-68). New York: Praeger.

Grossman, M. B., & Kumar, M. J. (1981). *Portraying the president: The White House and the news media.* Baltimore: Johns Hopkins University Press.

Groth, A. J. (1971). *Major ideologies.* New York: Wiley.

Grotjohn v. McCollar, 291 Minn. 344, 191 N.W. 2d 396 (1971).

Grove, L. (1988, Nov. 13). Attack ads trickled up from state races. *The Washington Post,* A1, pp. 18-19.

Grush, J. E. (1980). Impact of candidate expenditures, regionality, and prior outcomes on the 1976 Democratic presidential primaries. *Journal of Personality and Social Psychology, 38,* 337-347.

Grush, J. E., McKeough, K. L., & Ahlering, R. F. (1978). Extrapolating laboratory research to actual political elections. *Journal of Personality and Social Psychology, 36,* 257-270.

Guste v. Connick, 515 S1. 2d 436 (1987).

Hagstrom, J. (1992). *Political consulting: A guide for reporters and citizens.* New York: The Freedom Forum Media Studies Center, Columbia University.

Hagstrom, J., & Guskind, R. (1986). Selling the candidates. *National Journal, 18,* 2619-2626.

Haight, T., & Brody, R. (1977). The mass media and presidential popularity. *Communication Research, 4,* 41-60.

Hall, P. (1972). A symbolic interactionist analysis of politics. *Sociological Inquiry, 42,* 35-75.

Hall, P. (1977). *The presidency and impression management.* Paper presented at the annual meeting of the American Sociological Convention, Chicago.

Halpern, R. S. (1967). Application of pupil response to before-and-after experiments. *Journal of Marketing Research, 4,* 320-321.

Halverson, R. R., & Pallak, M. S. (1978). Commitment, ego-involvement, and resistance to attack. *Journal of Experimental Social Psychology, 14,* 1-12.

Hamilton, D. L., & Huffman, L. F. (1971). Generality of impression-formation processes for evaluative and non-evaluative judgments. *Journal of Personality and Social Psychology, 20,* 200-207.

Hamilton, D. L., & Zanna, M. P. (1972). Differential weighting of favorable and unfavorable attributes in impression formation. *Journal of Experimental Research in Personality, 6,* 204-212.

Harkins, S. G., & Petty, R. E. (1981). The multiple source effect in persuasion: The effects of distraction. *Personality and Social Psychology Bulletin, 7,* 627-633.

Harmon, R. R., & Coney, K. A. (1982). The persuasive effects of source credibility in buy and lease situations. *Journal of Marketing Research, 19,* 255-260.

Harrison, T. (1980). Impact polling: Feedback for a winning strategy. *Campaigns & Elections, 1,* 8-13.

Hart, R. (1987). *The sound of leadership: Presidential communication in the modern age.* Chicago: University of Chicago Press.

Haskins, J. B. (1968). *How to evaluate mass communications.* New York: Advertising Research Foundation.

Hawaii Code (1989),19-3 Election frauds (6).

Hedlund, R. D., Freeman, P. K., Hamm, K. E., & Stein, R. M. (1979). The electability of women candidates: The effects of sex role stereotypes. *The Journal of Politics, 41,* 513-524.

Heflin, D. T. A., & Haygood, R. C. (1985). Effects of scheduling on retention of advertising messages. *Journal of Advertising, 14,* 41-47.

Heller, D. J. (1987). In re Garvey v. Kasten: What happens when an attack ad is "wrong"? *Campaigns & Elections, 8,* 79.

Hellweg, S. (1979). An examination of voter conceptualizations of the ideal political candidate. *Southern Speech Communication Journal, 4,* 373-385.

Hennessey, B. C. (1970). A headnote on the existence and study of political attitudes. *Social Science Quarterly, 51,* 463-476.

Henry, J. (1963). *Culture against man.* New York: Random House.

Hermann, M. (1986). Political leadership. In M. G. Hermann (Ed.), *Political Psychology* (pp. 167-192). San Francisco: Josey-Bass Publishers.

Hershey, M. R. (1974). *The making of a campaign strategy.* Lexington, MA: Lexington Books.

Hickman, H. (1991). Public polls and election participants. In P. J. Lavrakas and J. K. Holey (Eds.), *Polling and presidential election coverage,* pp. 100-133. Newbury Park, CA: Sage.

Hiebert, R., Jones, R., Lotito, E., & Lorenz, J. (Eds.) (1971). *The political image merchants: Strategies in the NEW POLITICS.* Washington, DC: Acropolis Books.

Hill, D. (1984). Political campaigns and Madison Avenue: A wavering partnership. *Journal of Advertising, 13,* 21-26.

Himmelweit, H. T., Humphreys, P., Jaegers, M., & Katz, M. (1981). *How voters decide: A longitudinal study of political attitudes and voting extending over fifteen years.* London: Academic Press.

Hodges, B. H. (1974). Effect of valence on relative weighting in impression formation. *Journal of Personality and Social Psychology, 30,* 378-381.

Hoffman, L. W. (1977). Changes in family roles, socialization, and sex differences. *American Psychologist, 32,* 644-657.

Hofstetter, C. R., & Buss, T. F. (1980). Politics and last-minute television. *Western Political Quarterly,* 33, 24-37.

Hofstetter, C. R., & Zukin, C. (1979). TV network news and advertising in the Nixon and McGovern campaigns. *Journalism Quarterly, 56,* 106-115, 152.

Hofstetter, C. R., Zukin, C., & Buss, T. F. (1978). Political imagery and information in an age of television. *Journalism Quarterly, 55,* 562-569.

Hogan, J. M. (1984). Wallace and the wallacites: A reexamination. *The Southern Speech Communication Journal, 50,* 24-48.

Hollander, E. P. (1985). Leadership and power. In G. Lindzey & E. Aronson (Eds.), *The handbook of social psychology*, Vol. II (3rd ed., pp. 485-537). New York: Random House.

Holman, C. H. (1972). *A handbook to literature*, 3rd ed. New York: Odyssey Press.

Holsti, O. (1969). Content analysis for the social sciences and humanities. Reading, MA: Addison-Wesley.

Horton, D., & Wohl, R. (1956). Mass communication and para-social interaction: Observations on intimacy at a distance. *Psychiatry, 19*, 215-229.

Hovland, C. I., Janis, I. L., & Kelley, H. H. (1953). *Communication and persuasion.* New Haven, CT: Yale University Press.

Hughes, R. H. (1984). Voter behavior: Geopartisan v. geodemographic data. *Campaigns & Elections, 5*, 27-35.

Husson, W., Stephen, T., Harrison, T. M., & Fehr, B. J. (1988). An interpersonal communication perspective on images of political candidates. *Human Communication Research, 14*, 397-421.

Huston, T. L. (1973). Ambiguity of acceptance, social desirability and dating choice. *Journal of Experimental and Social Psychology, 9*, 32-42.

Illinois code of fair campaign practices, P.A. 86-873 (1990).

Ivengar, S., & Kinder, D. R. (1986). More than meets the eye: TV news, priming, and public evaluations of the president. In G. Comstock (Ed.), *Public communication and behavior*, Vol. 1 (pp. 135-171). Orlando, FL: Free Press.

Ivey, A., & Hurst, J. (1971). Communication as adaptation. *Journal of Communication, 21*, 199-207.

Jacobson, G. (1980). *Money in congressional elections.* New Haven, CT: Yale University Press.

Jacobson, G. C. (1975). The impact of broadcast campaigning on electoral outcomes. *Journal of Politics, 37*, 769-793.

Jamieson, K. H. (1984). *Packaging the presidency: A history and criticism of presidential campaign advertising* (2nd pr.), New York: Oxford University Press.

Jamieson, K. H. (1988). *Eloquence in an electronic age: The transformation of political speechmaking.* New York: Oxford University Press.

Jamieson, K. H. (1992). *Dirty politics: Deception, distraction, and democracy.* New York: Oxford University Press.

Jamieson, K. H., & Birdsell, D. S. (1988). *Presidential debates.* New York: Oxford University Press.

Jamieson, K. H., & Campbell, K. K. (1983). *The interplay of influence: Mass media and their publics in news, advertising, politics.* Belmont, CA: Wadsworth.

Janis, I. L., & Field, P. B. (1959). A behavioral assessment of persuasibility. In C. I. Hovland and I. L. Janis (Eds.), *Personality and persuasibility* (pp. 29-54). New Haven, CT: Yale University Press.

Janis, I. L., & Rife, D. (1959). Persuasibility and emotional disorder. In C. I. Hovland and I. L. Janis (Eds.), *Personality and persuasibility* (pp. 121-140). New Haven, CT: Yale University Press.

Janowitz, M. (1976). Content analysis and the study of sociopolitical change. *Journal of Communication, 26*, 10-21.

Jennings, M. K., & Niemi (1974). *The political character of adolescence: The influence of families and schools.* Princeton, NJ: Princeton University Press.

Jensen, R. (1968, May). *American election campaigns: A theoretical and historical typology.* Paper presented at the annual meeting of the Midwest Political Science Association, Chicago.

Johnson, J. T., & Taylor, S. E. (1981). The effect of metaphor on political attitudes. *Basic Applied Social Psychology, 2,* 305-316.

Johnson, K. S. (1981). Political party and media evolutions in the United States and Great Britain: A comparative functional analysis. In J. P. McKerns (Ed.), *Communications Research Symposium: Proceedings, 4,* 122-163.

Johnson, K. S. (1984). *Impression management during the presidential transitions of Nixon, Carter, and Reagan: A quantitative content analysis and thematic analysis.* Unpublished doctoral dissertation, University of Tennessee, Knoxville.

Johnson, K. S. (1985). The honeymoon period: Fact or fiction. *Journalism Quarterly, 62,* 869-876.

Johnson, K. S., & Copeland, G. A. (1987, May). *Setting the parameters of good taste: Negative political advertising.* Paper presented at the annual meeting of the International Communication Association Convention, Montreal, Canada.

Johnson, K. S., & Elebash, C. (1986). The contagion from the right: The Americanization of British political advertising. In L. L. Kaid, D. Nimmo, & K. Sanders (Eds.), *New perspectives on political advertising,* (pp. 293-313). Carbondale, IL: Southern Illinois University Press.

Johnson-Cartee, K. S., & Copeland, G. A. (1989a, May). *Alabama voters and the acceptance of negative political advertising in the 1986 elections: An historical anomaly.* Paper presented at the annual meeting of the International Communication Association Convention, San Francisco.

Johnson-Cartee, K. S., & Copeland, G. A. (1989b). Southern voters' reaction to negative political ads in the 1986 election. *Journalism Quarterly, 66,* 888-893, 986.

Johnson-Cartee, K. S., & Copeland, G. A. (1991a). *Negative political advertising: Coming of age.* Hillsdale, NJ: Lawrence Erlbaum.

Johnson-Cartee, K. S., & Copeland, G. A. (1991b, March). *Positivizing negative political advertising.* Presentation at the Conference on Professional Responsibility and Ethics in the Political Process, The American Association of Political Consultants, Colonial Williamsburg, VA.

Johnson-Cartee, K. S., & Copeland, G. A. (1997). *Manipulation of the American Voter: Political Campaign Commercials,* Westport, CT: Praeger.

Johnson-Cartee, K. S., Copeland, G. A., & Elebash, C. (1992, October) *Us versus them: George C. Wallace's negative political advertising,* Paper presented to the annual meeting of the Tennessee Speech Communication Association, Natchez Trace State Park, TN.

Johnson-Cartee, K. S., Elebash, C., & Copeland, G. A. (1992, August). *George C. Wallace's legacy: Thirty years of negative political advertising.* Paper presented at the annual meeting of the Association for Education in Journalism and Mass Communication, Montreal, Canada.

Johnston, A., & White, A. B. (1994). Communication styles and female candidates: A study of the political advertising during the 1986 senate elections. *Journalism Quarterly, 71,* 321-329.

Jordan, N. (1965). The "asymmetry" of "liking" and "disliking": A phenomenon meriting further replication and research. *Public Opinion Quarterly, 29*, 315-322.

Joslyn, R. (1986). Political advertising and the meaning of elections. In L. L. Kaid, D. Nimmo, & K. R. Sanders (Eds.) *New perspectives on political advertising* (pp. 139-183). Carbondale: Southern Illinois University Press.

Joslyn, R. A. (1980). The content of political spot ads. *Journalism Quarterly, 57*, 92-98.

Josyln, R. A. (1981). The impact of campaign spot advertising on voting defections. *Human Communication Research, 7*, 347-360.

Kahn, K. F. (1993). Gender differences in campaign messages: The political advertisements of men and women candidates for U.S. Senate. *Political Research Quarterly, 46*, 482-502.

Kaid, L. L. (1976). Measures of political advertising. *Journal of Advertising Research, 16*, 49-53.

Kaid, L. L. (1981). Political advertising. In D. Nimmo & K. R. Sanders (Eds.), *Handbook of political communication* (pp. 249-271). Beverly Hills: Sage.

Kaid, L. L. (1982). Paid television advertising and candidate name affiliation. *Campaigns & Elections, 3*, 34-36.

Kaid, L. L. (1991). Ethical dimensions of political advertising. In R. Denton (Ed.), *Ethical dimensions of political communication* (pp. 145-169). New York: Praeger.

Kaid, L. L., & Boydston, J. (1987). An experimental study of the effectiveness of negative political advertisements. *Communication Quarterly, 35*, 193-201.

Kaid, L. L., & Davidson, D. K. (1986). Elements of videostyle: Candidate presentation through television advertising. In L. L. Kaid, D. Nimmo, & K. R. Sanders (Eds.), *New perspectives on political advertising* (pp. 184-209). Carbondale, IL: Southern Illinois University Press.

Kaid, L. L., & Johnston, A. (1991). Negative versus positive television advertising in U.S. presidential campaigns, 1960-1988. *Journal of Communication, 41*, 53-64.

Kaid, L. L., Leland, C. M., & Whitney, S. (1992).The impact of televised political ads: Evoking viewer responses in the 1988 presidential campaign. *The Southern Communication Journal, 57*, 285-295.

Kaid, L. L., Myers, S. L., Pipps, V., & Hunter, J. (1985). Sex role perceptions and televised political advertising: Comparing male and female candidates. *Women & Politics, 4*, 41-53.

Kaid, L. L., & Sanders, K. R. (1978). Political television commercials: An experimental study of type and length. *Communication Research, 5*, 57-70.

Kamin, H. (1978). Advertising reach and frequency, *Journal of Advertising Research, 18*, 21-25.

Katz, D. (1960). The functional approach to the study of attitudes. *Public Opinion Quarterly, 24*, 163-204.

Katz, E., Blumler, J. G. & Gurevitch, M. (1974). Utilization of mass communication by the individual. In J. G. Blumler & E. Katz (Eds.), *The uses of mass communication: Current perspectives on gratifications research* (pp. 19-32). Beverly Hills: Sage.

Katz, E., & Feldman, J. J. (1962). The great debate in the light of research: A survey of surveys. In S. Kraus (Ed.), *The great debates* (173-223). Bloomington, IN: Indiana University Press.

Keating, J. P., & Latané, B. (1976). Politicians on TV: The image is the message. *Journal of Social Issues, 4,* 116-132.

Keeter, S. (1987). The illusion of intimacy: Television and the role of candidate personal qualities in voter choice. *Public Opinion Quarterly, 51,* 344-358.

Keeter, S., & Zukin, C. (1982). New romances and old horses: The public's images of presidential candidates. In D. Barber (Ed.), *The president and the public* (pp. 39-82). Philadelphia: ISHI.

Kellermann, K. (1984). The negativity effect and its implications for initial interaction. *Communication Monographs, 51,* 37-55.

Kelly, J. (1984, Nov. 12). Packaging the presidency. *Time, 36.*

Kelly, S., Jr. (1960). *Political campaigning: Problems in creating an informed electorate.* Washington, DC: The Brookings Institute.

Kendall, K. E., & Yum, J. O. (1984). Persuading the blue-collar voter: Issues, images and homophily. In R. N. Bostrom (Ed.), *Communication Yearbook 8* (pp. 707-722). Beverly Hills: Sage.

Kennedy v. Voss, 304 N.W. 2d 299 (1981).

Kern, M. (1989). *Thirty-second politics: Political advertising in the eighties.* New York: Praeger.

Kern, M., & Just, M. (1992). *The focus group method, ads, news and the construction of candidate images.* Paper presented to the annual meeting of the American Political Science Association, Chicago.

Kernell, S. (1977). Presidential popularity and negative voting: An alternative explanation of the midterm congressional decline of the president's party. *American Political Science Review, 71,* 44-66.

Kessel, J. H. (1965). Cognitive dimensions and political activity. *Public Opinion Quarterly, 29,* 377-389.

Key, V. O. (1961). *Public opinion and American democracy.* New York: Knopf.

Kinder, D. R., & Abelson, R. P. (1981). *Appraising presidential candidates: Personality and affect in the 1980 campaign.* Paper presented at the annual meeting of the American Political Science Association, New York.

Kinder, D. R., & Sears, D. O. (1985). Public opinion and political action. In G. Lindzey and E. Aronson (Eds.), *The handbook of social psychology,* Vol. 11 (3rd ed., pp. 659-741). New York: Random House.

King, B. T. (1959). Relationships between susceptibility to opinion change and child-rearing practices. In C. I. Hovland and I. L. Janis (Eds.), *Personality and persuasibility* (pp. 207-221). New Haven, CT: Yale University Press.

Kingdon, J. (1968). *Candidates for office: Beliefs and strategies.* New York: Random House.

Kitchens, J. T., & Powell, L. (1986). A critical analysis of NCPAC's strategies in key 1980 races: A third party negative campaign. *The Southern Speech Communication Journal, 51,* 208-228.

Kitchens, J. T., & Stiteler, B. (1979). Challenge to the "rule of minimum effect": A case study of the in man-out man strategy. *The Southern Speech Communication Journal, 44,* 176-190.

Kjeldahl, B., Carmichael, C., & Mertz, R. (1971). Factors in a presidential candidate image. *Speech Monographs, 38,* 129-133.

Klapp, O. (1964). *Symbolic leaders: Public dramas and public men.* New York: Minerva Press.

Klapper, J. T. (1960). *The effects of mass communication.* Glencoe, IL: Free Press.

Klein, J. G. (1991). Negativity effects in impression formation: A test in the political arena. *Personality and Social Psychology Bulletin, 17,* 412-418.

Knight, G., & Dean, T. (1982). Myth and the structure of news. *Journal of Communication, 32,* 144-161.

Kraus, S., & Davis, D. (1976). *The effects of mass communication on political behavior.* University Park, PA: Pennsylvania State University Press.

Krech, D., Crutchfield, R., & Ballachey, E. (1962). *Individual in society.* New York: McGraw-Hill.

Krueger, R. A. (1988). *Focus groups: A practical guide for applied research.* Newbury Park, CA: Sage.

Krugman, H. E. (1964). Some applications of pupil measurement. *Journal of Marketing Research, 1,* 15-19.

Krugman, H. E. (1965-1966). The impact of television advertising: Learning without involvement. *Public Opinion Quarterly, 29,* 249-356.

Krugman, H. E. (1971). Brain wave measures of media involvement. *Journal of Advertising Research, 11,* 3-9.

Krugman, H. E. (1972). Why three exposures may be enough. *Journal of Advertising Research, 12,* 11-14.

Kumar, M., & Grossman, M. (1981). The refracting lens: The president as he appears through the media. In H. Relyea (Ed.), *The presidency and information policy* (pp. 102-138). New York: Center for the Study of the Presidency.

Kurtz, D. L., & Boone, L. E. (1984). *Marketing* (2nd ed.). Hinsdale, IL: Dryden Press.

Lane, R. E. (1978). Interpersonal relations and leadership in a "society." *Comparative Politics,* 10, 443-459.

Lang, A. (1990). Involuntary attention and physiological arousal evoked by structural features and emotional content in TV commercials. *Communication Research, 17,* 275-299.

Lang, A. (1991). Emotion, formal features, and memory for televised political advertisements. In F. Biocca (Ed.) *Television and political advertising volume 1: Psychological processes* (pp. 221-243). Hillsdale, NJ: Lawrence Erlbaum.

Lang, K., & Lang, G. (1968). *Politics and television.* Chicago: Quadrangle.

Lashbrook, V. J. (1975). Leadership emergence and source valence: Concepts in support of interaction theory and measurement. *Human Communication Research, 1,* 308-315.

Lasswell, H. D. (1948). The structure and functions of communication in society. In L. Bryson (Ed.), *The communication of ideas* (pp. 37-51). New York: Institute for Religious and Social Studies.

Latimer, M. K. (1984). Political advertising for federal and state elections: Images or substance? *Journalism Quarterly, 62,* 861-868.

Lau, R. R. (1980). *Negativity in political perceptions.* Unpublished manuscript, Department of Psychology, University of California, Los Angeles.

Lau, R. R. (1982). Negativity in political perception. *Political Behavior, 4*, 353-378.

Lau, R. R. (1985). Two explanations for negativity effects in political behavior. *American Journal of Political Science, 29*, 119-138.

Lavrakas, P. J., Holley, J. K., and Miller, P. V. (1991). Public reactions to polling news during the 1988 presidential election campaign. In P. J. Lavrakas and J. K. Holey (Eds.), *Polling and presidential election coverage* (pp. 151-183). Newbury Park, CA: Sage.

Law of Political Broadcasting and Cablecasting, 69 F.C.C. 2d 78-523 (1978)

The Law of Political Broadcasting and Cablecasting: A Political Primer, 1984 Edition (1984). Washington, DC: Federal Communications Commission.

Lazarsfeld, P. F., Berelson, B., & Gaudet, H. (1948). *The people's choice.* New York: Columbia University Press.

Lazarsfeld, P. F., & Stanton, F. (Eds.). (1942). *Communication research.* New York: Harper.

Lazarsfeld, P. F., & Stanton, F. (Eds.). (1942). *Radio Research, 1941.* New York: Duell, Sloan & Pearce.

Lazarsfeld, P. F., & Stanton, F. (Eds.). (1944). *Radio Research, 1942-43.* New York: Duell, Sloan & Pearce.

Lebacqz, K. (1985). *Professional ethics.* Nashville: Abingdon Press.

Lee, D., Johnson, W., & Beld, J. (1979). The rhetorical challenge of the Carter transition: To build a governing majority. In D. Nimmo (Ed.), *Communication Yearbook 3* (pp. 475-489). New Brunswick: NJ: Transaction Books.

Leeper, M. S. (1991). The impact of prejudice on female candidates: An experimental look at voter inference. *American Politics Quarterly, 19*, 248-261.

Lehmann, S. (1970). Personality and compliance: A study of anxiety and self-esteem in opinion and behavior change. *Journal of Personality and Social Psychology, 15*, 76-86.

Lemert, J. B., Elliot, W. R., Bernstein, J. M., Rosenberg, W. L., & Nestvold, K. J. (1991). *News verdicts, the debates, and presidential campaigns.* New York: Praeger.

Leuthold, D. A., & Valentine, D. C. (1981). How Reagan "won" the Cleveland debate: Audience predispositions and presidential winners. *Speaker and Gavel, 18*, 60-66.

Leventhal, H., & Singer, D. (1964). Cognitive complexity, impression formation, and impression change. *Journal of Personality, 32*, 210-226.

Levin, I. P., & Schmidt, C. F. (1969). Sequential effects in impression formation with binary intermittent responding. *Journal of Experimental Psychology, 79*, 283-287.

Linton, H., & Graham, E. (1959). Personality correlates of persuasibility. In C. I. Hovland and I. L. Janis (Eds.), *Personality and persuasibility* (pp. 69-101). New Haven, CT: Yale University Press.

Lippmann, W. (1965). *Public opinion.* New York: Free Press.

Littlejohn, S. W. (1989). *Theories of human communication* (3rd ed.). Belmont, CA: Wadsworth.

Lorenz, J. D. (1978, Feb. 12). An insider's view of Jerry Brown. *Chicago Tribune.*

Luke, T. (1986-1987). Televisual democracy and the politics of charisma. *Telos, 70*, 59-79.

Maccoby, E. E., & Jacklin, C. N. (1974). *The psychology of sex differences.* Stanford, CA: Stanford University Press.

MacKenzie, S. B., & Lutz, R. J. (1989). An empirical examination of the structural antecedents of attitude toward the ad in an advertising pretesting context. *Journal of Marketing, 53,* 48-65.

Magill, A. (1982). Turning census data into meaningful information for political strategists. *Campaigns & Elections, 2,* 4-17.

Malchow, H. (1981). The use of adverse publicity to regulate campaign speech. *Pacific Law Journal, 12,* 811-828.

Mandel, R. B. (1981). *In the running: The new woman candidate.* New Haven, CT: Ticknor & Fields.

Mandese, J. (1992, October 19). Massive political buys lift Big 3. *Advertising Age,* 1, 3, 52.

Mansfield, M. W., & Hale, K. (1986). Uses and perceptions of political television: An application of Q-technique. In L. L. Kaid, D. Nimmo, & K. R. Sanders (Eds.), *New perspectives on political advertising.* Carbondale, IL: Southern Illinois University Press.

Markerson, L., & Goldstein, J. (1994). *Open secrets: The encyclopedia of congressional money & politics: The 1992 election* (3rd ed.). Washington, DC: Center for Responsive Politics, Congressional Quarterly.

Marshall, C., & Rossman, G. B. (1989). *Designing qualitative research.* Newbury Park, CA: Sage.

Marshall, T. (1983). The news verdict and public opinion during the primaries. In W. C. Adams (Ed.), *Television coverage of the 1980 presidential campaign.* Norwood, NJ: Ablex.

Martel, M. (1983). *Political campaign debates: Images, strategies, and tactics.* New York: Longman.

Martz, L., Warner, M. G., Fineman, H., Clift, E. & Starr, M. (1988, Oct. 31). The smear campaign. *Newsweek,* 16-19.

Mason, W. M. (1973). The impact of endorsements on voting. *Sociological Methods and Research, 1,* 463-495.

Matalin, M., & Carville, J. (1994). *All's fair.* New York: Random House.

Matthews, D. R. (1978). Winnowing. In J. D. Barber (Ed.), *Race for the presidency* (pp. 55-78). Englewood Cliffs, NJ: Prentice-Hall.

Mayo, C. W., & Crockett, W. H. (1964). Cognitive complexity and primacy-recency effects in impression formation. *Journal of Abnormal and Social Psychology, 68,* 335-338.

McBurney, J. H., & Mills, G. E. (1964). *Argumentation and debate: Techniques of a free society* (2nd ed.). New York: Macmillan.

McCabe, E. (1988, December 12). The campaign you never saw. *New York Magazine,* 33-48.

McCleneghan, J. S. (1980). Media and non-media effects in Texas mayoral elections. *Journalism Quarterly, 57,* 129-134, 201.

McClure, R. D., & Patterson, T. E. (1974). Television news and political advertising: The impact on voter beliefs. *Communication Research, 1,* 3-31.

McCombs, M. (1972). Mass communication in political campaigns: Information, gratification, and persuasion. In F. G. Kline & P. J. Tichenor (Eds.), *Current perspectives in mass communication research* (pp. 169-194). Beverly Hills: Sage.

McCombs, M. (1979). An address to the College of Communication at the University of Tennessee-Knoxville.

McCombs, M. E., & Shaw, D. L. (1972). The agenda-setting function of the mass media. *Public Opinion Quarterly, 36*, 176-187.

McCroskey, J. (1970). The effects of evidence as an inhibitor of counter-persuasion. *Speech Monographs, 37*, 188-194.

McCroskey, J. C., & Combs, W. H. (1969). The effects of the use of analogy on attitude change and source credibility. *Speech Monographs, 36*, 13-21.

McEwen, C. A. (1980). Continuities in the study of total and nontotal institutions. *Annual Review Sociology, 6*, 143-185.

McGann, A. F. (1984). Political advertising [Editorial]. *Journal of Advertising, 13*, 3.

McGinnis, J. (1969). *The selling of the president 1968.* New York: Trident Press.

McGrath, J., & McGrath, M. (1962). Effects of partisanship on perceptions of political figures. *Public Opinion Quarterly, 26*, 236-248.

McGuiness, C. (Ed.). (1986). *Elections '86.* Washington, DC: Congressional Quarterly.

McGuire, W. J. (1961a). The effectiveness of supportive and refutational defenses in immunizing and restoring beliefs against persuasion. *Sociometry, 24*, 184-197.

McGuire, W. J. (1961b). Resistance to persuasion conferred by active and passive prior refutation of the same and alternate counterarguments. *Journal of Abnormal and Social Psychology, 63*, 326-332.

McGuire, W. J. (1962). Persistence of resistance to persuasion induced by various types of prior belief defenses. *Journal of Abnormal and Social Psychology, 64*, 241-248.

McGuire, W. J. (1964). Inducing resistance to persuasion: Some contemporary approaches. In L. Berkowitz (Ed.), *Advances in experimental social psychology, Vol. 1* (pp. 191-229). New York: Academic Press.

McGuire, W. J. (1969). The nature of attitudes and attitude change. In G. Lindzey & E. Aronson (Eds.), *The handbook of social psychology, Vol. 3: The individual in social context* (2nd ed., pp. 136-314). Reading, MA.: Addison-Wesley.

McGuire, W. J. (1985). Attitudes and attitude change. In G. Lindzey & E. Aronson (Eds.), *The handbook of social psychology, Vol. II* (3rd ed., pp. 233-346). New York: Random House.

McGuire, W. J., & Papageorgis, D. (1961). The relative efficacy of various types of prior belief defense in producing immunity against persuasion. *Journal of Abnormal and Social Psychology, 62*, 327-337.

McGuire, W. J, & Papageorgis, D. (1962). Effectiveness in forewarning in developing resistance to persuasion. *Public Opinion Quarterly, 26*, 24-34.

McLeod, J., Becker, L., & Byrnes, J. (1974). Another look at the agenda-setting function of the press. *Communication Research, 1*, 131-167.

McLuhan, M., & Fiore, Q. (1968). *War and peace in the global village.* New York: McGraw-Hill.

Mead, G. H. (1934). *Mind, self and society: From the standpoint of a social behaviorist*. Chicago: University of Chicago Press.

Meadow, R. G., & Sigelman, L. (1982). Some effects and noneffects of campaign commercials: An experimental study. *Political Behavior, 4*, 163-175.

Mehrley, R. S., & McCroskey, J. C. (1970). Opinionated statements and attitude intensity as predictors of attitude change and source credibility. *Speech Monographs, 37*, 47-52.

Meiklejohn, A. (1948). *Free speech: And its relation to self-government*. New York: Harper & Brothers.

Melton, J. G., & Moore, R. L. (1982). *The cult experience: Responding to the new religious pluralism*. New York: Pilgrim Press.

Mendelsohn, H., & Crespi, I. (1970). *Polls, television and the new politics*. Scranton, PA: Chandler.

Mendelsohn, H., & O'Keefe, G. J. (1976). *The people choose a president: A study of vote decisions in the making*. Department of Mass Communication, Denver, CO: University of Denver.

Merritt, S. (1984). Negative political advertising: Some empirical findings. *Journal of Advertising, 13*, 27-38.

Meyer, T. P., & Donohue, T. R. (1973). Perceptions and misperceptions of political advertising. *Journal of Business Communication, 10*, 29-46.

Meyrowitz, J. (1985). *No sense of place: The impact of electronic media on social behavior*. New York: Oxford University Press.

Miami Herald Publishing Co. v. Tornillo, 418 U.S. 241 (1974).

Middleton, K. R., & Chamberlin, B. F. (1988). *The law of public communication*. White Plains, NY: Longman.

Miller, A. H., Wattenberg, M. P., & Malanchuk, O. (1986). Schematic assessments of presidential candidates. *American Political Science Review, 80*, 521-540.

Miller, G. R., & Basehart, J. (1969). Source trustworthiness, opinionated statements, and the response to persuasive communication. *Speech Mono-graphs, 36*, 1-7.

Miller, J. W., & Rowe, R. M. (1967). Influence of favorable and unfavorable information upon assessment decisions. *Journal of Applied Psychology, 51*, 432-435.

Miller, W. E., Miller, A. H., & Schneider, E. J. (1980). *American national election studies data sourcebook, 1952-1978*. Cambridge: Harvard University Press.

Mills v. Alabama, 3834 U.S. 214, 218 (1966).

Mississippi Corrupt Practices Law of 1935, 23-3-33, (1935).

Monge, P. (1977). The systems perspective as a theoretical basis for the study of human communication. *Communication Quarterly, 25*, 19-29.

Monitor Patriot Co. v. Roy, 401 U.S. 265, 271-272 (1971).

Montana Code Ann. 13-35-234 (1989).

Moore, D. W. (1994, December). Post-election bounce for Republican party. *The Gallup Monthly Report*, 14-15.

Moore, H. F., & Kalupa, F. B. (1985). *Public relations: Principles, cases, and problems* (9th ed.). Homewood, IL: Irwin.

Morreale, J. (1991a). *A new beginning: A textual frame analysis of the political campaign film*. Albany, NY: State University of New York Press.

Morreale, J. (1991b). The political campaign film: Epideictic rhetoric in a documentary frame. In F. Biocca (Ed.), *Television and political advertising: Signs, codes, and images*, Vol. 2 (pp. 187-201). Hillsdale, NJ: Lawrence Erlbaum.

Morris, D., & Gamache, M. (1994). *Handbook of campaign spending: Money in the 1992 congressional races*. Washington, DC: Congressional Quarterly.

Moshavi, S. D. (1992, November 2). Elections enter new television age. *Broadcasting*, 12-13.

Mulder, R. (1979). The effects of televised political ads in the 1975 Chicago mayoral election. *Journalism Quarterly, 56*, 336-340.

Mullen, J. J. (1963a). How candidates for the Senate use newspaper advertising. *Journalism Quarterly, 40*, 532-538.

Mullen, J. J. (1963b). Newspaper advertising in the Kennedy-Nixon campaign. *Journalism Quarterly, 40*, 3-11.

Mullen, J. J. (1968). Newspaper advertising in the Johnson-Goldwater campaign. *Journalism Quarterly, 45*, 219-225.

Napolitan, J. (1972). *The election game*. Garden City, NY: Doubleday.

Nasty ads are here again (1991, January 7). *U.S. News and World Report*, 50-51.

National Journal (1994, Nov. 12).

Negative advertising pro and con. (1986, Nov. 10). *Advertising Age*, 104.

NES Survey. National Election Study. Interuniversity Consortium for Political and Social Research. Ann Arbor, MI: University of Michigan.

Neustadt, R. (1980). *Presidential power*. New York: Wiley.

New Campaign Techniques. (1986). *Elections '86* (pp. 29-35). Washington, DC: Congressional Quarterly.

New York code of fair campaign practice, c. 8, (March 7, 1978).

New York Times v. Sullivan, 376 U.S. 254 (1964).

Newsom, D., & Scott, A. (1985). *This is PR: The realities of public relations* (3rd ed.). Belmont, CA: Wadsworth.

Nie, N. H., & Anderson, K. (1974). Mass belief systems revisited: Political change and attitude structure. *Journal of Politics, 36*, 540-490.

Nie, N. H., Verba, S., & Petrocik, J. R. (1976). *The changing American voter*, 2nd ed. Cambridge: Harvard University Press.

Nie, N., Verba, S., & Petrocik, J. (1979). *The changing American voter*. Cambridge: Harvard University Press.

Nielsen Media Research. (1993). *Nielsen tunes in to politics: Tracking the presidential election years (1960-1992)*. A. C. Nielsen Company.

Nimmo, D. (1970). *The political persuaders: The techniques of modern election campaigns*. Englewood Cliffs, NJ: Prentice-Hall.

Nimmo, D. (1978). *Political communication and public opinion in America*. Santa Monica: Goodyear.

Nimmo, D. (1986). Teleparty politics. *Campaigns & Elections, 6*, 75-78.

Nimmo, D., & Combs, J. (1980). *Subliminal politics: Myths and mythmakers in America*. Englewood Cliffs, NJ: Prentice-Hall.

Nimmo, D., & Combs, J. (1983). *Mediated political realities*. New York: Longman.

Nimmo, D., & Johnson, K. S. (1980). Positions and images in campaign communication: Newsmagazine labeling in the 1980 pre-primary presidential contests. In J. P. McKerns (Ed.), *Communications Research Symposium: Proceedings, 3*, 36-54.

Nimmo, D., & Savage, R. (1976). *Candidates and their images: Concepts, methods, and findings*. Pacific Palisades, CA: Goodyear.

Nimmo, D., & Swanson, D. L. (1990). The field of political communication: Beyond the voter persuasion paradigm. In D. L. Swanson and D. Nimmo (Eds.), *New directions in political communication* (pp. 1-47). Newbury Park, CA: Sage.

Nine key moments. (1988, November 21). *Time, 49.*

The 1988 delegate selection. (1988). *Elections '88* (pp. 33-42). Washington, DC: Congressional Quarterly.

Nisbett, R. E., & Gordon, A. (1967). Self-esteem and susceptibility to social influence. *Journal of Personality and Social Psychology, 5*, 268-276.

Noelle-Neumann, E. (1973). Return to the concept of powerful mass media. *Studies of Broadcasting, 9*, 67-112.

Noelle-Neumann, E. (1981). Mass media and social change in developed societies. In E. Katz & T. Szecsko (Eds.), *Mass media and social change* (pp. 137-165). Beverly Hills: Sage.

Noelle-Neumann, E. (1983). The effect of media on media effects research. *Journal of Communication, 33*, 157-165.

Nothstine, W., & Copeland, G. A. (1983). *Media criticism as argument: Conditions for defense of a judgment.* Paper presented at the annual meeting of the Eastern Communication Association, Ocean City, MD.

Nugent, J. H. (1987). Positively negative. *Campaigns & Elections, 2*, 25-30.

Nygren, T. E., & Jones, L. E. (1977). Individual differences in perceptions and preferences for political candidates. *Journal of Experimental and Social Psychology, 13*, 182-197.

Ogden, D. M., Jr., & Peterson, A. L. (1968). *Electing the president.* San Francisco: Chandler.

O'Gorman, H. J. (1975). Pluralistic ignorance and white estimates for racial integration. *Public Opinion Quarterly, 39*, 313-330.

O'Hara, R. (1961). *Media for the millions.* New York: Random House.

O'Keefe, T., & Sheinkopf, K. (1974). The voter decides: Candidate image or campaign issue? *Journal of Broadcasting, 18*, 403-412.

Ornstein, N. J., Mann, T. E., Malbin, M. J., Schick, A., & Bibby, J. F. (1986). *Vital statistics in Congress: 1984-1985 edition.* Washington, DC: American Enterprise Institute for Public Policy Research.

Orum, A. M. (1972). Religion and the rise of the radical white: The case of southern Wallace support in 1968. In D. Nimmo & D. Bonjean (Eds.), *Political attitudes and public opinion* (pp. 473-488). New York: McKay.

Osgood, C. E. (1957). *The measurement of meaning.* Urbana: University of Illinois Press.

Oskamp, S. (1991). *Attitudes and opinions* (2nd ed.). Englewood Cliffs, NJ: Prentice-Hall.

Ostrom, T. M. (1969). The relationship between the affective, behavioral and cognitive components of attitude. *Journal of Experimental Social Psychology, 5*, 12-30.

Owen, D. (1991). *Media messages in American presidential elections.* Westport, CT: Greenwood Press.

Packard, V. (1958). *The hidden persuaders.* New York: Pocket Books.

Page, B. I., & Shapiro, R. (1992). *The rational public: Fifty years of trends in Americans' policy preferences.* Chicago: University of Chicago Press.

Page, B., Shapiro, R., and Dempsey, G. (1985, May). *The mass media do affect policy preferences.* Paper presented at the annual meeting of the American Association for Public Opinion Research, McAfee, NJ.

Palda, K. S. (1975). The effects of expenditure on political success. *The Journal of Law and Economics, 18,* 745-771.

Palmgreen, P., & Clarke, P. (1977). Agenda-setting with local and national issues. *Communication Research, 4,* 435-452.

Palmgreen, P., & Clarke, P. (1991). Agenda setting with local and national issues. In D. Protess & M. McCombs (Eds.). Agenda setting: Readings on media, public opinion, and policy making (pp. 109-117). Hillsdale, NJ: Lawrence Erlbaum..

Papageorgis, D., & McGuire, W. J. (1961). The generality of immunity to persuasion produced by pre-exposure to weakened counterarguments. *Journal of Abnormal and Social Psychology, 62,* 475-481.

Papert, F. (1971). Good candidates make advertising experts. In R. Hiebert, R. Jones, E. Lotito, & J. Lorenz (Eds.), *The political image merchants: Strategies in the NEW POLITICS* (pp. 97-99). Washington, DC: Acropolis Books.

Park, R. (1940). News as a form of knowledge: A chapter in the sociology of knowledge. *American Journal of Sociology, 45,* 669-686.

Patterson, T. E. (1980). *The mass media election: How Americans choose their president.* New York: Praeger.

Patterson, T. E. (1983). Money rather than TV ads judged "root cause" of election costliness. *Television/Radio Age, 44,* 130-132.

Patterson, T. E., & McClure, R. D. (1976a). Television and the less interested voter: The costs of an informed electorate. *The Annals of the American Academy of Political and Social Science, 425,* 88-97.

Patterson, T. E., & McClure, R. D. (1976b). *The unseeing eye.* New York: Putnam.

Patti, C. H., & Frazer, C. F. (1988). *Advertising: A decision-making approach.* Chicago: Dryden.

Payne, J. G., Marlier, J., & Baukus, R. A. (1989). Polispots in the 1988 presidential primaries: Separating the nominees from the rest of the guys. *American Behavioral Research, 32,* 365-381.

Pearce, W. B., & Brommel, B. J. (1972). Vocalic communication in persuasion. *Quarterly Journal of Speech, 58,* 298-306.

Pence, O. M., & Scheidel, T. M. (1956). *The effects of critical thinking ability and certain other variables on persuasibility.* Paper presented to the annual meeting of the Speech Communication Association, Chicago.

The people for the American way: A pamphlet. (1990). Washington, DC: The People for the American Way.

Perlman, D., & Oskamp, S. (1971). The effects of picture content and exposure frequency on evaluations of Negroes and whites. *Journal of Experimental Social Psychology, 7,* 503-514.

Perry, J. M. (1968). *The new politics: The expanding technology of political manipulation.* New York: Clarkson N. Potter.

Petrocik, J. R., & Steeper, F. T. (1987). The political landscape in 1987. *Public Opinion, 10* (3), 41-44.

Pfau, M. (1990). A channel approach to television influence. *Journal of Broadcasting & Electronic Media, 34*, 1-20.

Pfau, M., & Burgoon, M. (1988). Inoculation in political campaign communication. *Human Communication Research, 15*, 91-111.

Pfau, M., & Kang, J. G. (1991). The impact of relational messages on candidate influence in televised political debates. *Communication Studies, 42*, 114-128.

Pfau, M., & Kenski, H. C. (1990). *Attack politics*. New York: Praeger.

Pfau, M., & Louden, A. (1994). Effectiveness of adwatch formats in deflecting political attack ads. *Communication Research, 21*, 325-341.

The poisoned cup. (1972, July 6). *The New York Times*, p. 6.

Political action committees. (1986). *Elections '86*, (pp. 47-55). Washington, DC: Congressional Quarterly.

Political advertising's hitmen. (1980). *Marketing & Media Decisions*, 15, 59-61, 180-182.

Political party campaigning. (1986). *Elections'86* (pp. 57-64). Washington, DC: Congressional Quarterly.

Pomper, G. M. (1975). Impacts on the political system. In S. A. Kirkpatrick (Ed.), *American electoral behavior: Change and stability* (pp. 137-143). Beverly Hills: Sage.

Pool, I. (1965). *Candidates, issues, and strategies*. Cambridge, MA: MIT Press.

Popkin, S., Gorman, J. W., Phillips, C., & Smith, J. A. (1976). Comment: What have you done for me lately: Toward an investment theory of voting. *American Political Science Review, 70*, 779-805.

Presidential primaries. (1988). *Elections '88* (pp. 27-32). Washington, DC: Congressional Quarterly.

Procter, D. E., Aden, R. C., & Japp, P. (1988). Gender/issue interaction in political identity making: Nebraska's woman vs. woman gubernatorial campaign. *Central States Speech Journal, 39*, 190-203.

Radio Act of 1927, 44 Stat. 1162-1165, 1168 (1927).

Railsback, C. C. (1983, April). *The rhetoric of the New Right: Ideas and consequences*. Paper presented at the annual meeting of the Southern Speech Communication Association Convention, Orlando.

Ranney, A. (1983). *Channels of power: The impact of television on American politics*. New York: Basic Books.

Ray, M. L. (1973). Marketing communication and the hierarchy-of-effects. In P. Clarke (Ed.), *New models for mass communication research* (pp. 147-176). Beverly Hills: Sage.

Red Lion Broadcasting Co. v. FCC, 395 U.S. (1969).

Reder, L. M., & Anderson, J. R. (1980). A comparison of texts and their summaries: Memorial consequences. *Journal of Verbal Learning and Verbal Behavior, 19*, 121-134.

Reeves, B., Thorson, E., & Schleuder, J. (1986). Attention to television: Psychological theories and chronometric measures. In J. Bryant & D. Zillmann (Eds.), *Perspectives on media effects* (pp. 251-279). Hillsdale, NJ: Lawrence Erlbaum.

Reeves, R. (1961). *Reality in advertising*. New York: Knopf.

Reid, L., & Soley, L. C. (1983). Is promotional spreading in high involvement elections: An examination of the voter involvement explanation. *Journal of Advertising, 12*, 43-50.

Reynolds, R. A., & Burgoon, M. (1983). Belief processing, reasoning, and evidence. In R. N. Bostrom, *Communication yearbook 7* (pp. 83-104). Beverly Hills: Sage.

Richey, M. H., Koenigs, R. J., Richey, H. W., & Fortin, R. (1975). Negative salience on impressions of character: Effects of unequal proportions of positive and negative information. *The Journal of Social Psychology, 97*, 233-241.

Richey, M. H., McClelland, L., & Shimkunas, A. M. (1967). Relative influence of positive and negative information in impression formation and persistence. *Journal of Personality and Social Psychology, 6*, 322-327.

Riggio, R. (1987). *The charisma quotient: What it is, how to get it, how to use it.* New York: Dodd, Mead.

Riker, W. (1986). *The art of political manipulation.* New Haven, CT: Yale University Press.

Robbin, J. (1980). Geodemographics: The new magic. *Campaigns & Elections, 1*, 25-45.

Roberts, C. (1973). Voting intentions and attitude change in a congressional election. *Speech Monographs, 40*, 49-55.

Robertson, T. S. (1976). Low-commitment consumer behavior. *Journal of Advertising Research, 16*, 19-26.

Robinson, M. (1976). Public affairs television and the growth of political malaise: The case of the "selling of the Pentagon." *American Political Science Review, 70*, 409-432.

Robinson, M. J. (1981a). The media in 1980: Was the message the message? In A. Ranney (Ed.), *The American elections of 1980* (pp. 171-211). Washington, DC: American Enterprise Institute.

Robinson, M. J. (1981b). Three faces of congressional media. In T. E. Mann & N. J. Ornstein (Eds.), *The new Congress,* (pp. 55-96). Washington, DC: American Enterprise Institute.

Robinson, M. J., & Sheehan, M. (1984). *Over the wire and on TV.* New York: Russell Sage.

Roddy, B. L., & Garramone, G. M. (1988). Appeals and strategies of negative political advertising. *Journal of Broadcasting & Electronic Media, 32*, 415-427.

Rogers, R. W. (1975). A protection motivation theory of fear appeals and attitude change. *The Journal of Psychology, 91*, 93-114.

Roper, B. (1969). *A ten-year view of public attitudes toward television and other mass media, 1959-1968.* New York: Morrow.

Rosenberg, M. J., & Hovland, C. I. (1960). Cognitive, affective, and behavioral components of attitudes. In M. J. Rosenberg, C. I. Hovland, W. J. McGuire, R. P. Abelson, & J. W. Brehm (Eds.), *Attitude organization and change: An analysis of consistency among attitude components* (pp. 1-14). New Haven, CT: Yale University Press.

Rosenberg, S. W., Bohan, L., McCafferty, P., & Harris, K. (1986). The image and the vote: The effect of candidate presentation on voter preference. *American Journal of Political Science, 30*, 108-127.

Rosenberg, S. W., & McCafferty, P. (1987). The image and the vote: Manipulating voters' preferences. *Public Opinion Quarterly, 51*, 31-47.

Rothschild, M., & Ray, M. (1974). Involvement and political advertising effect: An exploratory experiment. *Communication Research, 1*, 264-284.

Rothschild, M. L. (1975). The effects of political advertising on the voting behavior of a low-involvement electorate. (Doctoral dissertation, Stanford University, 1975. *Dissertation Abstracts International, 35*, 7473A-7474A.

Rothschild, M. L. (1978). Political advertising: A neglected policy issue in marketing. *Journal of Marketing Research, 15*, 58-71.

Rubin, A. M., & Windahl, S. (1986). The uses and dependency model of mass communication. *Critical Studies in Mass Communication, 3*, 184-199.

Rubin, B. (1967). *Political television*. Belmont, CA: Wadsworth.

Rudd, R. (1986). Issues as image in political campaign commercials. *Western Journal of Speech Communication, 50*, 102-118.

Rusk, J. G., & Weisberg, H. G. (1972). Perceptions of presidential candidates: Implications for electoral change. *Midwest Journal of Political Science, 16*, 338-410.

Ryder, J. (1986). On the docket: Mudslinging "remedies" not new. *Campaigns & Elections, 7*, 72-74.

Sabato, L. (1981). *The rise of political consultants: New ways of winning elections*. New York: Basic Books.

Sabato, L. (1984). *Pac power*. New York: Norton.

Sabato, L. (1991). *Feeding frenzy: How attack journalism transformed American politics*. New York: Free Press.

Salmore, S. A., & Salmore. B. G. (1985). *Candidates, parties, and campaigns: Electoral politics in America*. Washington, DC: Congressional Quarterly.

Sampson, E. E., & Insko, C. A. (1964). Cognitive consistency and conformity in the autokinetic situation. *Journal of Personality and Social Psychology, 68*, 184-192.

Sarbin, T. R., & Coe, W. (1972). *Hypnosis: A social psychological analysis of influence communication*. New York: Holt, Rinehart & Winston.

Scarrow, H. A., & Borman, S. (1979). The effects of newspaper endorsements on election outcomes: A case study. *Public Opinion Quarterly, 43*, 388-393.

Schaffner, P. E., Wandersman, A., & Stang, D. (1981). Candidate name exposure and voting: Two field studies. *Basic and Applied Social Psychology, 2*, 195-203.

Scheidel, T. M. (1963). Sex and persuasibility. *Speech Monographs, 30*, 353-358.

Schiller, H. (1973). *The mind managers*. Boston: Beacon Press.

Schneider, E. J. (1983). Geodemographics refined: An alternative to standardized clustering. *Campaigns & Elections, 3*, 62-73.

Schram, S. F. (1991). The post-modern presidency and the grammar of electronic electioneering. *Critical Studies in Mass Communication, 8*, 210-216.

Schramm, W., & Carter, R. F. (1959). Effectiveness of a political telethon. *Public Opinion Quarterly, 23*, 121-126.

Schudson, M. (1982). The politics of narrative form: The emergence of news conventions in print and television. *Daedalus, 11*, 97-112.

Schutz, A. (1970). *On phenomenology and social relations*. Chicago: University of Chicago Press.

Schwartz, T. (1972). *The responsive chord.* Garden City, NY: Anchor.

Schwartz, T. (1976). The inside of the outside. In R. Agranoff (Ed.), *The new style in election campaigns* (pp. 344-358). Boston: Holbrook.

Scott, R. (1981). You cannot not debate: The debate over the 1980 presidential debates. *Speaker & Gavel, 18,* 28-33.

Sears, D. O. (1975). Political socialization. In F. I. Greenstein & N. W. Polsby (Eds.), *Handbook of political science, Vol. 2* (pp. 96-136). Reading, MA: Addison-Wesley.

Sears, D. O., & Chaffee, S. H. (1979). Uses and effects of the 1976 debates: An overview of empirical studies. In S. Kraus (Ed.), *The great debates: Carter vs Ford, 1976* (pp. 237-239). Bloomington, IN: Indiana University Press.

Sego, M. A. (1977). *Who gets the cookies? III.* Brunswick, OH: King's Court Communications.

Semetko, H. A., Blumler, J. G., Gurevitch, M., Weaver, D. H., Barkin, S., & Wilhoit, G. C. (1991). *The formation of campaign agendas: A comparative analysis of party and media roles in recent American and British elections.* Hillsdale, NJ: Lawrence Erlbaum.

Seymour-Ure, C. (1974). *The political impact of the mass media.* Beverly Hills: Sage.

Shapiro, M. A., & Rieger, R. H. (1989). Comparing positive and negative political advertising on radio. *Journalism Quarterly, 69,* 135-145.

Shapiro, R. Y., Young, J. T., Patterson, K. D., Blumenfeld, J. E., Cifu, D. A., Offenhartz, S. M., & Tsekerides, T. E. (1991). Media influences on support for presidential candidates in primary elections: Theory, method, and evidence. *International Journal of Public Opinion Research, 3,* 340-365.

Shaw, D., & Bowers, T. (1973). *Learning from commercials: The influence of TV advertising on the voter political agenda.* Paper presented to the annual meeting of the Association for Education in Journalism.

Shaw, D. L., & McCombs, M. E. (Eds.). (1977). *The emergence of American political issues: The agenda-setting function of the press.* St. Paul, MN: West.

Sheinkopf, K. G., Atkin, C. K., & Bowen, L. (1972). The functions of political advertising for campaign organizations. *Journal of Marketing Research, 9,* 401-405.

Sheinkopf, K. G., Atkin, C. K., & Bowen, L. (1973). How political party workers respond to political advertising. *Journalism Quarterly, 50,* 334-339.

Sherif, M., Sherif, C. W., & Nebergall, R. E. (1965). *Attitude and attitude change.* Philadelphia: Saunders.

Shotter, J. (1984). *Social accountability and selfhood.* Oxford, England: Basil Blackwell.

Shyles, L. C. (1983). Defining the issues of a presidential election from televised political spot advertisements. *Journal of Broadcasting, 27,* 333-343.

Shyles, L. (1986). The televised political spot advertisement: Its structure, content, and role in the political system. In L. L. Kaid, D. Nimmo, & K. R. Sanders (Eds.), *New perspectives on political advertising* (pp. 107-138). Carbondale, IL: Southern Illinois University Press.

Shyles, L. (1988). Profiling candidate images in televised political spot advertisements for 1984: Roles and realities of presidential jousters at the height of the Reagan era. *Political Communication and Persuasion, 5,* 15-31.

Sigal, L. (1978). Newsmen and campaigners: Organization men make the news. *Political Science Quarterly, 93*, 465-470.

69 Op. Atty. Gen. 278, Dec. 30, 1986. California Election Code, 12520.

Skibinski v. Tadych, 142 N.W.2d 838, 31 Wis. 2d 189 (1966).

Smith, A. (1976). A maturing telocracy: Observations on the television coverage of the British general elections of 1974. In L. Maisel (Ed.), *Changing campaign techniques: Elections and values in contemporary democracies,* (pp. 195-215). Sage electoral studies yearbook, Vol. 2. London: Sage.

Smith, L. D., & Golden, J. L. (1988). Electronic storytelling in electoral politics: An anecdotal analysis of television advertising in the Helms-Hunt Senate race. *The Southern Speech Communication Journal, 53*, 244-258.

Smith, P. B. (1983). Social influence processes in groups. In J. Nicholson & B. Foss (Eds.), *Psychology survey* (pp. 88-108). Herts: British Psychology Society.

Smith, R. E., & Hunt, S. D. (1978). Attributional processes and effects in promotional situations, *Journal of Consumer Research, 5*, 149-158.

Snow, C. P. (1959). *The two cultures.* London: Cambridge University Press.

Sohn, D. (1980). Critique of Cooper's meta-analytic assessment of the findings on sex differences in conformity behavior. *Journal of Personality and Social Psychology, 39*, 1215-1221.

Sonquist, J. A., & Dunkelberg, W. C. (1977). *Survey and opinion research: Procedures for processing and analysis.* Englewood Cliffs, NJ: Prentice-Hall.

Sorauf, F. (1992). *Inside campaign finance: Myths and realities.* New Haven, CT: Yale University Press.

Spero, R. (1980). *The duping of the American voter.* New York: Lippincott & Crowell.

Squier, R. (1987, May). Unpublished lecture at the School of Communication, University of Alabama, Tuscaloosa, AL.

State political action legislation and regulations: Index and directory of organizations (1984). Westport, CT: Quorum Books.

State v. Burgess, 543 So. 2d 1332 (1989).

Steeper, F. (1995, Feb., 8). This swing is different: Analysis of 1994 election exit polls. *The Cook Political Report,* 6.

Stephenson, W. (1953). *The study of behavior: Q-technique and its methodology.* Chicago: University of Chicago Press.

Stokes, D. E. (1966). Some dynamic elements of contests for the presidency. *American Political Science Review, 60*, 19-28.

Strand, P. J., Dozier, D. M., Hofstetter, C. R., & Ledingham, J. D. (1983). Campaign messages, media usage, and types of voters. *Public Relations Review, 9*, 53-63.

Strong, E. C. (1974). The use of field experimental observations in estimating advertising recall. *Journal of Marketing Research, 11*, 369-378.

Strong, E. K. (1925). *The psychology of selling.* New York: McGraw-Hill.

Strouse, J. C. (1975). *The mass media, public opinion and public policy analysis.* Columbus, OH: Merrill.

Sullivan, A. (1965). Toward a philosophy of public relations: Images. In O. Lerbinger & A. Sullivan (Eds.), *Information, influence, and communication* (pp. 240-249). New York: Basic Books.

Swanson, D. (1973). Political information, influence and judgment in the 1972 presidential campaign. *Quarterly Journal of Speech, 59*, 130-142.

Swanson, D. L. (1972). The new politics meets the old rhetoric: New directions in campaign communication research. *Quarterly Journal of Speech, 58*, 31-40.

Swinyard, W. R., & Coney, K. A. (1978). Promotional effects on a high versus low-involvement electorate. *Journal of Consumer Research, 5*, 41-48.

Tannenbaum, P. H. (1967). The congruity principle revisited: Studies in the reduction, induction and generalization of attitude change. In L. Berkowitz (Ed.), *Advances in experimental social psychology, Vol. III* (pp. 271-320). New York: Academic Press.

Tarrance, V. L., Jr. (1982). *Negative campaigns and negative votes: The 1980 elections.* Washington, DC: Free Congress Research & Education Foundation.

Taylor, P. (1986, October 5). Negative ads becoming powerful political force. *The Washington Post*, pp. A1, A6-A7.

Technology, strategy bring new campaign era. (1985, Dec. 7). *Congressional Quarterly* (pp. 2559-2565). Washington, DC: Congressional Quarterly.

Theis, P. (1968). Publicity and politics. *Public Relations Journal, 24*, 8-10.

Tichenor, P. J., Donohue, G. A., & Olien, C. N. (1970). Mass media flow and differential growth in knowledge. *Public Opinion Quarterly, 34*, 159-170.

Time (1979, April 23), 42.

Tobe, F. (1984). New techniques in computerized voter contact. *Campaigns & Elections, 5*, 56-64.

Tomei v. Finley, 512 F. Supp. 695 (N.D. Ill. 1981).

Traugott, M. (1992a). The impact of media polls on the public. In T. E. Mann & G. R. Orren (Eds.), *Media polls in American politics* (pp. 125-149). Washington, DC: The Brookings Institution.

Traugott, M. W. (1992b, Sept.). *The use of focus groups to supplement campaign coverage.* Paper presented to the annual meeting of the American Political Science Association, Chicago.

Trent, J. S., & Friedenberg, R. V. (1983). *Political campaign communication.* New York: Praeger.

Trent, J., & Sabourin, T. (1993). Sex still counts: Women's use of televised advertising during the decade of the 1980s. *Journal of Applied Communication Research, 21*, 21-40.

Tuchman, G. (1976). Telling stories. *Journal of Communication, 26*, 93-97.

Tuchman, G. (1981). Myth and the consciousness industry: A new look at the effects of the mass media. In E. Katz & T. Szecsko (Eds.), *Mass media and social change* (pp. 83-100). Beverly Hills: Sage.

Tucker, L. A., & Heller, D. J. (1987). Putting ethics into practice. *Campaigns & Elections, 7*, 42-46.

Vanasco v. Schwartz, 401 F. Supp. 87 (S.D. N.Y. 1975).

Vanneman, R., & Pampel, F. C. (1977). The American perception of class and status. *American Sociological Review, 42*, 422-437.

Vatz, R. (1973). The myth of the rhetorical situation. *Philosophy and Rhetoric, 6*, 154-161.

Vatz, R. (1976). Public opinion and presidential ethos. *Western Speech Communication, 40*, 196-206.

Virginia State Board of Pharmacy v. Virginia Citizens Consumer Council , 425 U. S. 760 (1976).

Vogel, S. R., Broverman, I. K., Broverman, D. M., Clarkson, F. E., & Rosenkrantz, P. S. (1970). Maternal employment and perception of sex roles among college students. *Developmental Psychology, 3*, 384-391.

Wadsworth, A. J., Patterson, P., Kaid, L. L., Cullers, G., Malcomb, D., & Lamarind, L. (1987). "Masculine" vs. "feminine" strategies in political ads: Implications for female candidates. *Journal of Applied Communication Research, 15*, 77-94.

Wakshlag, J. J., & Edison, N. G. (1979). Attraction, credibility, perceived similarity, and the image of public figures. *Communications Quarterly, 27*, 27-34.

Wamsley, G., & Pride, R. (1972). Television network news: Re-thinking the iceberg problem. *The Western Political Quarterly, 25*, 433-450.

Wanat, J. (1974). Political broadcast advertising and primary election voting. *Journal of Broadcasting, 18*, 413-422.

Ward, S. D., McGinnies, E. (1974). Persuasive effects of early and late mention of credible and non-credible sources. *Journal of Psychology, 86*, 17-23.

Warner, W. L. (1976). Mass media: The transformation of a political hero. In J. E. Combs & M. W. Mansfield (Eds.), *Drama in life: The uses of communication in society* (pp. 200-211). New York: Hastings House.

Warr, P., & Jackson, P. (1976). Three weighting criteria in impression formation. *European Journal of Social Psychology, 6*, 41-49.

Wattenberg, M. P. (1986). *The decline of American political parties, 1952-1984.* Cambridge: Harvard University Press.

Wattier, M. J. (1982). Voter targeting using the Q-method. *Campaigns & Elections, 2*, 31-41.

Wattier, M. J. (1986). Discovering campaign themes: Reinforcement with Q method. *Election & Politics, 3*, 20-23.

Watzlawick, P. (1976). *How real is real?* New York: Random House.

Watzlawick, P., Beavin, J. H., & Jackson, D. D. (1967). *Pragmatics of human communication: A study of interactional patterns, pathologies, and paradoxes.* New York: Norton.

Weaver, P. H. (1976, August 29). Captives of melodrama. *The New York Times Magazine, 6*, 48-51, 54, 56-57.

Weaver-Lariscy, R. A., & Tinkham, S. F. (1987). The influence of media expenditure and allocation strategies in congressional advertising campaigns. *Journal of Advertising, 16*, 13-21.

Weaver-Lariscy, R. A., Tinkham, S. F., & Nordstrom, K. E. (1988, May). *The use and impact of polling as a strategic planning tool in congressional campaigns.* Paper presented to the annual meeting of the International Communication Association Convention, New Orleans, LA.

Weber, M. (1978) *Economy and society*, Vol. 1. Berkeley: University of California Press.

Weisberg, H. F., & Bowen, B. D. (1977). *An introduction to survey research and data analysis.* San Francisco: Freeman.

Weiss, W. (1966). *Effects of the mass media of communication.* New York: Hunter College, Center for Research & Social Psychology.

West, D. M. (1992, March). Reforming campaign ads. *PS: Political Science & Politics*, 74-77.

Wheeless, L. R., & Grotz, J. (1977). The measurement of trust and its relationship to self-disclosure. *Human Communication Research, 3*, 250-257.

Whillock, R. K. (1991). *Political empiricism*. Westport, CT: Praeger.

Whitehead, A. N. (1925). *Science and the modern world*. New York: Macmillan.

Whitehead, A. N. (1930). *Process and reality*. New York: Macmillan.

Whitehead, A. N. (1933). *Adventures of ideas*. New York: Macmillan.

Whorf, B. L. (1956). *Language, thought, and reality*. New York: Wiley.

Why America doesn't vote. (1988). *Elections '88* (pp. 139-147). Washington, DC: Congressional Quarterly.

Wilcox, D. L., Ault, P. H., & Agee, W. K. (1986). *Public relations: Strategies and tactics*. New York: Harper & Row.

Will, G. (1989, Nov. 6). The pollution of politics. *Newsweek*, 92.

Williams, L. (1994). Political advertising in the "year of the woman": Did X mark the spot? In E. A. Cook, S. Thomas, & C. Wilcox (Eds.), *The year of the woman: Myths and realities* (pp. 197-215). Boulder, CO: Westview Press.

Williams, W., Jr., Shapiro, M., & Cutbirth, C. (1991). The impact of campaign agendas on perceptions of issues. In David L. Protess and Maxwell McCombs (Eds.), *Agenda setting: Readings on media, public opinion, and policymaking* (pp. 251-259). Hillsdale, NJ: Lawrence Erlbaum.

Wilson, P. O. (1987). Presidential advertising in 1988. *Election Politics, 4*, 17-21.

Wimmer, R. D., & Dominick, J. R. (1991). *Mass media research: An introduction*. Belmont, CA: Wadsworth.

Winneg, K. M. (1986). Verbal and visual information found in televised political advertisements from the 1984 general presidential election campaign (Master's thesis, University of Pennsylvania, 1985). *Journalism Abstracts, 24*, 97.

Winsbro, J. (1987). Misrepresentation in political advertising: The role of legal sanctions. *Emory Law Journal, 36*, 853-916.

Wirthlin, R. B. (1995, June/July). Politics of the nineties; campaign 1996: Searching for its structure. *The Public Perspective,* The Roper Center for Public Opinion Research, 6 (4), 43.

Witherspoon, J. (1984, Summer). Campaign commercials & the media blitz. *Campaigns & Elections, 5*, 6-20.

Wolfson, L. W. (1972a, Feb. 13). The media masters: Part one. *The Potomac Magazine, The Washington Post*, 15-19, 34-37.

Wolfson, L. W. (1972b, Feb. 20). The media masters: Part two. *The Potomac Magazine, The Washington Post*, 13-15, 20-21, 24.

Wolfson, L. W. (1972c, March 5). The media masters: Part three. *The Potomac Magazine, The Washington Post*, 17-21, 38-39, 45-46.

Wood, G. S. (1978). The democratization of mind in the American Revolution. In R. H. Horowitz (Ed.), *The moral foundations of the American republic* (pp. 102-128). Charlottesville, VA: University Press of Virginia.

Wyckoff, G. (1968). *The image candidate*. New York: Macmillan.

Wyer, R. S. (1970). Information redundancy, inconsistency, and novelty and their role in impression formation. *Journal of Experimental Social Psychology, 6*, 111-127.

Wyer, R. S., & Frey, D. (1983). The effects of feedback about self and others on the recall and judgments of feedback-relevant information. *Journal of Social Psychology, 19*, 540-559.

Zajonc, R. B. (1968). Attitudinal effects of mere exposure. *Journal of Personality and Social Psychology Monograph Supplement, 9*, 1-27.

Zajonc, R. B. (1980). Feeling and thinking: Preferences need no inferences. *American Psychologist, 35*, 151-175.

Zajonc, R. B., & Rajecki, D. W. (1969). Exposure and effect: A field experiment. *Psychonomic Science, 17*, 216-217.

Zajonc, R. B., Shaver, P., Tavris, C., & Van Kreveld, D. (1972). Exposure, satiation, and stimulus discriminability. *Journal of Personality and Social Psychology, 21*, 270-280.

Zellner, M. (1970). Self-esteem, reception, and influencibility. *Journal of Personality and Social Psychology, 15*, 87-93.

Zucker, H. G. (1978). The variable nature of news media influence. In B. D. Ruben (Ed.), *Communication Yearbook 2* (pp. 225-240). New Bruns-wick, NJ: Transaction Books.

Zullow, H. M., Oettingen, G., Peterson, C., & Seligman, M. E. P. (1988). Pessimistic explanatory style in the historical record: CAVing LBJ, presidential candidates, and East versus West Berlin. *American Psychologist, 43*, 673-682.

Index

Media age and declining voter
    participation, 17
Media age politics, 7-17; candidate
    style, 8; consequences, 15-17;
    declining voter participa-
    tion, 17; dominance of tele-
    vision, 13-14; journalists,
    14; media, 12-15; para-social
    interaction, 8; political
    parties, 8-9, 15; presidential
    primaries, 11-12;
Media effects, agenda setting, 97-
    98; conditional powerful ef-
    fects, 97-100; limited effects
    theory, 93-95; minimal ef-
    fects, 105; reinforcement, 94;
    selective exposure, 94; selec-
    tive perception, 94; selective
    retention, 94
Mere exposure theory, 152
Message research, 120-121
*Miami Herald Publishing Co. v.
    Tornillo*, 211
Mikulski, Barbara, 159
Mills v. Alabama, 186
Mondale, Walter, 10, 11, 72
Monitor Patriot Co. v. Roy, 186
Murray, Patti, 159
Muskey, Edmund, 41

National Rifle Association
    (NRA), 180
Negative candidate evaluation,
    85-86
Negative information, 101-102
Negative political advertising, 28-
    29, 33-34, 35-36, 42-43, 146,
    160-161, 167-168, 197-198;
    direct attack ads, 168-170;
    direct comparison ads, 170-
    171; implied comparison ads,
    171-172; refutation ads, 36;
    responses to, 36
New York Times Co. v. Sullivan,
    186, 193
News, as melodrama, 63; as story
    telling, 63; dramatic evalua-
    tions of candidates, 86;

dramatization, 62-73; nega-
    tivity, 64-66; of the cam-
    paign, 66-68; power of de-
    fined 63
Newspaper independent partici-
    patory stage, 12
Nixon, Richard, 45, 156
Nominal group technique, 125

O'Leary, Bradley S., 204
Opposition research, 118-119,
    127-129; content analysis,
    144
Organizational politics era, 5-7;
    machine politics, 5-6; news-
    papers, 6-7; party identifica-
    tion, 7

Packaging, 41
Party identification, 26-27, 59-60
Perot, Ross, 45-46
Peterson, Donna, 169-170
Physiological response research,
    139-140
Political Action Committees
    (PACs), 10-11, 29, 217, 222-
    224; growth in, 222-223; in-
    dependent, 222; independent
    expenditures, 221-222; spon-
    sored ads, 222;
Political advertising, broadcast
    protection from libel, 213-
    214; buying schemes, 49-50;
    buying strategy, 45-50; can-
    didate's responsibility, 196-
    197; defined, 31; dissimilari-
    ties with commercial adver-
    tising, 43-45; distorting vot-
    ing records, 201-202; donut
    ads, 221; effective lengths,
    45, 46; effectiveness, 153-
    154; effects, 149-150; effects
    affective, 151-153; effects
    behavioral, 153; effects cog-
    nitive, 150-151; expendi-
    tures, 214-215, 216; expo-
    sure effects, 48; goals, 154-
    155; image, 157-159; issues,

About the Authors

KAREN S. JOHNSON-CARTEE is Professor of Advertising and Public Relations and Speech Communication at The University of Alabama.

GARY A. COPELAND is Professor of Telecommunication and Film and Speech Communication at The University of Alabama.

Heterick Memorial Library
Ohio Northern University

	DUE	RETURNED		DUE	RETURNED
1.			13.		
2.			14.		
3.			15.		
4.			16.		
5.			17.		
6.			18.		
7.			19.		
8.			20.		
9.			21.		
10.			22.		
11.			23.		
12.			24.